WOMEN, SUBALTERNS, AND ECOLOGIES
IN SOUTH AND SOUTHEAST ASIAN WOMEN'S FICTION

Women, Subalterns, and Ecologies in South and Southeast Asian Women's Fiction

Chitra Sankaran

THE UNIVERSITY OF GEORGIA PRESS
ATHENS

© 2021 by the University of Georgia Press
Athens, Georgia 30602
www.ugapress.org
All rights reserved

Set in Adobe Garamond Pro by TIPS Publishing Services, Carrboro, NC

Most University of Georgia Press titles are available from popular e-book vendors.
Printed digitally

Library of Congress Control Number: 2021936877

ISBN 9780820360874 (hardback)
ISBN 9780820360881 (paperback)
ISBN 9780820360898 (ebook)

For
Arjun, Anika, Layana, and Aarav,
with all my love.

Contents

Acknowledgments ix

Introduction 1

CHAPTER ONE
Colonial, Postcolonial, and Neocolonial Ecologies 21

CHAPTER TWO
Women, Animals, and Animality 55

CHAPTER THREE
Feminized Rivers, History, and Enchantment 89

CHAPTER FOUR
Women, Pasts, and the Apocalypse 115

CHAPTER FIVE
The Sacred, the Subalterns, Women, and Literary Legacies 151

Postscript 189

Notes 193

Bibliography 201

Index 223

ACKNOWLEDGMENTS

I would like to register my sincere thanks to my editor, Bethany Snead of UGA, who has been a source of great support and strength. I am very grateful to Professors Helen Tiffin, Adeline Johns-Putra, and Yuki Masami for sparing their valuable time to read through my manuscript and for providing detailed reader-responses. I would like to thank John Ryan for sending me the essay on "Tawlar Ratu," which has been so useful for understanding certain literary traditions of Myanmar. I would also like to thank Jane Nardin for her suggestions for revising the introduction and chapter 1. Finally, my grateful thanks to my husband and my family for their enthusiasm, support, and endless patience in backing my book project.

INTRODUCTION

> The human population can no longer be allowed to grow in the same old uncontrolled way. If we do not take charge of our population size, then nature will do it for us and it is the poor people of the world who will suffer most.
> —Sir David Attenborough
>
> May peace radiate throughout, across the sky as well as in the vast ethereal spaces everywhere!
> May peace reign over all of this earth, in water and in all herbs, trees and creepers!
> May peace flow over the whole universe.
> May peace be in the Supreme Being, The Brahman [Universal Consciousness]!
> And may there always exist peace in everyone and peace alone!
> OM peace, peace and peace to us and all beings!
> —"Hymn to Peace," *Yajur Veda*

The epigraph from the *Yajur Veda*, which expresses the desire for peace to reign everywhere, not only all over Earth but in the sky and in "vast ethereal spaces," intuits a harmony that coheres all elements, within and beyond our planet. Scholarly consensus dates the bulk of the *Yajur Veda* hymns to the early Indian Iron Age, after circa 1200 and before 800 BCE.[1] It is deeply disheartening that, despite the extensive passage of time from the Vedic age to contemporary times, Asians are no closer to finding peace or harmony with their surroundings and if anything, have moved further away from it. The several natural disasters and the current pandemic we face are living proof of our disharmony with our planetary ecology.

Moreover, the COVID-19 pandemic has sadly proven the accuracy of Sir David Attenborough's prediction above in the most draconian way possible, causing worldwide anguish. Two important lessons among many that the pandemic has taught us is that human conduct directly impacts planetary ecology at so many incalculable levels and that all of humanity, regardless of class, race, or nation, is irrevocably embedded in natural ecologies and hence cannot escape their impacts. The pandemic has decimated populations globally, and Attenborough's lines in the epigraph appear pertinent to the world at large but especially to Asia, where population explosion has reached its zenith.

The discrepancy between ancient Asian wisdom and current practices is one reason among many why, in many Asian spaces, there is an ongoing, silent, but resolute rebellion that strives to relearn, recreate, and reinstate the sanctity and significance of Planet Earth and its determinants, its ecosystems, its natural resources and the environment, while paying heed to the perils of excessive exploitation of our planet. Green activists and philosophers are part of this rebellion, but also its creative writers and indeed ecocritics, whose careful attention to ways in which humans have imaged, imagined, and interacted with the nonhuman world has opened up for study the turbulent and exploitative relationship that humanity has adopted toward nature over the millennia. In this study, I argue that a strong ecological awareness is apparent in Asian women's fictions. The writers discussed in this book are responding in thought-provoking ways to environmental perils and connecting them to human cultures and conduct. In doing so, they are harnessing many Asian re/sources to either augment or realign mainstream (read Western) positions. In this study of fictions by South and Southeast Asian women writers, I focus on the ways that these narratives—in describing ecological crises in these two regions, particularly in their gendered aspects—emerge, and examine their significance.

This pioneering study, which introduces a new corpus of more than thirty ecofictions, examines how recent global threats to ecosystems, both in nature and culture, impact subdominant groups, including women. The corpus depicts the diverse ways in which women (and subalterns) engage with various aspects of their environments. I argue that these writers present unique perspectives that describe Asian women's relationships to non/human worlds and hence project their interventions in social and natural ecologies. This study is urgent and significant for several reasons. First, as Amitav Ghosh observes in his book on the environmental crisis, "[t]o look at the climate crisis . . . is to recognize, first, that the continent of Asia is conceptually critical to every aspect of global warming: its causes, its philosophical and historical implications, and the possibility of a global response to it. Yet . . . the discourse around the Anthropocene, and climate matters generally, remains largely Eurocentric" (*The Great Derangement* 87).

My study redresses the balance. It examines not only the role and impact of global warming on the hugely populous Asian nations, but also ways in which these are entangled with history and culture; it does so by displaying an analysis of literary ecofictions that present these entanglements. Second, it is important to note how, in recent decades, East Asia has become "overdetermined" as Asia, which has meant that South and Southeast Asia have been subsumed under it. This imbalance has meant that significant aspects of the global ecological crisis as they affect these two regions have been overlooked. The differences between East

Asia and Southeast Asia or ASEAN (*The Association of Southeast Asian Nations*, often discussed without sufficient differentiation from East Asian nations) are significant—culturally, politically, and in the management of natural resources. It is important to note these differences. This study refocuses the global lens on these two rapidly developing regions of Asia. Third, while in the past decade, in recognition of a gap in scholarship, a few edited volumes on ecocriticism have emerged (which include South and/or Southeast Asia), none of these center women and/or the subalterns. This is unacceptable since in terms of numbers, it is estimated that more than half a billion Asians will be seriously impacted by climate change, rising sea levels, desertification, and so forth. The burden of these impacts will inevitably be borne by the poorest in these regions and, amongst them, disproportionately by women. So, it is imperative that this is a demographic upon which studies focus. Finally, existing studies treat these two regions separately, never combining them, despite the common historical and cultural antecedents they share, which are important to compare and contrast. This book addresses these manifold and important gaps in scholarship.

The study centers an ecofeminist perspective. Unlike some other ecocritical approaches, which treat both humans and nature as separate and monolithic entities, ecofeminism emphasizes the fact that women's devaluation in nearly every society, and its degree, is conceptually related to the devaluation of the natural environment and its members. Therefore, in order to evaluate the latter, we need to engage with the former. This study makes connections that foreground an awareness of how entrenched *cultural* attitudes are imbricated in human relationships with nature, and that a separation of the two is conceptually and ideologically reductive. As social ecologist Murray Bookchin points out, humans are "beings, who are divided by the oppressions of race, sex, material means of life, culture and the like" (Chase 4). It is important to acknowledge that humans bring the impact of these oppressions into their relationships with the non-human world. We also need to examine *how* these occur. Patriarchal oppression of women and racial oppression of other races therefore form an integral aspect of investigating human separation from the rest of nature. Since most of South Asia and Southeast Asia were formerly colonies, the literatures of the region reveal the impact of this historical oppression. Thus, an ecofeminist approach augmented by a postcolonial approach becomes necessary. This study adopts this combined approach in examining South and Southeast Asian fiction by women.

Global Literatures and Ecocriticism in South and Southeast Asia

For several millennia, literature from around the world has referenced nature. As long as there are humans and there is nature, it is inevitable that the two will interact and these interactions will be registered in texts and communities in multitudinous ways. Asian literary traditions are amongst the oldest; although rich and diverse, they have (in varying degrees and in a variety of ways) engaged with the *idea* and the *reality* of nature. It is not surprising that, more often than not, there has been a disjunction between idealistic conceptions of nature in Asian literature and philosophy, and exploitative engagements with them in practice. Despite an explicit acknowledgement of this disconnect by Asian ecocritics like Vandana Shiva (*Staying Alive*), Huey-li Li ("A Cross-Cultural Critique of Ecofeminism"), and others, the importance of literature in building ecological awareness, which may in turn help change practice, has never been disputed. As Lawrence Buell remarks:

> For technological breakthroughs, legislative reforms, and paper covenants about environmental welfare to take effect, or even to be generated in the first place, requires a climate of transformed environmental values, perception, and will. To that end, the power of story, image, and artistic performance and the resources of aesthetics, ethics, and cultural theory are crucial. (vi)

Human-nature interactions have been represented widely, either overtly or subtly, in literary and cultural texts across South and Southeast Asia, and in congruence with Buell's view, may be collectively said to have been a powerful shaping force in these societies. However, it is inevitable that the ways in which environmental awareness has been registered and recorded would vary from one linguistic community to another. Therefore, to anchor this study, it is important to briefly trace the foundations of Western ecocritical traditions before expanding on contemporary Asian ecocritical studies.

The Western environmentalist movement emerged in the late nineteenth century with its rich nature writings. In the 1960s, there was again a renewed ecological consciousness. The first significant ecocritical study by Joseph Meeker was published in the 1970s (*The Comedy of Survival*), which was also when the term "ecocriticism" was coined by William Rueckert ("Literature and Ecology") and gradually came into vogue. According to Rueckert, ecocriticism is "the application of ecology and ecological concepts to the study of literature" (*Literature and Ecology* 107). Ecology, or ecological science, can be defined as "the scientific study of the distribution and abundance of living organisms and how the[se] . . . are affected by interactions between the organisms and their environment" ("Ecology"). Ecological criticism, plural and multiform in its evolution in the past few decades, has now come to embrace not just the science of ecology but all possible relations between literature and the non-human world, and hence has branched out into various subfields such as ecofeminism, eco-spiritualism, material ecocriticism, and postcolonial ecocriticism, to name a few, focusing on diverse areas that impact human-nature interactions. In this study, while ecofeminism is the dominant perspective, individual chapters employ in tandem other significant concepts from within the humanities to analyze the corpus and augment the central thesis.

In "The Hitchhiker's Guide to Ecocriticism," Ursula Heise clarifies how "ecocriticism in its first stage differed sharply from other forms of 'postmodern' thought in that it sought to redefine the human subject not so much in relation to the human others that subjecthood had traditionally excluded as in relation to the nonhuman world" (507). This points to how the various strands of ecocriticism cohere around a shared political goal that has led to a reevaluation of the human/nonhuman binary. A focus on this enduring binary is important to this study, which examines ecological approaches in the fictions of South and Southeast Asian women writers, marking their cultural specificities that overlap with, but also differ from, Western approaches. The ecological landscapes described in these works are often against the backdrop of extreme scenarios such as natural disasters, civil riots, wars, toxins in the air, water pollution, terrorism, and economic imperialism through corporate globalization. The texts often redefine or challenge boundaries, showing the limitations of Benedict Anderson's "imagined communities" of the nation to produce what Ulrich Beck terms "imagined cosmopolitan communities of global risk" ("Cosmopolitanism as Imagined Communities of Global Risk" 1347).

The recent interest within ecocritical studies in global literatures, indigeneity, and, crucially, the intersections between ecocriticism and postcolonialism[2] has prompted the examination of non-Western literary works to arrive at an enhanced understanding of how humans and environments have interacted for centuries in these other(ed) traditions and continue to do so. However, as Laura Wright points out, even when there is mention of Asian literatures, these studies,

> tend to pay lip service to the third world by using binary rhetoric to point out the similarities between the othering of nature and the othering of non-Western peoples without examining conceptions of nature that do not originate in the West and *without examining environmental issues that are unique to populations in formerly colonized cultures* . . . Such rhetorical explorations continue to consider Western notions of nature without discussing the environmental issues that are unique to formerly colonized cultures. (Wright 8, emphasis added)

This dearth of material on the East, as Wright highlights, is indeed puzzling because in philosophical traditions within these regions, such as Hinduism and

Buddhism, there has, for longer than a millennium, been a deep cognizance of nature as an autonomous as well as ideological realm. Furthermore, within Indian literary traditions, Sanskrit, for example, has extant literatures dating back to the twelfth century BCE,[3] which present sustained and coherent narratives that engage with nature, acknowledging its primordiality but also engaging anthropocentrically, exposing sociopolitical agendas. The concept of the Aranyakas (or forest literatures) in Sanskrit—where the forests function paradoxically as both abodes of contemplative peace and sites of ecological carnage—displays the dynamic engagements that these literatures have recorded or constructed between nature and "man." It is inevitable, therefore, that my analyses of novels and short stories, which are often embedded in Asian philosophies and rich native traditions that have been cross-pollinated by colonialism and globalization, will be enabled by these various perspectives.

There are many emerging postcolonial-ecocritical studies with at least the odd chapter on South Asian fictions. Upamanyu Pablo Mukherjee's *Postcolonial Environments*, for example, includes fairly detailed readings of several South Asian texts. But sustained ecocritical studies on South Asia are rare, and on women's literature, negligible and even non-existent.

The paucity of scholarship in the field of South and Southeast Asian ecocriticism has been widely noted. As Ursula Heise points out, "[c]ritics such as Patrick Murphy and Slovic have . . . made sustained efforts to spread ecocritical analysis to the study of other cultures and languages, though their success has been limited" (513). There is truth in this observation, and its implied West-centric model of intellectual diffusion can be turned to advantage while analyzing Asian ecofictions. Sophisticated ways of thinking about ecology have long been part of South and Southeast Asian literary and philosophical traditions. The point is to bring ecocriticism, with its North American intellectual heritage, into dialogue with these traditions and to, if not challenge, at least qualify some of these mainstream assumptions.

Some Ecological/Feminist Concepts of South and Southeast Asia

One of the most dynamic subfields to emerge from ecological studies has been ecofeminism. It is premised on the view that under patriarchy, the exploitation of nature and that of women are ideologically linked. Sherry Ortner's famous essay, "Is Female to Male as Nature is to Culture?" began an important field of enquiry. Several groundbreaking books that examine women-nature connections have appeared in the past few decades. However, again, there is *no* sustained study that explores the links between women, land, and literary traditions in South and

Southeast Asia.[4] Hence ecofeminist perspectives become central to my literary explorations. Pioneering ecofeminist Karen J. Warren observes,

> Just as there is not one feminism, there is neither one ecofeminism nor one feminist philosophy. 'Ecological feminism' is the name of a variety of different feminist perspectives on the nature of the connections between the domination of women (and other oppressed humans) and the domination of nature . . . Given the newness of ecofeminism as a theoretical position, the nature of ecofeminist ethics is still emerging. (111)

Warren's perception is still timely and relevant. In South and Southeast Asia, philosophical perspectives and indigenous myths link women with earth and nature in empowering ways, details of which can be mined from the works of contemporary women writers. At first sight, I may appear to be accusing these writers of viewing the women-nature relationship in a reactionary mode.

Women's conventional association with the natural world in Western culture which, as ecofeminists like Carolyn Merchant point out, is ubiquitous (*Earthcare* 3–26), received approval from writers such as Aldo Leopold (*A Sand County Almanac*) and continued to be celebrated by writers like Sharon Doubiago (*Hard Country*). But the woman-nature association has been contested by contemporary ecofeminists. Janet Biehl, Catriona Sandilands, and several others have been troubled by this essentializing of both woman and nature, which they see as being reductive of the diversity of women, collapsing various ecological predicaments into one; they see this as ultimately disempowering to women and not useful for ecological preservation. However, some alternative relationships, such as between the goddess and nature in some traditions within my two regions of study, have us review what would ordinarily appear an entirely justifiable stand against essentialism.

The unique traditions within Hinduism, for instance, perceive/deify the Earth as Bhooma Devi (Earth Goddess), "who" is not only agentic but often comes to the rescue of vulnerable women, liberating them from patriarchal excesses. The most famous instance of this is from the *Uttar Ramayana*[5] where the pregnant Sita, finally abandoned by Rama, brings up their twin sons in Sage Valmiki's ashram in the forest. When the boys are grown and reunited with their father, Sita rejects Rama's call for her return, preferring instead to return to her mother, Bhooma Devi, who enfolds her in her bosom and whisks her away to safety. Given the pervasive regional influence of the Ramayana, such beliefs undergird the social persuasions of many non-Hindu cultures as well.

Similarly, pervasive in both South and Southeast Asia is the worship of Kuan Yin,[6] who is adulated as the patron goddess of both farmers and fisherfolk. She is deified in Nepal, Thailand, Sri Lanka, Myanmar, Cambodia, and other South and Southeast Asian nations. In at least two of the texts in the corpus are poor Chinese women, who, abjuring "first and second obeying" to "father or husband," take the vow of obedience to Kuan Yin instead. These women emerge as feminist models, defying gender norms, class, and other trajectories of power that work to subjugate them.

Again, insights from Asian philosophies such as *Sāṃkhya*, common to both Hindu and Buddhist belief systems, where nature (*prakṛti*) is said to mold the human soul/self (*puruṣa*) to attain nirvana or *mokṣa* (terms that refer to salvation and eternal bliss in Buddhism and Hinduism, respectively), may qualify mainstream perceptions. Since *prakṛti* is also associated with the goddess (hence the femininity), this again reveals potential paths for reconceptualizing female eco-empowerment. The goddess immanent as nature but *also* as *vāc* or speech complicates traditional patriarchal binaries that associate empowered speech with culture, specifically with males and the public domain, and nature with silence. Based on these perspectives, therefore, Christopher Manes' persuasive argument in "Nature and Silence" that modern societies have silenced nature, can be revisited. By using native modes of narrativizing, such as the *sutra* or *tawlar ratu*, contemporary South and Southeast Asian women writers, such as Gita Mehta in *The River Sutra* and Khin Mya Zin in "Heartless Forest," render agentic the river, forest, and animals. These fictional texts conceptualize the relationships between women and the non-human world differently.

These ideas resonate with Stacy Alaimo's notion of "transcorporeality" and her assertion in *Bodily Natures* that human bodies and non-human natures are open to one another and have been mutually affected through interaction. Rosemary Ruether links this idea to feminist politics when she asserts, "[W]omen throughout history have not been particularly concerned to create transcendent, overarching, all-powerful entities." Instead, "women's spirituality has focused on the immanent and intricate ties among nature, body, and personal intuition" (Salleh, "The Ecofeminism/Deep Ecology Debate" 202). In many South and Southeast Asian traditions, although goddess worship is an intricate part of life, the goddess herself is a celebration of these material bonds. Goddess faiths, therefore, also function as cultural conduits that help channel sociopolitical protests against ecological rampage and thus challenge globalized patriarchal corporatization.

Finally, there is the concept of dharma, which, though foundational to all dharmic religions,[7] can in fact be understood as a secular concept, for it revolves around the idea of cosmic balance. Troy Wilson Organ, one of the foremost scholars of Hinduism, describes it as the "foundation of law and morality . . .

which developed in India *before* Hinduism or Brahminism came into being" (210, emphasis added). Dharma, which has multiple meanings, is predominantly understood as cosmic law and order and/or as "righteous or assigned" conduct. It signifies behaviors that are considered to be in accord with *Rta*, the order that makes life and universe possible. The root of the word dharma is *dhri*, which means "to support, hold, or bear." It is the thing that regulates the course of change by not participating in change, but that principle which remains constant. Therefore, the concept of dharma insists that for the smooth functioning of the universe, *every* entity within the material and spiritual cosmos should act in accordance with its dharma. If any entity acts *out* of its dharmic role, cosmic balance is overturned.[8]

This concept can productively enter the discursive space explored by ecofeminists like Kate Soper, who, citing John Stuart Mill's essay on "Nature," points out how he "denounces the immorality of following the course of nature and rejects any consecration of instinctual action" (272). But it is this central dualism between "instinctual and deliberative" that the concept of dharma has the potential to resolve for; as Organ observes, dharma encompasses *both* instinct and conscious virtue. Bhagavan Das defines it as that which "makes the world-process what it is and holds all its parts together as One Whole . . ." (49). Organ states that in humans, to show dharma is "to order one's thoughts, passions, and affections in accordance with a rule of a place for everything and everything in its place" (211–12).

Since few ecocritical studies discuss them, dharma and related concepts not only need to be explored in themselves, but also need to be re-examined from the point of view of contemporary feminist literatures emerging from these regions, because women writers are responding to these ideas in ways that actively contribute to ecofeminist debates.

The critical essays on Asian women writers thus far have tended to focus on a few prominent authors from these regions, one such being Mahaswetha Devi. But here too, her fiction—made famous in the Anglophone world by Gayatri Chakravorty Spivak's translations—has mostly been analyzed from the postcolonial angle. There are fewer critical works generated from the ecological angle except sporadically (as, for instance, articles by Jennifer Wenzel ["Epic Struggles"; "Reading the Politics"] and Alan Johnson ["Sacred Forest]). Also, there are no book-length ecocritical studies on South and Southeast Asian literatures, let alone on women's fiction from an ecofeminist angle. This is very much a field in formation. Interestingly, however, several comprehensive ecocritical studies about East Asia, such as Karen Laura Thornber's *Ecoambiguity: Environmental Crisis and East Asian Literatures* and Simon C. Estok and Won-Chung Kim edited volume *East Asian Ecocriticisms: A Critical Reader* have emerged in recent years. Indeed, Scott Slovic, in his *Critical Insights: Nature and the Environment*, notes the increasingly international nature of ecocriticism. The book is the result of extensive research, incorporating Chinese, South African, Japanese, and Korean ecocritics' contributions. But due to the paucity of local scholarship, there is justifiably no mention of South or Southeast Asian ecocritical materials. More recently, Slovic, Swarnalatha Rangarajan, and Vidya Sarveswaran co-edited a volume, *Ecocriticism of the Global South*, which successfully fills this gap in scholarship. It has essays by individual contributors about several developing countries from around the world. But again, there is little on *women's* fiction in South Asia and none on Southeast Asian women's writing, although both regions have representative chapters on select male authors. This reveals how, despite diligent efforts made by committed international scholars, women's contributions in these two regions remain under-examined. John Ryan's *South East Asian Ecocriticism: Theories, Practices, Prospects* is the first sustained study of ecocriticism of this region, though again, understandably, the focus is mainly on male authors.[9] The most recent study, *Ecologies in Southeast Asian Literatures: Histories, Myths and Societies* by Chi Pham et al. is another foray into studying the ecocritical traditions of this complex region. Thus, when Southeast Asian ecocriticism is gradually gaining global attention, this study becomes critical in foregrounding work *by* and *on* women from these two Asian regions.

Why South and Southeast Asia?

One question that might emerge would be the usefulness of studying these two distinct regions together. Aside from the palpable fact that being geographically adjacent, natural hazards (like the tsunami) and manufactured risks (such as world wars) often affected South and Southeast Asia in largely similar or comparable ways, there are several cultural reasons for examining them together. First, these regions have interacted for over 2,000 years and there have been many cultural crossovers and social interactions that continue in the present. Both Tamil and Sanskrit influences are pervasive in the regions: in India, needless to say, and in Sri Lanka, where Tamil and Indo-Aryan Sinhala are mainstream languages; in Singapore, where Tamil is one of the four official languages, and in Malaysia, where there is also a strong Tamil presence (while Bahasa, the Malay language as it is known in Singapore and Malaysia, is powerfully influenced by Sanskrit culture and literature). This is graphically evidenced by the fact that despite being a Muslim culture, Malay indigenous traditions consider the Ramayana as part of their own culture. Vālmīki's (Sanskrit) *Rāmāyana*, or "the progress of Rama," is the source from which other versions have emerged through the centuries in Southeast Asia, from the Thai *Ramakien* to the Malay *Hikayat Seri Rama* or the Javanese *Ramayana*.[10] Again, Buddhism is the majority religion in Sri Lanka,

Vietnam, Laos, and Singapore. A consciousness of the ways in which this religion has impacted people's relations to nature that emerges through examining specific national literatures yields valuable insights. Through examining these two regions alongside each other, such connections can be teased out while acknowledging the fact that these two regions are exposed to the very same or similar environmental and sociopolitical crises, such as deforestation, militarization, soil erosion, and socioeconomic impoverishment. Studying the role and impact of global warming on the hugely populous Asian ecologies cannot be overstated.

Thus, my study, while not laying claim to any broad ahistorical or holistic tradition for the entire region—its Indic cultural substratum notwithstanding—nevertheless attempts to focus on ecological issues that are common across the two regions. Each chapter examines a few contemporary texts from South and Southeast Asia which resonate with a prominent theme within ecofeminism, and in that sense are discrete. But each chapter forms a link in the chain that ties together ecofictions with important ecofeminist themes to provide an overview of an emerging ecofeminist consciousness in two prominent regions of Asia.

In the ensuing chapters, I examine around thirty ecofictions by women writers from eleven countries: India, Sri Lanka, Pakistan, and Bangladesh in South Asia; and Singapore, Malaysia, Indonesia, Laos, Vietnam, Myanmar, and the Philippines in Southeast Asia. True to the tenets of ecofeminist thought, I discuss how these fictions reveal links between nature and culture. These connections, for example, can occur between disappearing lakes and political corruption in Indonesia; polluted rivers and rights of marginal groups in Singapore; Agent Orange and the treatment of "ugly" women in Vietnam; earthquakes, tsunamis, and the benefits of narrativizing, and so forth. Thus, I bring together cultural narratives that grapple with the larger implications of seemingly disparate events centered on sociopolitical disruptions and environmental problems, all of which together illuminate a common thematic.

Aims of the Study and Some Conceptual Frameworks

The aim of this book is not to identify or trace one overarching tradition or theme in Asian women's conceptions of nature. There is no central narrative, pervasive metaphor, or underlying ideology that unites these texts emerging from distinctive cultures and nations or is tied to different religious belief systems within South and Southeast Asia. Attempting to find one would be reductive of the rich and diverse Asian heritage. However, one interesting point that does emerge is that these women writers are attuned to the increasing disharmony that exists between their cultures and non-human nature. Their writings reveal the diverse ways through which they have signaled their awareness of (the need for) human embedment in natural ecologies. In their efforts to depict the predicament of women and the subaltern in their communities—inevitably the first to suffer the ill effects of the environmental crisis—they engage with the local and the global in their fictional depictions. Even as they are focused on the peculiar dynamics of their specific ecologies and how these affect vulnerable groups, they are also (sometimes distantly) aware of the global connections, of what Heise labels "eco-cosmopolitanism" (*Sense of Place*). Gathering up these narratives, my study strings them coherently together in order to obtain a perspective on how they connect with emerging ecofeminist discourses.

My critical analyses of the texts are undertaken with close attention to the central philosophies and perspectives upon which the texts themselves expound. One can identify a range of Asian perspectives and philosophies that emerge: *Sāṃkhya* philosophy with *Prakṛti* as agentic nature; the spiritual and material in Buddha's Fire Sermon; animistic features from ancient texts such as the Panchatantra, and traditions like *Bonbibi*; *tawlar ratu* poetics of Myanmar that portray a "speaking nature"; *sutra* traditions; examples of an ideology-infused nature from the epics, the Mahabharata and the Ramayana; agentic females in the Baromashi folk tradition and, of course, dharma. In viewing these ecofictions through one or other of these lenses, I strive to highlight the various Asian perspectives that link non-human natures to human cultures. However, in negotiating these Asian philosophies and myths, I try to strike a balance. Even as I delve into pertinent Asian philosophies and traditions, I link these analyses to relevant contemporary debates within the ecocritical field by referencing various Western theorists.

Within ecofeminism, my study, attentive to the textual patterns that emerge, foregrounds eco-spiritual and eco-material approaches. The indigenous religions of both South Asia and Southeast Asia, including Buddhism and Hinduism, are often invoked in these texts and, therefore, I allude to pertinent aspects of these in my analysis. Similarly, Catholic beliefs are often explicitly advanced in the texts emerging from the Philippines, which too are discussed. The corpus, however, does not refer to Islamic beliefs per se, even in texts emerging from Pakistan, Bangladesh, Malaysia, or Indonesia, since these writers are either secular in their approach or, indeed, use folk traditions in their texts rather than referring to a religious paradigm. This affords me little or no opportunity to foreground this important and influential religion in Asia.

Timothy Clark describes material ecocriticism as "a loose amalgam of various positions held together by the common theme of affirming the view that non-human matter has an incalculable agency of its own" (*The Value of Ecocriticism* 111–12). One realizes that the pervasive influence of dharmic religions—which assert the "inspirited" aspect of nature, be it a rock or an animal or indeed a human, all of which are seen as possessing *differing degrees* of consciousness—is still influential in Asia. Or again, the central idea in Taoism (or Daoism), that Tao pervades everything and in order to live an ethical life we have to live in harmony with it, does not sit awkwardly with material ecocritical speculations. The Vedic postulations about *nirguna brahman*[11] as the substratum of all things, material and spiritual, once again render this particular binary less definitive in Asian thought. All these influences can be identified in the ecofictions that are examined in this book. This leads us to speculate whether perhaps the strong secular trend that was the post-Enlightenment legacy in the West applies in quite the same measure in Asia where, it appears from these eco-texts at least, that traditional attitudes to a "mystical nature" are not entirely discredited despite the influx of "modernity" and "globalization."

Based on these ideas, a few common concepts that run through several of these ecofictions are briefly discussed here to avoid repetition in individual chapters. In these writings that emerge from erstwhile European colonies, Ulrich Beck's idea of a second modernity or risk society (where risk is pervasive and ever-present) also appears quite pertinent because Asian modernity cannot be easily disentangled from colonial rule. Next, *Sāṃkhya* philosophy, with its notion of an agentic "feminine" nature, is an idea that emerges in several primary texts. Finally, another useful concept is the idea of the Third Space. This liminal space that bridges the gap between the "real" and the "imaginary" is significant since these authors are attempting to depict local ecological realities in their fictional imaginings. For these reasons, I will discuss these concepts briefly below.

Risk Society

Risk as an intellectual framework was constructed by German sociologist Ulrich Beck in the 1980s. As Simon Cottle points out, "Ulrich Beck has placed ideas of 'risk society' on the intellectual map; his social theory of late modern society and its endemic production of potentially catastrophic risks has attracted, rightly, considerable academic interest in Europe and beyond" (5). Beck identifies some features of *first modernity*, a term that he uses to indicate an industrialized society with an emphasis on nation-states. The features of first modernity include "programmatic individualization," heavily reminiscent of premodern structures where status is determined by birth and under which the sexual division of labor is subsumed; gainful employment with males predominantly contributing to the labor force; and a binary division of nature as other to culture with an instrumental view that reduces nature to a resource. In first modernity, rationality becomes a monopoly of science and is primarily used to exercise power over nature (Beck et al. 4). But later, as Mads Peter Sørensen and Allan Christiansen clarify, these "securities, wisdoms and core institutions of first modernity" are gradually eroded. So, all the institutions and beliefs—nation-states, predetermined communities (such as class and the nuclear family), traditional gender divisions of labor, monopoly of science on truth and rationality, the view of nature as external and separate from society—come to be questioned (31).

Beck sees these as symptomatic of a transition from first to second or "reflexive" modernity that is also the onset of a risk society, where the awareness of risk has seeped into society as a whole and is ever-present (Sørensen and Christiansen 1–6). In *Risk Governance*, Ortwin Renn judiciously reminds us that "[r]isks are created and selected by human actors"[12] (2). Risk theorists do not cognize tsunamis that lashed periodically against uninhabited shores in the prehistoric era as risk since these events did not enter human narrative. Therefore, risk as an anthropocentric concept emerges at climactic moments in the national and/or personal histories that these authors describe. Thus, the link between human society and risk emerges as important to many texts in the corpus that describe critical ecologies. In Asia, in recent times, with tsunamis, hurricanes, and recently the pandemic, the idea of risky ecologies has gained prominence. This in turn has permeated the themes of Asian ecofictions. This becomes another useful rubric used in this study.

Sāṃkhya Philosophy

As Bina Gupta explains in *An Introduction to Indian Philosophy: Perspectives on Reality, Knowledge, and Freedom*, *Sāṃkhya* is one of the six philosophical schools in Hinduism known as *Darśana*s *or* insights (from the Sanskrit *drish*, that is, "to see"). *Sāṃkhya* is perhaps the most ancient of the systems and was very influential in antiquity. Historical antecedents of this school can be traced to the Upanishads, especially the *Svetasvatara* and the *Maitrayanya*. Scholars point out that the Bhagavad Gita is substantially influenced by *Sāṃkhya*. The main developments of this school occurred in the period extending from the first to the eleventh century CE (Gupta 130–34).

Sāṃkhya is also fairly central to Buddhism. *Duḥkha* or suffering is foundational to *Sāṃkhya*, which asserts that liberation comes from knowing how to free oneself from *duḥkha*. *Sāṃkhya* has often been categorized, not without controversy, as an atheistic spirituality (Radhakrishnan and Moore).

Sāṃkhya is a dualistic system and the dualism is between *puruṣa* (*purusha*) and *prakṛti*, where *puruṣa* stands for pure consciousness and *prakṛti* is variously interpreted as "manifest energy," "non-conscious substance energy," and more commonly as "manifest nature." *Prakṛti* is the first "uncaused cause" of all objects, gross and subtle (Gupta 135–38). *Puruṣa* or consciousness is considered to be the masculine principle and *prakṛti* the feminine principle, which is also linked to the Hindu goddess Shakti in "practiced" faith.

According to *Sāṃkhya*, *puruṣa*s are many. This is due to the diversity of births, deaths, and faculties and because of actions and functions at different times. Thus, *Sāṃkhya* advocates a dualism between *prakṛti* and (many) *puruṣa*s, a dualism that is unlike the Cartesian dualism between matter and mind. In *Sāṃkhya*, *prakṛti*, being the first cause, is always there. *Puruṣa* is a witness of *prakṛti*. In Cartesian dualism, on the other hand, *res cogitans* (*puruṣa*) and *res extensa* are completely separate and it is only when *res cogitans* and *res extensa* meet that they come to know each other (Gupta 137–38).

In *Sāṃkhya*, *puruṣa* can see but cannot act as it has no agency; *prakṛti* has agency but has no path to walk since it just "is." Prior to the emergence of the world and its infinite concrete objects, *puruṣa* has nothing to see. *Prakṛti*, being active, leads *puruṣa* to the goal of liberation. When the goal is reached —that is, when *puruṣa* becomes free—their provisional cooperation ends. *Puruṣa* is liberated and *prakṛti* returns to its original state of pure undifferentiated homogeneity (Gupta 138–43). Thus, it is *prakṛti* that is agentic in the evolution of *puruṣa*. *Prakṛti* in common understanding is often parsed as nature or the goddess. In many ecofictions analyzed in this book, individual natural entities like rivers and forests are cognized by authors as aspects of *prakṛti*.

Sāṃkhya is useful for ecocritical study for it is noteworthy that its concepts can productively interact with new ideas emerging in the subfield of material ecocriticism. They resonate first with Jane Bennett's concept in *Vibrant Matter: A Political Ecology of Things*, where she explains "vitality" as "the capacity of things . . . not only to impede or block the will and designs of humans but also to act as quasi agents or forces with trajectories, propensities, or tendencies of their own" (viii) and second with Rosi Braidotti's "vital materialisms," which she discusses in *The Posthuman*. Indeed, Serenella Iovino and Serpil Oppermann's "search for new conceptual models apt to theorize the connections between matter and agency on the one side, and the intertwining of bodies, natures, and meanings on the other side" (450) could conceivably lead them to *Sāṃkhya* and *prakṛti*.

Thus, to summarize, contrary to most mainstream conceptions of the masculine and feminine, in *Sāṃkhya*, it is nature or the feminine principle that is agentic. In other words, *prakṛti* works to bring *puruṣa* to "awareness." Asian women writers have used this idea of "agentic nature" in productive ways in their ecofictions, which I present in several chapters in this study.

Third Space

I argue that several of these primary texts depict a Third Space, a term used by both Homi K. Bhabha in *The Location of Culture* and Edward Soja, who, borrowing from Henri Lefebvre's spatial thinking, understands it as a "third dimension" that breaks up binary modes of thought and/or first and second space duality ("Third Space" 52). This term has subsequently been adopted in many disciplines and emerges as highly complex and multifaceted. The Third Space is liminal and transformative. It is subversive in that it challenges binary categorizations and oppositional positionings. It "initiates new signs of identity, and innovative sites of collaboration and contestation" (Bhabha, *The Location of Culture* 1). Bhabha calls this "the realm of the beyond" (1). He describes "the beyond" as a contested space, "the borderline of the 'present'" (7), "the moment of transit where space and time cross to produce complex figures of difference and identity, past and present, inside and outside, inclusion and exclusion." This Third Space prompts "a sense of disorientation, a disturbance of direction, in the 'beyond'" (2).

The Third Space between fiction and history is explored in Meira Chand's *A Different Sky*, Christine Suchen Lim's *The River's Song*, Merlinda Bobis' *Fish-Hair Woman*, and Jean Arasanaygam's *All Is Burning*. These are classified as historical "fictions," but the authors are keen to ally them with specific historical periods or incidents in their respective national histories. Through interviews or an afterword, the novelists establish firm links with history. Sometimes the texts are biographical, as for instance, *Wave: A Memoir of Life after the Tsunami* by Sonali Deraniyagala, while "Lake" by Lily Yulianti Farid, an activist and journalist, is about the dark days in Indonesia in the 1960s when activists went missing under Suharto's rule. But even where such obvious connections between fiction and fact are not forthcoming, I argue that these texts hinge their content in a hinterland where real, hyperreal, and surreal collapse into a space that is precisely Bhabha's Third Space of liminality and subversion.

Since I use all the three concepts above intermittently across chapters in examining the corpus, it becomes useful to clarify these terms here. Finally, I present a summary of the chapters.

Summary of Chapters

This introductory chapter presents the relevant critical debates and explores the scope and significance of this book with regard to the larger ecocritical field. It explains why ecofeminism is the most salient theoretical framework to use in this context along with insights from postcolonial studies, material, and spiritual ecocriticism. It presents the reasons for engaging in a comparison of South Asia and Southeast Asia. Some common concepts that appear in different chapters are briefly discussed. I also present reasons for why this particular project is unique, important, and timely in filling a vital gap in scholarship in ecocriticism, global literatures, and gender studies.

Chapter 1: Colonial, Postcolonial, and Neocolonial Ecologies begins with colonial, postcolonial, and neocolonial encounters because the classic industrial society as the harbinger of a global modernity came to Asia via colonial rule. This chapter examines four ecofictions: two novels from Singapore, and short stories from Sri Lanka and Pakistan, which present the multifaceted roles that women played during World War II, civil unrest, land mining, and governmental acquisition of "the commons" in resisting environmental injustice. It explores how the complicity between patriarchy and capitalism has facilitated the occurrence of historical events that have destroyed families, communities, and nations in these two regions of Asia which, in turn, have had a direct impact on natural ecologies here. Rob Nixon's idea of "slow violence" becomes pertinent in examining the gradual unfolding of Asian nations from colonial to postcolonial and neocolonial societies (*Slow Violence*).

Meira Chand's *A Different Sky*, set in World War II Singapore, rewrites the role of Asian women and minorities. It highlights how perceptions about "natural environments" have impacted history and vice versa. Suchen Christine Lim's *The River's Song* debates the River People's rights during the "Clean River Campaign" in Singapore of the 1970s and 1980. Women and other subdominant groups and their differential experiences of local ecosystems are contrasted with more distantly located and centralized meta-institutions.

Jean Arasanayagam's *All Is Burning* depicts a civil war-torn Sri Lanka. Here, I examine the colonial politics of "divide and rule" and the impact of corporate globalization that coerces countries into export-dependent economies and the ways in which these shred the fabrics of local ecologies in nature and culture. Finally, "The Zemindar's Wife" by Qaisra Shahraz portrays a greedy feudal lord in modern Pakistan, whose vulnerable but feisty wife fights to safeguard villagers' lands from being acquired for Bauxite mining. These texts traverse through colonial, postcolonial, and neocolonial terrain, foregrounding women's roles within different national spaces. The fight for the rights of the subdominant to preserve their lands and their cultures is highlighted.

Chapter 2: Women, Animals, and Animality examines the man versus woman-animal binary and its interesting manifestations in Asia in four fictions from Malaysia, the Philippines, Vietnam, and Myanmar, all of which are concerned with the dehumanizing of the subdominant and the concomitant devaluation of nature. The risks of ignoring a biocentric ethic—one that extends moral rights to the non-human world—are underscored by focusing on the endangered spaces inhabited by animals, as also women and the subalterns. Michel Foucault's idea of "biopower"—which he describes as power over life that becomes politicized, that is, biopolitics—is useful. The underside of biopolitics is "thanatopolitics." All four texts revolve around the politics of death, and are usefully linked to Asian cultural perceptions.

Beth Yahp's *The Crocodile Fury*, which is engagingly postmodernist, approaches the imperialist project from the angle of animality, while simultaneously describing certain Asian utilitarian approaches to nature. The idea of the "death of nature" emerges as distinctly gendered and linked to Asian women. In "Maharlika" by Irene Carolina A. Sarmiento, the increasing economic and cultural distance between the rich and the poor in Asia is taken to its extreme. A scenario akin to that depicted in Suzanne Collins' *The Hunger Games* is enacted, with the rich hunting the poor. This seems aligned to predictions about Second Modernity, where risk raises levels of suspicion between different classes of humans. The Vietnamese "Blood of Leaves" by Thi Hao Vo examines cultural fallouts from the "American War" and Agent Orange, that lead to the animalization of "deformed"/"ugly" women. "Heartless Forest" from Myanmar, by Mya Zin Khin, is an example of the quintessential Asian genre of Bonbibi stories. It imbues animals and the forest with agency. The gaze exchanged between humans and non-humans becomes important in this genre.

These ecofictions, while favoring ecofeminist concerns about women and animals, who are constructed as the symbolic other, focus on "man-made" environmental catastrophes. My analysis of these texts presents ideological interconnections between women and animals, while exploring their histories.

In Chapter 3: Feminized Rivers, History, and Enchantment, I study another central theme in ecofeminist politics, namely, the feminization of nature. I examine texts from India, the Philippines, and Bangladesh that center the river. *A River Sutra*, *Fish-Hair Woman*, and "The Immersion" by Dilara Hashem explore the interplay between myth and trauma. For some time now, the aesthetic value of enchantment has come to be gradually acknowledged and assessed in ecocritical studies. I discuss "enchantment" and its use by Asian women writers. Female dis/empowerment in history, negotiated through invocations of indigenous myths and philosophies, challenge some "mainstream" assumptions.

Rivers across Asia are polluted. Access to clean water is increasingly difficult for the poor in Asia. These women authors, known for their sociopolitical awareness, choose to present their narratives as centered around rivers, obliquely, through myths and metaphors. It is important to understand why. No doubt, subalterns, women, and myths have a long and close relationship. Aside from constructing solidarity among the disenfranchised, myths introduce enchantment and enable existence in extreme conditions. They construct alternate worlds that credibly and usefully reveal the failures of the real one. Thus, myths aid in undermining corporate perspectives that are dismissive of subdominant classes. Finally, further exploration uncovers some interesting connections between sociopolitical landscapes, the treatment of rivers, and the time of publication of these texts.

Having engaged with the idea of "enchantment" and its usefulness in ecofeminist analysis, in Chapter 4: Women, Pasts, and the Apocalypse, I turn to what may be considered a mode that is in direct opposition to it, namely, apocalypse. Frederick Jameson's idea that futuristic fiction enacts and enables "a structurally unique 'method' for apprehending the present as history" (153) becomes useful here. I argue that "apocalypse" itself is differently narrativized in these texts, which holds larger implications for Asian and Western positionings vis-à-vis power. This chapter explores five apocalyptic narratives from Laos, Sri Lanka, Pakistan, Indonesia, and India, which center women's voices *in extremis* during tsunamis, earthquakes, war, and other environmental and social catastrophes.

"The Roar of a Distant War" by Viliya Ketavong describes the traumas of the "American War" from the perspective of a Laotian child. *Wave: A Memoir of Life after the Tsunami* is set in the aftermath of the devastating Asian tsunami and is a biographical account of a Sri Lankan academic who lost her entire family to the sea. Shaila Abdullah's *Rani in Search of a Rainbow*, that is set during the Pakistani floods of 2010, also recounts the climate crisis from a child's point of view. "Lake" links the sudden disappearance of Lake Beloye in central Russia with the disappearance of the narrator's sister, Fayza, in Jakarta. Finally, *One Amazing Thing* by Chitra Banerjee Divakaruni depicts seven survivors of an earthquake, who spend their last hopeless hours narrating "one amazing thing" from their lives. The (in)congruence between the apocalyptic and the pastoral, which makes for interesting interventions with risk, is also explored.

Chapter 5: The Sacred, the Subalterns, Women and Literary Legacies focuses on the relationship between traditions and representations. Four authors, one each from India and Bangladesh, and two from the Philippines, present religious legacies and their influence on how women, subalterns, and nature are narrativized in Hinduism, Islam, and Catholicism, as they pertain to Asia. This chapter examines how the "logic of domination" that has justified the oppression of women, subalterns, "othered" races, animals, and nature for millennia, has been constructed in these cultures.

I explore cultural legacies and their impact on societies. Several of the little explored short stories of the Indian writer Mahasweta Devi, such as "The Hunt," "Arjun," and "Seeds," which discuss the predicaments of the tribal populations in India, make interesting links to two major Hindu epics, the Ramayana and the Mahabharata. The author uses these to expose covert ideologies of the status quo in order to speak up for "tribal" rights. Next, I analyze the works of two Filipino writers: Rosario Cruz Lucero's "The Death of Fray Salvador Montano, Conquistador of Negros" juxtaposes the meta-narrative of Catholicism—with its legacies of sin and redemption—with the lives of two hapless priests in a remote province of the Philippines. Their poststructuralist dilemma of fixing meaning to words, though comical at one level, has darker implications. I also analyse Nita Umali-Berthelsen's "The Money-Makers," in which the first-person narrative of the Catholic child underscores the significance of voice and perspective. Last, the Bangladeshi writer Niaz Zaman negotiates, in *The Baromashi Tapes*, interesting connections between the contemporary women of Bangladesh and the famous Baromashi folk songs that are central to Bangla culture. These subversive narratives highlight how women and subalterns are marginalized through mainstream ideologies. The emergence of Bhabha's Third Space in these texts is also explored.

Foundational religious and cultural texts are interwoven as subtexts in all three narratives to trace the close allegiance between ideology and the treatment of nature. The implicit message that emerges from all three texts is that ideology dictates whose lives can be put at risk or preserved.

The Postscript—a brief concluding chapter—brings together the perspectives reached in the individual chapters to speculate on the mosaic of natural and cultural ecologies that emerge in contemporary Asia. It shows how an analysis of South and Southeast Asian cultural and literary productions helps reassess the many ecological perspectives that have emerged in Anglo-American scholarship, especially pertaining to women, the subdominant, and the non-human, offering a (counter) view from the East.

CHAPTER ONE

Colonial, Postcolonial, and Neocolonial Ecologies

❧

> I think the economic logic behind dumping a load of toxic waste in the lowest-wage country is impeccable and we should face up to that . . . I've always thought that countries in Africa are vastly under polluted; their air quality is probably vastly inefficiently low compared to Los Angeles. . . . Just between you and me, shouldn't the World Bank be encouraging more migration of the dirty industries to the Least Developed Countries?
> —Lawrence Summers, confidential World Bank memo, 12 December 1991 (when he was President of World Bank); cited in Nixon, *Slow Violence*

> If you want to awaken all of humanity, then awaken all of yourself. If you want to eliminate the suffering in the world, then eliminate all that is dark and negative in yourself.
> —Lao Tzu

Texts and Contexts

The epigraph, where a World Bank President thinks that shifting "the dirty industries" to less polluted, underdeveloped nations is a clever way of managing toxic waste, opens up many themes central to this chapter. This directly contradicts the tenet by Lao Tzu cited above which, indeed, compares with the famous Biblical aphorism, "Physician, heal thyself." In light of these sentiments, I explore eco-justice issues and highlight the different ways that these texts present Asian ecologies as being preyed upon by global capitalists and Western power bases from the colonial era onwards. I examine ecofictions that present social and natural ecologies at critical historical junctures in some Asian countries, and locate how the agency of women and the subdominant raises the bugle call for action. The treatment of natural environments—jungles, rivers, and the soil itself—these texts reveal, cannot be separated from the ideological and cultural mindsets that surround them. Thus, these narratives meld environmental awareness with national and personal histories, projecting ecofeminist perspectives.

Another significant feature of the texts examined in this chapter is that they engage with what Rob Nixon identifies as "slow violence." This is "a violence that occurs gradually and out of sight, a violence of delayed destruction that is dispersed across time and space, an attritional violence that is typically not viewed as violence at all" (*Slow Violence* 2). Long-term historical occurrences like colonial or neocolonial rule and civil dissensions often bequeath "incremental violence," its "calamitous repercussions playing out across a range of temporal scales" (2). Deforestation, soil acidification, and desertification are only some of the natural catastrophes that are associated with slow violence. Nixon associates these "long dyings" with the "environmentalism of the poor," borrowing the term from Ramachandra Guha (2).

It is well established that the British Empire had a huge impact on the sociopolitics and cultures of Asia. What is less well known is that the Empire also initiated a global ecological moment in world history. As Deepak Kumar et al. observe, "[b]etween 1600 and 1960, through economic expansion, political strategy, military conquest, and territorial control, it held and linked separate lands and varied peoples" (1). This involved major changes in both social and natural ecologies in Asia. Rubber plantations in Malaya, not to mention the planting and harvesting of vast swathes of poppy fields on the Indo-Gangetic Plain, are only two examples of these revolutionary socio-environmental changes.

The classic industrial society as the harbinger of a global modernity came to Asia via colonial rule. In Robert J. C. Young's words, "by the end of the First World War, European or European derived powers controlled or occupied around four-fifths of the globe . . . The domination of western perspectives today is still based on that structure of power, originally developed through the course of European colonial expansion" (*Postcolonialism* 19). Although colonialism—as in the direct control of colonies by European powers—came to an end around the mid-twentieth century in most Asian countries, its influence is enduring. We talk about postcolonial governments and neocolonial regimes. In contemporary Asia, most postcolonial nations, many of them part of the British Commonwealth, largely base their constitution and judiciary on colonial legacies and follow democratic rule. Neocolonial rule, understood as existing in countries where the hierarchical power structures of colonial regimes are replicated in the newly independent nations, has penetrated many Asian countries. The term "neocolonialism" was first coined by Kwame Nkrumah, the first post-independence president of Ghana. Neocolonial regimes use capitalism, globalization, and the local hegemonic class to control the population. In Asia, at least, often there is a considerable overlap between the so-called postcolonial democracies and neocolonial regimes since neocolonial power structures shape both.

The texts examined in this chapter mark important historical events in Asian societies which link imperial and postimperial affects to environmental issues, foregrounding the plight and agency of the powerless. These fictions portray ways in which agentic women and subalterns intervene to make a difference. Thus, the focus is on "the environmentalism of the poor." Nature and its related politics are central concerns in all of them, and are shown to be inextricable from sociopolitics. Though the authors are narrating histories contained within national spaces, these narratives, read together, reveal a chronological yet panoramic cosmopolitan perspective of Asian history by focusing on key historical moments: World War II in *colonial* Malaya (Singapore and Peninsular Malaysia); the civil war of 1980s and 1990s *neocolonial* Sri Lanka; a near civil strife during nation-building efforts in 1970s and 1980s *"postcolonial"* Singapore that divided the country along economic lines (which lingers on), and a conflict over Bauxite mining in feudal, *neocolonial*, rural Pakistan in the early twenty-first century that moves beyond the specific to become representative. This panoramic Asian history is projected from below, where the focalizers are women and/or subalterns, who are tied to local ecologies.

These "histories from the underside"[1] (Alcoff and Mendieta) are concerned with issues of "slow violence": displacement of the marginalized, soil acidification, global capitalism's predatory theft of Asian natural resources (like prawns), denying the subaltern villagers their daily sustenance and, ironically, "modern environmental schemes" that appear to replicate colonial hegemonies. None of these issues is simple. They all present the complex, convoluted sociopolitical and natural environmental problems of contemporary Asia. Overall, the texts promote Homi K. Bhabha's imagining of a cultural space that gives voice to the subalterns and the subdominant other. This "Third Space," to use Edward Soja's phrase (*Thirdspace*) that is also theorized by Bhabha (*The Location of Culture*), acknowledges the hybridity of cultures defying ethnocentric traditions and/or other privileged locations. There is an insistence on the significance of diverse cultural conditions and differentiated historical perspectives that interrogate official histories. Bhabha writes of "the inscription and articulation of culture's hybridity" and of a "Third Space of enunciations," which is a useful lens through which to examine these texts (Ibid. 56). Inevitably, therefore, all four texts focus on the victims of history.

The first of these, the historical fiction *A Different Sky*, is by Meira Chand, a well-known novelist of Swiss-Indian parentage. An author with six previous novels, her multicultural heritage is reflected in her works, which explore issues of identity and cultural dislocation. Set during World War II, *A Different Sky* is probably the first historical fiction to emerge from Singapore. More than Philip Jeyaratnam's novel *Abraham's Promise*, a thinly veiled political satire, or historical accounts by Singapore's first prime minister Lee Kuan Yew such as *From Third World to First* or *The Singapore Story: Memoirs of Lee Kuan Yew*, *A Different Sky* approximates to Sarah Johnson's definition of historical fiction as "set before the middle of the last [20th] century [. . .] in which the author is writing from research rather than personal experience" (S. Johnson 1). It deals with a relatively little explored segment of World War II history: The Southeast Asian war theatre viewed through the eyes of subdominant civilians. The novel begins with the well-documented communist riot of 1927 under British rule and ends with pro-independence rallies during the Malayan emergency in the mid-1950s, framed at both ends by highly tense and volatile political situations. The plot is divided into four parts dealing with significant historical periods. The plotline traces the lives of three families caught up in the turbulent events of the Japanese occupation and the fall of British rule. It is during the communist riots that all the principal players—Rose Burns and her son Howard, of Eurasian descent; Mei Lan, a Chinese girl with her *amah* (nanny), Ah Siew; a young Indian trader, Raj Sherma, and an urbane Chinese entrepreneur, Joseph Ho, come together as passengers seated in a trolley brought to a standstill by angry demonstrators. These characters' fluctuating fortunes during this historical period also tells the Singapore story through the eyes of the disenfranchised.

All Is Burning, a collection of nineteen short stories, is by Jean Arasanayagam, née Solomon, a Dutch-Burgher from Sri Lanka. A well-known poet and author, she has been publishing for over four decades. *All Is Burning* explores the common theme of the ravaging impact of the Sri Lankan civil war on its citizens but with a noticeable difference: that in all the stories, the narrative perspective is consciously non-partisan, never specifying ethnicity, a singular example of Third Space consciousness. Each short story depicts a vignette of life with a variety of protagonists—from a sensitive schoolmaster caught in the cross fire between the Tamils and the Sinhalese, an old woman searching a field of assassinated men for her daughter's young fiancé, a group of illegal Sri Lankan immigrants being smuggled into Germany, and even a mercenary killer on his way to fulfill a "professional assignment"—capturing both cultural and environmental devastation during the long civil war.

The third novel is by Suchen Christine Lim, winner of the inaugural Singapore Literature Prize (1992) and the Southeast Asian Writers Award (2012). *The River's Song* is a sympathetic account of the hardships faced by the "river people," who were forcibly rehoused during the Clean River Campaign of the 1970s and 1980s, an "environmentally friendly" scheme to clean up the much-polluted river and upgrade its banks. The novel focuses on two children, Wong Ping Ping and Wong Fook Weng, who live on the river's banks and whose musical talent unites them. It explores the community of people who live around the river, providing an insight into the social history and privations of a little-known segment of Singapore society that has since been erased from history. The novel opens up two opposing viewpoints. The first is held by "well-intentioned" government officials and corporate visionaries, who feel the need to clean the polluted river. The other is held by the river people, who view this "developmental vision" as an infringement of their rights and a form of neocolonialism. The narrative thus uncovers an epoch in Singapore's national history that reveals the economic fault lines that are still patent.

The final text is by Pakistani-British writer Qaisra Shahraz, a well-known novelist, scriptwriter, and freelance journalist. Her short story, "The Zemindar's Wife," is set in rural Pakistan and investigates the relationship between a feudal lord, his wife, and his vassals. The conflict that arises between them relates to land deeds. The wife strives to protect the land from her husband's mining interests and avarice, which would result in soil acidification and threaten the livelihood of the poor farmers, who grow cash crops in their small farms. She struggles to articulate the destruction she foresees that would wreck both the rural landscape and the traditions of the people. Hence while land conservation becomes a central theme, the narrative simultaneously opens up highly volatile situations in both culture and nature that could potentially destroy the marriage, the community, and the soil.

The texts in this chapter, taken collectively, address a theme that is vital to conceptualizations of the universe from the perspective of dharma. The awareness that everything is linked and needs to be kept in fine balance; also, that human conduct and nature's flow are deeply interconnected. The five great elements or *panchabhūta*s are distinct elaborations of primal energy or *prakṛti*. Seshagiri Rao lists these elements sequentially according to their decreasing subtlety: space (sometimes called ether), air, fire, water, and earth (that is, *ākāsa*, *vāyu*, *tejas*, *ap*, *pṛthvi*). Rao discusses the association between the individual and the cosmic body (25–26). Strong manifestations of these interconnections emerge from these eco-fictions.

I begin by examining *A Different Sky* and *All Is Burning* before proceeding to *A River's Song* and "The Zemindar's Wife" to uncover ways in which these ecologies reinforce both the dharmic, and Avner de-Shalit's, view that sociological and ecological unevenness reinforce each other. The colonial trope that links natives with nature is explored, and also, in two of the texts, the colonial trope of the "unmanageable and evil" tropical jungle is *reworked* to either reverse some colonial perspectives or add new ones. It therefore becomes necessary to first trace and establish these colonial perspectives.

Colonial Tropes of Natives and Jungles

Tropical jungles have long been *ideologically* branded in colonial narratives. The depiction of the tropics as an exotic, albeit hazardous, environment for Europeans began long before the actual conquest of the East. One of the earliest texts from which postcolonial scholars trace colonial attitudes is *The Tempest*. As early as 1818, William Hazlitt in his *Characters of Shakespeare's Plays* argues that Prospero is an imperialist. In the "Introduction" to the Arden edition of *The Tempest*, Frank Kermode points out that the *True Declaration of the State of the Colonie in Virginia* "defends colonizing, on the ground that . . . in any case the natives cannot be regarded as civilized people." It states that "[t]here is no trust in the fidelitie [*sic*] of human beasts" (xxxi). Thus, one of the central aspects of the "trope of the tropics" involves the conflation of natives and animals, and has a hoary past. Throughout the colonial enterprise, these associations, and indeed the "othering" of natives, became even more entrenched.

This conflation, once established within colonial discourse, gave the European colonizers the latitude to denigrate the natives with impunity. Therefore, it is no surprise to come across William Roff's mention of the dismissive attitude to Malays that was prevalent in 1880s. He remarks that the "unregenerate Malay" was a term much favored by Victorian colonial administrators, thus qualifying them for "the assistance and blessings of British rule." In the mid-nineteenth century, the typical Malay state was held to be "manifestly a morass of misrule, inefficiency and social injustice." There was a firmly held belief that probably because of the "enervating climate," Oriental races "were simply incapable of ordering their affairs competently" (Roff xi). "Frederick Weld, spoke for many of his kind when he wrote in 1880: 'I doubt if Asiatics can ever really be taught to govern themselves. Good government seems not to be a plant congenial to the soil'" (xi). These lines explain the ways in which the "enervating" tropical climate and Asian incapacity for self-rule were yoked together in colonial discourse in order to establish colonial rule as a "civilizing mission." It was also couched as a brave and honorable enterprise for Europeans, the heroic course that made for the emergence of an *exemplar virtutis*. In Victorian England, popular "Boys' Own magazines" were full of heroes who dared to venture into the evil tropics on a noble mission. Hence for the colonizers, tropical landscape and accompanying "nature," both human and environmental, are hazardous entities to be tamed and civilized.

Colonial literature is replete with themes of tropical decadence, incorporating both natives and land. Joseph Conrad in "The Lagoon" reveals how the average white, male colonizer routinely made this unconscious link between natives and animals, exposing the racism that informed colonial interactions:

> He [The white man] had known Arsat years ago, in a far country in times of trouble and danger, when no friendship is to be despised. And since his Malay friend had come unexpectedly to dwell in the hut in the lagoon . . . he had slept many times there . . . *He liked the man . . . not so much perhaps as a man likes his favourite dog—but still he liked him well enough to help and ask no questions.* (47; emphasis added)

This association of natives, land, and animals leads imperialists to extrapolate from the perceived feelings of antagonism emanating from the natives to the landscape. Hence, they cognize the land as hostile and malignant.

The idea that jungles and lush rainforests across the sweep of Empire from the Caribbean to Burma appeared symbolic of a malignant force is captured in Jean Rhys' novel *Wide Sargasso Sea*, in the way the unnamed male "hero," nominally Rochester, the quintessential Victorian, patriarchal, protagonist of Charlotte Brontë's *Jane Eyre*, responds to the lush Jamaican landscape. His words to Antoinette encapsulate the misgivings of the imperial subject unused to the tropical landscape. "I feel very much a stranger here . . . I feel that this place is my enemy and on your side" (45). Earlier he exclaims, "What an extreme green!" (39) and records his ennui, which he blames on the landscape: "Everything is too much. I felt as I rode wearily after her. Too much blue, too much purple, too much green. The flowers too red, the mountains too high, the hills too near . . ." (39). The colonial self's cultural alienation is projected onto the land. The confusions that were rife in the minds of even the more thoughtful of imperial subjects is spelt out by George Orwell in his short narrative "Shooting an Elephant." Here, the first-person narrator records his regret at being "coerced" into shooting an elephant, which had killed an Indian coolie while it was "in must" but was no longer dangerous. The protagonist was "forced" to kill it only in order to preserve, before a crowd of natives, the imperialist image of "being in charge." The British officer's confusions are made visible. He affirms that despite knowing that "imperialism was an evil thing," he could "get nothing into perspective." With one part of his mind, he thought of the British Raj as "an unbreakable tyranny" but with another part, he felt that "the greatest joy in the world would be to drive a bayonet into a Buddhist priest's guts." He confesses that "(f)eelings like these are the normal by-products of imperialism; ask any Anglo-Indian official, if you can catch him off duty." The tale reveals that colonial guilt can often transform into violence against animals and natives. Characteristic colonial attitudes are revealed in the words of the younger British officials, who, commenting on the incident, later exclaim that "it was a damn shame to shoot an elephant for killing a coolie, because an elephant was worth more than any damn Coringhee [Indian] coolie."

Val Plumwood and other ecofeminist scholars argue that the definition of the "human" in Western culture is predicated on the presence of the non-human, the uncivilized, and the animalistic. This civilized/savage binary entrenched in the colonial enterprise was augmented and justified by cognizing non-European lands as spaces unused, underused, or empty, dismissing the people and animals that inhabited them as non-entities ("Decolonising Relationships with Nature" 53). As a result, violence against them was not only legitimized but rationalized. Thus, in colonial ideology, "Eurocentrism," that othered non-European lands and their inhabitants, and "anthropocentrism," that othered all non-human species, were linked.

In a similar vein, Doris Lessing, in her insightful fiction "Old Chief Mshlanga," which probes the cultural arrogance that prevents the white child from breaching the social gap with Africans, shows how, to the girl, a tall African mountain feels like a looming threat to her personhood. Lessing explores how colonial guilt is projected onto the landscape, which is associated with the natives and experienced as malignant: a threat to the imperial race.

Sharae Deckard elaborates on these troubling literary tropes that are recurrent images in Sri Lankan colonial and postcolonial texts, and which are then imprinted on the nation's eco-imaginary (32–48). For instance, in Leonard Woolf's *Village in the Jungle* set in colonial Ceylon, the narrator declares unequivocally, "All jungles are evil but no jungle is more evil than that which lay about the village of Bedagama" (40). As Deckard observes, "the rainforest is personified as a metaphysical force" (36). The fecundity of the forest itself becomes a threat to the village: "The jungle surrounded it, overhung it, continually pressed upon it. It stood at the door of the houses, always ready to press in upon the compounds and open spaces, to break through the mud huts, and to choke up the tracks and paths" (Woolf 39). In "The East Coast," Hugh Clifford registers a similar sense of oppression as emanating from the Malayan rain forests: "The air 'hangs heavy as remembered sin', and the gloom of a great cathedral is on every side. Everything is damp, and moist and oppressive. The soil, and the cool dead leaves underfoot are dank with decay, and sodden to the touch" (16-17). It is uncanny how, despite the vast spread of the Empire, jungles, whether in Jamaica, Malaya, or Ceylon, seem to incite fear in the white male, reducing the natural world to an ideological theatre. In "Lagoon," which is set in the Malay Peninsula, Conrad's omniscient narrator trails the white hero traversing the forests in a boat steered by natives. In an interesting deployment of "pathetic fallacy," the menace and oppression of the jungle foreshadow the dark events to follow. "Immense trees soared up, invisible behind the festooned draperies of creepers." Nearby is "the glistening blackness of the water" and "a twisted root of some tall tree" which is "black and dull, writhing and motionless, like an arrested snake." We are told: "Darkness oozed out from between the trees, through the tangled maze of the creepers, from behind the great fantastic and unstirring leaves; the darkness, mysterious and invincible; the darkness scented and poisonous of impenetrable forests" (44). Many of these descriptions of geographical spaces with repetitive use of words like "blackness," "darkness," "sombre," "black and dull" are suffused with ideological undertones. As Deckard points out, these ideas were often used by colonial regimes "to justify the eradication of the rainforest" and its "lethal miasmas" (34). This is also the reason why the forests and wilderness are heavily *gendered*. In colonial texts, the wilderness is an almost exclusively male domain. Man is the master of the wilderness, wielding his power over it, subjugating it, meeting its dangers with courage and determination. There are no white women in the jungles. The only women are natives, who, unlike white women, are conflated with the wilderness.

The natural landscape in many parts of the Empire was radically altered through the centuries. Amitav Ghosh's *Sea of Poppies*, which narrates the ecological damage caused to the Indo-Gangetic Plain when the East India Company forced the cultivation of poppies and prohibited that of food crops, a policy continued by the British Crown, and Romesh Gunasekara's investigation into the ecological crisis precipitated by coral mining in *Reef*, are only two examples of narratives that record the end result of colonial and neocolonial reordering and exploitation of natural landscapes. Natives and nature are mere resources necessary to undergird Western modernity. Ulrich Beck et al. observe that a distinct characteristic of industrialized modernity is that nature is seen as separate from society and an instrumental view reduces it to a resource. Also, rationality becomes a monopoly of science and is primarily used to exercise power over nature (4). The white man's alienation from nature led to many problems, which we will examine below.

Jungles and Civic Spaces in Singapore and Sri Lanka

Tracing colonial ideologies is necessary for comparing how jungles and civic spaces are presented in *A Different Sky* and *All Is Burning*. One repetitive theme that emerges in both texts is the extensive deforestation caused by overpopulation. Hence, in "Sand Serpents" (*All Is Burning*), the maid, returning home to her beloved Sri Lanka from Doha, indulges in a nostalgic description, which encapsulates this theme:

> It was very different in the past . . . the jungles full of bear, deer, leopard. The thalagoyas, the giant lizards, used to crawl into the garden at night and the jungle cocks would crow in the garden . . . The jungle was close to the property but it has now been cleared and the animals have had to go far into what's left of the jungle. (54)

Interestingly, both texts blur entrenched colonial binaries. *A Different Sky* displays an awareness of colonial attitudes and as historical fiction, at times, even deliberately reenacts them. However, its overarching postcolonial perspective adds a subversive dimension to these colonial reenactments. *All Is Burning*, set in civil war-torn Sri Lanka, explores neocolonial predicaments. Thus, colonial tropes are interestingly refracted in altered ways.

One telling difference between colonial texts and these novels is that the forests are described by central characters who are Asian and have been positioned, through colonial and neocolonial histories, *on the opposite side of the power equation* as victims. In *A Different Sky*, almost all the characters who contribute to the story of Singapore are disenfranchised, whether it is Rose Burns, who is driven out from her lodging-house by Japanese soldiers; her son, Howard, who, as Eurasian, realizes that he exists in the margins of both British and Asian societies; Raj, the Indian trader, who acts as a middleman between the Japanese and the Chinese; or Leila, his illiterate sister. Even Mei Lan, from a wealthy Chinese family, we discover, is vulnerable both politically and in her personal life, with a mother married to an adulterous man, her father, who cares little for her, while her footbound grandmother with her gangrenous feet has to be carried around like a baby.

Ironically, Mei Lan's impoverished maid, her *amah* Ah Siew, appears stronger than these wealthy women. Ah Siew had refused the first or second obeying, namely to a father or husband, respectively. Instead, having taken a vow to Kuan Yin, the Goddess of Mercy, to abjure men, she has formed a sisterhood with other like-minded women, who remain single. They have undergone the age-old *sor-hei*, the "comb-up" ceremony, which is akin to a wedding. Ah Siew explains to a young Mei Lan, "[W]e sisters are married to each other and our work" (Chand 31). These are the subdominant characters from whose perspective history unfolds. They do not have the luxury of sheltering behind illusions, and neither are they blinded by power.

This is the key difference between the British officers and the Eurasian, Howard Burns, or his brother-in-law, Wilfred Patterson, a journalist who, though white, is in touch with Asians, bred among them, and married to one. When Captain Jenkins comments nonchalantly that there is "[n]o need to worry—those Japs have only ever fought the Chinese. If they come up against British steel, I predict they will fall flat on their faces" (173), Wilfred realizes that this patronizing attitude toward the natives has considerably compromised British war preparations. When Wilfred points out that a "Japanese Zero aircraft is far in advance of the British Brewster Buffaloes," Jenkins scoffs at him (173). Shortly after, across the water a short distance away, Wilfred sees the Malay Peninsula. "As he surveyed the empty beach, Wilfred was filled with unease. He saw that these northern Singapore beaches lay open to attack; no pillboxes, guns or landmines, no searchlights—not even the deterrent of barbed wire stood as fortification against an enemy landing" (Chand 177). Wilfred realizes that Singapore is not the impregnable fortress that the British fondly believe it to be. He remembers his interview with Brigadier Simson, who, to the annoyance of Jenkins's "top brass," held an opinion contrary to all others. Simson declares unequivocally: "In my view the jungle is not impassable for determined infantry, even during the monsoon. Our troops are not trained for jungle warfare, nor do we possess any tanks, for they are not thought to be necessary. Any defenses we have are built entirely to meet a seaward attack" (177). When the main Japanese force moved rapidly down the western flank of Malaya on "motorized" cycles and bicycles, using the narrow footpaths of the rubber plantations, it took the British completely by surprise. The Allied troops, mainly British and poorly trained, lacking in experience and equipment, were forced to retreat. In less than two months, the Japanese had eliminated British naval and air capabilities, and captured Malaya.[2] The "male power fantasy," to use Edward W. Said's phrase (207), conceptually distanced European males from nature. *A Different Sky* reveals how these perspectives led to the decimation of Singapore. There is no greater testament to the white man's alienation from his land and the "natives" than this historic defeat that is labelled "the fall of Singapore."

Howard, conscripted to fight against the Japanese, is badly wounded. He regains consciousness to find that he is in the dense jungle being cared for by a Malay couple, Ayesha and Abdulla, who inform him of the Japanese invasion of Singapore. It is ironic but entirely fitting that, sheltered in the "peace" of the forest, Howard fears going back to his house in the city. "Fireflies lit up the trees, while the moon shed its empty light on the dark jungle, illuminating the shapes of flitting bats. The night was noisy with crickets. Howard absorbed the peace with some unease, aware of how near the violent reality the war really was" (Chand 211). The colonial tropes of the "malign jungle" and the "safe city" are completely reversed and the hierarchical dualism of culture/nature is turned on its head.

Indeed, a sardonic acknowledgement of imperial binaries of "savage/civilized" forms the leitmotif against which historical events unfold in Chand's novel. The description of the neighboring houses of Howard and Mei Lan—the two central characters—mimics and mocks this entrenched imperial trope. Bougainvillaea House, that belonged to Howard's family, "had been left half wild with papaya trees, mango, wild orchid, spider lilies and an abundance of the bougainvillaea after which the house was named . . . At the back was a wide storm canal that channelled torrential rain and prevented flooding" (71). In contrast, Mei Lan's "Lim Villa" is ferociously ordered by "an army of gardeners" (71). Chand positions cultivated landscapes and wild vegetation antithetically, and this opposition is later extrapolated to the whole cityscape of Singapore during the Japanese occupation in contrast to the dense jungles that exist just beyond its boundary.

"Singapore had become a vegetable garden: the slogan everywhere was GROW MORE FOOD" (271; emphasis in original). This trope is meant to ironically satirize the colonial binary, for "civilized" European nations were, paradoxically, the harbingers of the greatest barbarity to Asia through the world wars.[3]

In Japanese-occupied Singapore, nature remains an equally contested site, paradoxically existing as *unheimlich* space, as exterior and separate but also as refuge. We are told that "[t]he Japanese were constantly searching for guerrilla camps in the jungle and the campers lived in perpetual risk of an attack, alert to every crack of a falling branch, every rustle of a passing animal" (282). Howard is aware that he is watched by the communist leader Wee Jack and his men, and realizes that they see him "as soft, indulged and decadent and that they are waiting to deride him, to break him down" (282). For them, Howard appears to be an example of Theodore Roosevelt's "overcivilized man, who has lost the great fighting masterful virtues" (150). When Brokentooth, a stooge of Wee Jack, leads Howard in a boat to the communist camp in the jungle, Howard "was sweating profusely, and his limbs, covered by insect bites, itched unbearably" (Chand 277). The essential inhospitableness of the forest—his refuge from the punitive Japanese army—is brought home to him in no uncertain terms. "[H]e saw the black leeches clinging to his legs, fat slugs the size of his thumb, bloated with his blood" (278). "Mosquitoes kept their distance while the fire smoked, but when it died down and they lay in the hut, the insects swarmed viciously about them" (279). The perils of the jungles are overwhelming: "Wee Jack had several suppurating jungle sores on his arms and legs" (280). Also, Howard had learned from his sister Cynthia, a nurse, about the ailments of the jungle, "malaria, beriberi, scabies and other uncomfortable skin diseases . . . Howard examined everyone and saw that without exception all of them had malaria, besides a variety of other afflictions" (283). But these tribulations are real, not ideological, and to be expected. Not so the perils of the city.

In World War II Singapore, civic spaces are ruled by "jungle laws" that make them more terrifying than the tropical forests. It is deeply ironic that this "vegetable-garden city" where the wilderness has been tamed (271) is also the scene of human carnage, where men are shot without reason, and their heads, stuck on poles, are left by the roadside for passersby to view. It is also not just the Japanese who resort to savagery. Factions within the city resort to mindless violence in the name of self-preservation. All residents, regardless of race, are shown to engage in inhuman acts. It is no wonder that Wee Jack is adamant in believing that "[t]he jungle protects us" (262). The carefully preserved culture/nature dualism unravels along with colonial rule.

Neat binaries that hold jungles and gardens distinct from each other also fall apart in Arasanayagam's *All Is Burning*. Jungles are infinitely preferable to the distraught citizens in civil war-torn Sri Lanka.

It was a time of crisis and as they had done before, the villagers, with mats, pots of water, some food and a few of their precious belongings, took refuge in the jungles at night. In spite of the snakes and death from their venom, they preferred this uncertain safety. (31)

Repeatedly, we see that human violence overrides the dangers of the jungles. For example, in "The Journey," the lone Sinhala male in a group of Tamil illegal refugees, treks through the Grunewald forest, attempting to enter unnoticed into Berlin (Germany) in the thick of night: "The trees are silent and watchful sentinels. Yet they offer us protection too. Oak, Birch. Beech. Pines" (2). Unlike colonial fictions, here it is not the jungle that is seen as the malign force but humans, with their power to imprison, torture, and deport refugees. Thus, malign nature versus benign culture does not hold much meaning in the midst of the intense risk of discovery and repatriation they face as a group.

At this point, it is worth noting the differences that emerge between colonial depictions of the natural world (as discussed above) and these Asian fictions by women. In the former, nature is painted *ideologically* whereas in these narratives, the brutality of nature, though acknowledged, is aligned with reality. Second, in colonial literature, forests are a malignant force to be tamed and conquered. Here, forests are often a feared and respected ally that offer refuge when human society becomes unendurable. Furthermore, here nature cannot be separated from culture; the one feeds into the other. These resonate with the concept of dharma, which drives the idea that the spiritual and the material, the abstract and the concrete, human conduct and universal stability, are all interconnected.

Therefore, non-human ecology is also co-opted into human drama in "I am an Innocent Man," where the schoolmaster, Das, cycling down a lonely road, observes his surroundings and feels that the clamor for survival is pervasive:

The mangroves flourish and grow dense and dark, a thick screen of leaves and succulent stems swollen with water. Their aerial roots grow and spread above the surface of the lagoon as if struggling to reach the light and breathe the air. A wild tangle of thick, rope-like roots traps the sediment that flows from the water . . . Small armoured steel-grey crabs scuttle about in the rich mud. And in turn, all these forms of life are prey to water snakes and iguanas. (Arasanayagam 28)

Here nature (read non-humans) and humans become competitors for survival. The idea feeds into Alan Weisman's rueful sentiments expressed in *The World without Us,* when he speculates that were the human species to become extinct, perhaps nature would "heave a huge biological sigh of relief" (3–5). Indeed, at

Wee Jack's communist camp, Howard dispassionately observes the constant strife between him and Wee Jack, who fears his education and detests the liberalism he advocates. He finds this enmity ironic when it is the jungle that is their current foe, with its potential to destroy their health and life. Thus, humans are pitted against each other and against "nature." A telling image brings this truth home to the readers. While at his cousin Lionel's house, Howard recalls "staring silently at a swollen body washed up under the palms. The man's hands were tied behind his back, sharks had savaged his torso and a bullet hole scarred his forehead" (Chand 254). The corpse, ravaged by both man and nature, and bearing the imprint of deliberate human malevolence as well as nature's involuntary molestation, both antagonistic forces, is truly emblematic of the perennial power struggle.

Therefore, nature and culture cannot be disentangled. Howard's cultural moorings are shown to dictate his response to the jungle. As a dark-skinned Eurasian, Howard is a liminal figure. An early incident clearly signals his racial and social marginality, where even spending a day with his father, Charles Burns, at the "Great World Amusement Park" opens him up to abuse. Father and son wend their way to a lavatory. Inside, as Howard follows his light-skinned father to the urinals, a tall Englishman turns around and looks past the Caucasian-looking Charles, his eyes alighting on Howard. Stepping forward with a frown and grasping Howard by the scruff of the neck, he begins to shout, "You are not allowed in here, you dark-skinned rascal. If you were older, I'd call the police." Shocked by the sudden attack, Howard cowers in terror. The man, dragging Howard roughly forward, ejects him brutally into the din and racket of *Great World*. When Howard turns in mute appeal to his father, "Charlie Burns stood rigid at the urinal, his face turned away, his eyes on the wall before him and uttered not a word" (18).

His father's betrayal scars Howard deeply and a feeling of solitariness dogs him all his life. As an adult, he is intensely aware of the disparity between the treatment of British subjects and that meted out to colonized underdogs like himself. The condescension that is shown by Europeans to his mother, the poverty that makes it impossible for him to pursue his studies, and his direct encounter with discrimination at work, all result in a heightened awareness of the social injustice of the colonial order. The many incidents featured in the narrative always position Howard as decentered from power and hovering in the margins. After the fall of Singapore, when Howard seeks refuge in the jungle at Wee Jack's communist camp, his Eurasian roots are treated with suspicion by the other Asians. The cerebral Howard, unable to bear the hardships of the jungle, becomes an alien there too. Thus, the feeling of *unheimlich* dogs him in both the civic space of the city and in the jungle.

In another, equally significant narrative movement, the female focalizer, Mei Lan, begins life as the heiress and legatee of a Chinese dynastic family. But she becomes conscious of the many constraints facing Chinese women and rebels against them from an early age. Mei Lan's family is killed by the Japanese for supporting the China Relief Fund. Mei Lan is imprisoned, tortured, and repeatedly raped by Japanese soldiers. The angst-ridden Howard, harboring a sense of "un-belonging," and the traumatized Mei Lan, who were originally neighbors, form a natural alliance. Later, Mei Lan becomes an active figure in transforming the social lives of the troubled women of the newly emerging republic. As a lawyer, she fights for their rights, challenging polygamy—relatively common at that time—and sheltering the battered wives. Though herself a victim, she fights for other victims of abuse. In making these powerless characters the main focalizers, Chand echoes Walter Benjamin's sentiments: "Not man or men but the struggling oppressed class itself is the depository of historical knowledge" (xii, 260).

Curiously, however, even courageous women like Mei Lan or Cynthia never operate outside the city. There is no mention of women who reside in the jungle camp except for shadowy "serving women" in the background. It appears that Wee Jack's communist egalitarianism stops short of gender equality. This exclusion creates a literary topos that aligns these sections of *A Different Sky* to the "American Western" genre. As ecofeminists point out, this quintessentially "male genre" works on certain sublimated assumptions that ally woman to nature, unproblematically bestowing "success" on the man who subordinates both. In such narratives, "man" emerges as the (only) agent of change. This trope is entirely predictable given *A Different Sky's* colonial setting because, as postcolonial critics like Anne McClintock have discussed, colonial powers both feminized and eroticized the tropics, constructing the "pornotropics" with the male as the sole master (22). Thus, nature and women were both eroticized and considered legitimately exploitable.

This segregation of sexes is *not* identifiable in the titular story of *All Is Burning*. This story opens with Alice, a single mother, who has raised her daughter, Seela, by working as a maid with dreams of resting in her old age, her labors done. One terrible night, after every man in their village has been dragged out and shot dead by guerrillas seeking out informers, she goes out to search for Sena, her daughter's fiancé, in the faint hope that he might still be alive. Nature, as always, is impersonal to human activities. Earth's diurnal rhythm bringing light and darkness becomes useful to the killers: since they had stopped at the entrance to the village, "*the darkness had moved like an open door to admit them. And they had entered*" (Arasanayagam 169).

Alice's walk through the "valley of death" emphasizes the ephemeral nature of human life and parallels its casual annihilation to the gradual destruction of the planet. Her fortitude as a victim is contrasted with the ruthlessness of the warmongers, and ironically also with the dispassion of nature. The stoicism of the Asian woman as subaltern is foregrounded through her. Paradoxically, though, one cannot escape the fact that in both *A Different Sky* and *All Is Burning*, Asians, whether Japanese or Sri Lankan, are portrayed as violent and barbaric. There is verisimilitude in these depictions. But the question may arise as to whether these writers, unconsciously and/or unintentionally, are reifying the colonial trope of the "savage native." But a careful examination of the texts will disabuse us of this idea since the insistence is on how these people's lives have been *systematically mis/directed and oppressed by hegemonic forces*, thus pushing for a strong ecojustice awareness to emerge. In *A Different Sky*, both the Japanese and the British are primarily identified as colonizing forces; they are bracketed together, overriding their racial identity. As events unfold, the cultural space of the island city is rendered passive through repeated conquests and it emerges as dormant, where imperialism and racism are practiced. In *All Is Burning*, neocolonial forces, driven by global capital's profiteering schemes, whether through arms sales or other rapacious ventures, are shown to prey on vulnerable Asians, driving them to extreme violence. Hence these texts offer sociohistorical explanations for both the construction and/or the dismantling of the civilized/savage binaries that abound in colonial and neocolonial descriptions.

The context therefore becomes all-important. For example, anchoring "All Is Burning," the titular story, to its social and religious context enables some peculiarly empowering Asian insights to emerge. Its epigraph is a famous passage from the Buddha's *Fire Sermon*:

> Bhikkus, all is burning. And what is the all that is burning? Bhikkus, the eye is burning, visible forms are burning, visual consciousness is burning, visual impression is burning ... Burning with what? Burning with the fire of lust, with the fire of hate, with the fire of delusion; I say it is burning with birth, ageing and death, with sorrows, with lamentations, with pains, with griefs, with despairs. (Arasanayagam 166)

The Buddha refers to the inner fires that feed our negative drives and emotions. The passage below ironically echoes the sermon while referring to fires caused by the civil war:

> The country was on fire. Everything was on fire. All was burning, burning. Yes, the fires were burning. Fires that burnt down the huts. These and hundreds of other villages burning. The Self burning. The unconscious, the visual impressions, burning. The fire of lust and hate, the fire of delusion. (Arasanayagam 169)

In contrast to the *Fire Sermon*, which focuses on the spiritual inner fires that discipline the *atman* (Self, which loosely approximates to the Christian "soul"), the fires that rampage the land cause widespread environmental devastation. This reference to two different kinds of fires—one referring to the effacement of human ego and the other caused by it—creates a deliberate dissonance and hints at the fundamental failure of religion to regulate human conduct and, by extension, civic society. The shift from "*ego*-centric" to "*eco*-centric" that ecologists urge is the way forward, has clearly not come to pass.

Furthermore, the characters play into Eastern philosophical visions like *Sāṃkhya*, which is foundational to Buddhism and one of the six schools of philosophy in Hinduism[4] and is discussed in the Introduction. Alice can be read as *prakṛti*, the feminine principle in *Sāṃkhya*, and is also equated to nature and understood as the elemental power of the manifest world. In *Sāṃkhya*'s dualistic vision, *prakṛti* supports the evolution of *puruṣa*, the masculine principle, which is understood as the *atman* (human soul, Self), to evolve in its path of self-realization to attain *nirvana* or *mokṣa*. In this view, *nature is agentic*, working to save the lost, rudderless *atman* (human self). According to *Sāṃkhya*, the *atman*'s only teacher is nature (*prakṛti*) and the material world associated with it.

Alice's death walk, and a dying man's final words requesting water, mistaking her for his mother, symbolically make her the embodiment of *prakṛti* or Bhooma Devi (Mother Earth) and allied to nature in *agentic* ways. Alice's words near the end of the story, conflating myth, religion, and her predicament further associates her with *prakṛti*. "When can I ever complete this journey? Yama [Hindu and Buddhist God of Death] told me—somewhere—that this is my first journey into the darkness of the underworld" (174–75). Acknowledging this Asian philosophical association highlights ways in which connecting women with nature—despite the legitimate problems identified in Western ecofeminist theory with such associations that render women passive—can be parsed in ways that create *agency* for the woman, countering mainstream perceptions. Also, identifying this symbolism takes nothing away from Alice's actual achievements and stoicism. So, when she remarks, "What can a village do without all its men? We will have to take their place now, we women" (175), she speaks as both *prakṛti (*nature*)* and Alice (woman), and she speaks to a nature and a culture that is disintegrating. Once again, indisputable nature/culture entanglements emerge. Thus, Chand and Arasanayagam's narratives echo Upamanyu Pablo Mukherjee's conviction on the importance of viewing politics and environment, nature and culture as necessarily and mutually interpenetrated, eschewing the still entrenched dogma that sees human politics as a part of the cultural world and the environment as being synonymous with "nature" ("Arundhati Roy" 18).

All Is Burning persuades us that social and environmental justice are equally, deeply enmeshed. In "I am an Innocent Man," Das ponders if silently and helplessly witnessing cruelty makes one complicit in the crime. Not only is the vulnerability of members of subdominant groups highlighted, but their suffering in the face of a predatory environmental colonialism cannot be overstated. As he cycles past the recently hatched prawn farms in his village the teacher realizes that, to the foreign investors, "the prawns appeared to have an even greater price than that placed on human life. They were being reared for profit" (Arasanayagam 23). This becomes a classic instance of the ways in which global capitalism can indulge in not just political and economic but also environmental colonizing. The emergence of vast stretches of prawn ponds that are fenced in and guarded by guerrilla groups, cutting off villagers from their traditional sources of sustenance, leads to complaints and deaths that bring in the army, resulting in a civil war in the village that decimates the hapless villagers. The similarity between the views of several erstwhile colonizers and the neocolonials—the corporate warlords—who *both* appear to devalue native life, appears to be stark.

Ecological justice issues are prioritized. The prawns that for centuries had flourished in the communal ponds are privatized overnight and are now the property of wealthy global capitalists. Guerrillas have been hired to guard them from locals who are branded "thieves" if they attempt to net the prawns for their daily meal: a vivid example of the ecological imperialism that Vandana Shiva and Andrew Ross label "biopiracy" and "planetary management," in which ecological riches are mined and managed for self-serving ends by the global elite. Das's description of the prawn farms graphically illustrates this idea of predation: "[. . .] there was this feeling that the ponds were seething, alive, and that the prawns were trapped in their aquatic prisons from which they could not escape until they grew large enough to be caught, netted, packed and sent away to titillate the appetites of the wealthy gourmets . . ." (Arasanayagam 22–23). Both the prawns and the villagers are exploited by global capital. Nature, animals, racial and gendered "others" are in permanent service to wealthy humans on a planet that is teeming with conflict. The arrogant insularity of global capitalists causes widespread ecological destruction. The prawn farms symbolize not only the success of the projects of global capital, but also of the devolution of post-independence Sri Lanka, hailed the "pearl in the Indian Ocean," the "Venice of the East" before the civil war, and its steady descent into chaos.

Das' "dispassionate" rhetoric recounting trauma is symptomatic of his shocked state of mind. His observations are clinical: just as the prawns are "caught, netted, packed and sent away," the prawn stealers, the villagers, are also "caught, beaten up, even killed" (22–23). The capitalists' merciless treatment of the prawns parallels the military's dehumanizing treatment of the villagers. Like "wily prawns," the guerrillas slip away. As the war escalates, the prawn farms are neglected. Again, Das perceives the similarities growing between prawn and human habitats:

> No one would come to net the prawns for a long time now and they would grow and procreate in their underwater world . . . They would crowd the ponds and jostle each other as their numbers grew and soon, perhaps, they too would begin to war against one another and turn cannibalistic as the space that contained them became small. (Arasanayagam 36)

This encapsulates Nixon's views about "the environmentalism of the poor," because "slow violence" neglects the long-term needs of both subalterns and non-humans. The metaphors of concealment and violence described in the passage yoke human and crustacean predicaments together.

The "cannibalism" of man's ruthlessness against man is also exposed in "Man without a Mask," where a mercenary narrates his next killing mission. Interestingly, his impersonal killings are directly proportional to his distance from nature.

> I'm given orders to silence a voice . . . I want to dwell in a vast and endless space where a landscape will have no impediments. Cascading waterfalls, rivers rushing headlong in spate, a sky rent apart by tissues of lightening, a dull boom of thunder—all this would lead to a disturbance of the mind. My world would be uniformly grey, silent . . . No echoes. (99)

There is no sense of guilt in the mercenary killer. His amoral attitude is not dissimilar to human attitudes to the non-human world, while what distinguishes Das is precisely his capacity to feel guilt and anxiety. Das then becomes the lonely surviving voice that cognizes guilt. His reiterative statement, "I am an innocent man" (27), repeated with escalating nervousness, in fact, paradoxically serves to increase his feelings of guilt. His intermittent query, "And where do I fit in?" (27) is a search for a space untainted by guilt, which he discovers does not exist. His assertion that he is not "a terrorist, or a militant, or a guerrilla" (27), his active distance from global capitalists and gourmet consumers, all of whom he groups under one accusing label as the perpetrators of violence, reveals the sad fact that few humans escape all these categories. Hence his unceasing attempt to reify the binaries between innocence and guilt, predator and prey actually serves to muddle them, showing that there is no escape from taint. The very title of the book, *All Is Burning*, brackets together socioreligious culpabilities and ecological devastation. It also captures the enduring misery in "the environmentalism of the poor" and points to the fact that in the face of abject penury, eco-justice parameters need to be stretched.

Thus, in recounting human wars in Singapore and Sri Lanka, both authors force us to reflect on social and natural ecologies and their interconnections. They demonstrate how nature and culture are endlessly intertwined in both colonial and neocolonial regimes. They raise pressing eco-justice questions and point to the consequences of irresponsible environmentalism. They leave us with the message that inaction with regard to our ecological and cultural perils equates to culpability.

The ensuing text, set in postcolonial Singapore, demonstrates how even so-called "responsible environmentalism" can be perceived as a form of colonization, which impacts the poor.

The Environment versus Subalterns in Postcolonial Singapore: *The River's Song*

Suchen Christine Lim's novel *The River's Song* opens up a historical moment that ties in with environmental management, when "well-intentioned" national developmental schemes can be perceived as harmful by subsistence-based communities. It focuses on the Clean River Campaign of Singapore of the 1970s and 1980s, passionately pleading the cause of the "river people." The book describes a complicated moment in Singapore's national history where political risk, environmental hazard, and eco-justice issues are enmeshed in ways that Molly Wallace believes is typical in contemporary "post-industrial" societies which habitually and inadvertently generate hazards that we can neither imagine nor control (31).

In ecological disputes around the globe binaries appear, which place governments on one side and committed environmental activists on the other. Rebecca Solnit, in *Hope in the Dark: Untold Histories, Wild Possibilities,* remarks that, "The United States is the most disproportionate producer of global warming, governed by the most disregarding administration" (11). Such clearly marked dichotomies between governments and activists are easily understood and the lines of divisions are plainly drawn. *The River's Song*, however, depicts a political situation of 1970s Singapore where the government promotes an environmental cleanup, while the river people resent the interference in their lives. The situation is far from simple.

Lim narrates how the terrible hardships faced by nearly 5,000 river people—those dependent on the river in various ways, who were forcibly evicted from the river and rehoused from 1977–87—inspired her to write this novel. She calls them the "unsung heroes" of Singapore. In an interview with Damyanti Biswas she remarks:

> The image of a wiry, bare-chested, sun-browned man crouched among his pots of wilting chilli plants, his lost and vacant eyes gazing through the railings of a 12-storey apartment block, had haunted me for a long time. This memory of a squatter farmer evicted from the Singapore River in the 1970s led me to write *The River's Song*. (Biswas)

Lim's advocacy on behalf of the "River People" places her in the category of Nixon's "combative writers," whose works focus on the "environmentalism of the poor" (Nixon, *Slow Violence* 5). The narrative describes the suffering faced by the river people during the "clean river campaign." All the central characters who are vivid, sensitive, and appealing are part of the river community, while the government personnel are distant, impersonal, and appear unfeeling and patronizing with little or no understanding of the way of life they are destroying. They are similar to the British colonial administrator who, after butchering Nigerians, writes about *The Pacification of the Primitive Tribes of the Lower Niger* that Chinua Achebe satirizes in *Things Fall Apart*. Like the imperialists, the government is shown to take recourse to a position which, as Judith Butler observes, places these powerful blocs "beyond the play of power, and which seeks to establish the metapolitical basis for a negotiation of power relations." Here the metapolitics revolves around environmental sanitation. Butler believes metapolitical positioning is "perhaps the most insidious ruse of power" (6). Paradoxically, even as the surface text draws our sympathies toward the sad plight of the displaced river people, the subtext points to the risks of ignoring what historian Dipesh Chakrabarty points out as the ineluctable fact that "humans are [now] a force of nature in the geological sense" (206). Or, as Naomi Oreskes clarifies: "To deny that global warming is real is precisely to deny that humans have become geological agents, changing the most basic physical processes of the earth" (73, 74). Therefore, the text, even as it raises the political and social issue of the displacement of the river people, also simultaneously projects the larger issues of environmental hazards and a planet at risk.

The novel's central focalizers are Ping and Weng, two children living in squalor in Singapore's Chinatown. The central thread of the plot traces Ping's childhood friendship and, later, her mature love for Weng. This is social history narrated from the underside, stressing the heterogeneity of a world order that always/already privileges the status quo. It can also be read as "protest literature" that challenges the superior claims of what Wolfgang Sachs terms a "global ecocracy," whose environmental management relies on methods of control that devalue the rights and opinions of subsistence-based local communities.

The dialectics of *The River's Song* revolves around a problem and defining historical moment, tracing a sociopolitical, economy-centered environmental problem that occurs as the city-state is transforming into a modern metropolis. The central characters are all subalterns or members of subdominant groups. Weng, the son of a pipa[5] master, has lost his mother and now lives with his father, stepmother, and stepsisters as one of the "boat people" along the "polluted" Singapore River. Ping's mother Yoke-Lan, through her grit and determination, elevates her status from being the mistress of an effete older man to marrying "respectably." Ping, however, lives as the unacknowledged (because illegitimate) daughter in the margins of her mother's life. Moreover, Ping's dusky complexion also belies her half-Indian heritage. At first abandoned by her mother who moves to Hong Kong, Ping is befriended by Weng. Together the two children roam the streets selling vegetables. Later, beckoned to her mother's new home, Ping is forced to address her mother by the kinship term Ah Ku, meaning "paternal aunt." She is precluded from getting close to her kindly stepfather by her mother's suspicion and jealousy. But interestingly, businesses resembling Ping's stepfather's shipping conglomerate are the ones allied with the government and pitted against the river people.

Therefore, the dialogic heart of the novel opens up the environmental question and the impassioned debate at its center. It foregrounds what Nixon terms "attritional distress" (*Slow Violence* 5) in the environments of the poor. For the government, the river is a precious national resource. From the corporate perspective as well, the mission to clean the Singapore River is necessary and the project is welcomed both as an environmentally and economically sound venture. The prologue quotes the official statement plucked from a *Straits Times* report: "Today the Prime Minister had declared his Clean River Campaign a success. Ten thousand tons of flotsam and jetsam, two thousand tons of rubbish and forty-one thousand cubic meters of putrid mud had been removed from this river, along with the squatters and hawkers" (Lim 12). This statement highlights two contentious aspects of this governmental scheme, namely, the cavalier bracketing of humans ("squatters and hawkers") with "rubbish and putrid mud" and the contrary effect of statistical data on the masses, a problem that has been identified by Scott Slovic and Paul Slovic as pervasive, especially in relation to environmental risks.

In their edited volume *Numbers and Nerves: Information, Emotion and Meaning in a World of Data*, Slovic and Slovic note that "despite the compelling power of quantification, despite our sense of the usefulness of numbers, there persists an underlying skepticism toward numbers as a medium of communication and as a gauge of reality" (4). This problem lies at the core of the Singapore Clean River Campaign. In spite of the relentless statistics that the government throws at the nation and at the river people, their displacement, when they are served a "quit notice" with arrangements made for them to be rehoused in the new government-built multistoried apartments, is portrayed as unfeeling. It meets with strong opposition from the river people and emotional resistance from other members of the public. The government's arguments are viewed with suspicion, illustrating what Scott Slovic terms "the role *asymmetry of trust* plays in a democratic society and in policy formations" (118; italics in original). The river people believe that the governmental attempt to rehouse them is a ploy to remove them from the source of their livelihood. Used to living in the open air, the built-up, enclosed, high-rise apartments are alien spaces to them. Weng fondly remembers the colorful scene at the river as opposed to the isolation in the apartments:

> At the crack of dawn, the river had stirred to life. Fires were lit in the stoves in his neighbours' huts. Bare-chested boatmen squatted on the decks of their bumboats brushing their teeth with a bit of coconut husk, gargling into their tin mugs like hundreds of tenors and baritones in the choir. This was the music Weng had heard since he was a toddler on his parents' boat, when they still lived on a boat then. (Lim 57)

The warmth and conviviality conveyed in this passage stands in strong contrast to the dispassionate government communication. It is not surprising that many, including Weng's father, fall into depression and meet a speedy death. "The memory of his father's listless figure crouched in the common corridor outside their flat, gazing vacantly down at the car park below through the bars of iron railing tore his heart" (177). The narrative is haunted by the plaintive voices of the river people. They gather in coffee shops to voice their outrage. Weng's impassioned address at their informal gathering reflects their deep hurt:

> We who were born on the river have lived here all our lives. Some of you for generations. We're the river people. We work here, live here, and hope to die here. But today, this is not allowed. We have to move out. Last year, they evicted my family. Now, they're evicting you. The government people say we have turned this river into a rubbish dump. It's an open sewer. A national disgrace. They want to clean it up. Clear us out as if we're part of the rubbish. The riffraff who pollute this river. Squatters! Polluters! They shout at us from their newspapers, their radios and television. (Lim 196)

Weng's speech advocates the idea that social justice should be prioritized over ecological agendas. This runs counter to government propaganda. The government's stand is overtly paternalistic ("We know what is best for your future better than you do") and rather ominously patriarchal ("Those who disagree with our view will regret their decision"), an unvoiced sentiment that nevertheless hangs over the heads of the river people. It comes as no surprise that Weng's rousing speech is seen as "trouble making." Weng is sought out by the Internal Security Department and jailed.

In his *Society Must be Defended: Lectures at the Collège de France, 1975–1976*, Michel Foucault argues that the politics and practices of war, colonialism, border control, and homeland security are fundamentally embedded in biopolitical racial logic (Bigo; Jabri), where some races are deemed "worthy" and others not. As David Macey observes, "tropes of race became aligned with the sciences and technologies of the social that were emerging as part of biopolitics" (186). If we extend this view and marry it to Chakrabarty's, then a very interesting perspective emerges. Chakrabarty points out how in the era of the Anthropocene, it is logical to trace how anthropogenic factors that contribute to global warming—the burning of fossil fuel, industrialization of animal stock, clearing of tropical and other forests, and so on—can all be linked to the larger story of the unfolding of capitalism in the West and its domination of the rest of the world in modes of capital. The ambitions of the elite of the East draw inspiration from the Western model. Therefore, Chakrabarty queries rhetorically:

> [D]oes not the talk of species or mankind simply serve to hide the reality of capitalist production and the logic of imperial—formal, informal, or machinic in a Deleuzian sense—domination that it fosters? Why should one include the poor of the world—whose carbon footprint is small anyway—by use of such all-inclusive terms as species or mankind when the blame for the current crisis should be squarely laid at the door of the rich nations in the first place and of the richer classes in the poorer ones? (216)

This important perspective angles a critical lens on eco-justice altercations, emphasizing the uneven placements of environmental crisis and its causes. It drives home the point that, in developmental discourses, only if the requests of the marginal groups are aligned with so-called ideals of national progress will they be heeded. This brings up another contentious point: that ecological ideals need not always coincide with humanitarian principles. As Graham Huggan and Helen Tiffin remind us, "allegedly egalitarian terms like 'postcolonial' and 'ecological' are eminently co-optable for a variety of often far-from-egalitarian (national) state interests and (transnational) corporate-capitalist concerns" (2).

These words encapsulate the way the river people comprehend the government's move to clean the river. Governmental efforts to pacify and compensate the river people are not understood as such by the community. For the boat-people, governmental force and oppression approximates to a neocolonial mentality, which (to paraphrase Huggan and Tiffin) overvalues the potential for industrialization and engages in a parallel devaluation of subalterns (2). As political ecologist Arturo Escobar points out, governments in general do not believe that marginalized communities may work with their own very different set of ecological principles. They instead are quick to believe in the "tragedy of the commons," where subsistence communities are often perceived as trashing the environment from which they wrest a living as applying to every case. Escobar describes the government's viewpoint as symptomatic of "the resignification of nature as environment" and the "reinterpretation of poverty" as an "effect of destroyed environment"(203). This becomes an aspect of "slow violence" in that the affect is gradual, not spectacular, and the subalterns, lacking resources and existing outside discursive zones, become casualties.

Partha Chatterjee's sardonic perspective regarding the role of the government, which he hails as "the sarkar,[6] the omnipotent and supremely enlightened state," becomes pertinent here:

> The fiction of national progress demands that government be "abstracted" out of the messy business of politics thereby releasing it for the utopian task of "receiving inputs" from all parts of society, processing them and finally allocating the optimal values for the common satisfaction and preservation of society as a whole. (160)

But this utopian ideal, according to Chatterjee, rarely occurs in reality. The problem is also that disempowered pockets of people within the nation space are deeply sceptical about the government's professed "neutrality." The river people refuse to believe that it can operate independent of the interests of "big businesses." The fact that very often these two sectors do find natural alliances adds to the problem and discredits the *sarkar*'s assumed stand of lofty neutrality in relation to all segments of the population. *The River's Song* thus asks whether anti-pollution environmental campaigns should be perceived as forms of *environmental colonialism* practiced under the guise of ecological activism combined with protective humanitarianism. The issue is complicated.

The text persuades the critic to balance a stance at once critical and credulous of these developmental schemes since ironically, despite the voiced intention of the author to tell the story from the underside of history and out of a deeply felt sympathy for the river people, the narrative is equally persuasive about the benefits of the Clean River Campaign. The descriptions of the sorry plight of the displaced boat people are undoubtedly emotionally compelling. But the measured rationality of the government's stand is a parallel discourse that strongly qualifies the emotional scenes. No doubt the government is shown to be a behemoth, relentless in steam-rolling the populace. Despite the fact that the authorial stand is allied firmly on the side of the river people, the government's "rational" claim that the polluted river is both an economic handicap and environmental hazard is a refrain that runs through the narrative and cannot be discounted. The prime minister's voice, which argues that it is in the nation's long-term interests to clean the river and that it is definitely in the nation's ecological interests too, echoes through its pages. This might be disquieting for readers looking to find an uncompromising message of sympathy for the underdog.

Lim's narrative is not a straightforward or simple history from the margins but the unconscious surfacing of two or indeed plural discourses that were competing for space at a critical point in Singapore's history. It becomes an example of the complications that surround environmental and social management in Asia, where human-rights issues sometimes clash with environmental agendas. One narrative strand passionately foregrounds the rights of subaltern groups to live without interference from governments or mega corporations. But the other, willy-nilly, co-opts the idea of advocating development that will clean up a polluted river and promote national interests. As Akshita Nanda, a reviewer, comments, "*The River's Song* is no one-sided rhapsody over the past but a clear-sighted chronicle of what one gains and loses with change" (16).

The book unravels a complex national discourse that was, and still is, in circulation and prioritizes the interests of the nation over that of individuals or groups. But it is relevant that the novel was published a quarter-century after the historical period reviewed. This means that its Singaporean readers have lived with at least twenty-five years of prosperity and comfort that the Clean River Campaign has brought to their lives; their vantage point would be informed by this historical hindsight. The erased history and privations of the river people would have been forgotten by the majority of the citizens. In this case, Lim's narrative could be viewed as a "consciousness-raising" effort.

We remind ourselves that the interests of capital can, paradoxically at times, coincide with environmental responsibility. Singaporean sociologist Chua Beng Huat scripts the national discourse of Singapore as habitually interlacing idealism and pragmatism in its construction of the national narrative, which is both ideological and hegemonic: an interesting echo of colonial attitudes. Chua argues that a "set of prerequisite cultural values and appropriate attitudes had to be inculcated in the population of Singapore in order for the economy to take off and for subsequent sustained growth" (1). This meant that the "meeting of the government and the governed at the ideological level should result in a high degree of legitimacy for the former and a high degree of social stability, where specific but effective coercion is used only against those who do not share the same normative values" (3). I contend that the text operates within this prescribed discursive path, where the contrasting views of the activists (the river people and their sympathizers) and the government are in circulation in what Louis Althusser has called a "closed ideological system" (*For Marx* 233–34). Despite only wanting to foreground the plight of the river people, *The River's Song* also unconsciously lends credence to the pragmatic ideology of the government that has been internalized by the populace. This "measure of a difference" emerges, reminding us of the "eloquent silence" that leads Pierre Macherey to postulate that "the text says what it does not say." Thus a fictional text is "decentered," that is, not centered on authorial intention. Instead, there is a clash between several discourses: "explicit, implicit, silent and absent," all of which are in circulation and the novel participates in either deliberately or unconsciously ("The Text Says What it Does Not Say" 252).

The River's Song straddles two primary discursive zones, one of which is explicitly foregrounded by the author. This view, which supports the "river people," is articulate, impassioned, fighting for the rights of subsistence-based, marginalized communities within the nation-space. But an alternative discourse emerges from what Louis Althusser has termed "a determinate absence" that adjudicates a nationalistic and economy-driven rhetoric ("Cremonini" 1). This opposing dialectic of commerce and pragmatism, even rationality, combined strategically with an environmentalist idealism that pushes for combating the pollution of a precious natural resource is an echo—as in E. M. Forster's Marabar Caves in *A Passage to India*—that just will not go away. The discourses undercut each other. Neither overwhelms the other. These opposing testimonies emerge as equally convincing. The energy of the text derives precisely from these dual and unresolved discursive perspectives. These opposing perspectives reveal the complications involved in speaking about the rights of the subalterns and environmental agendas in rapidly modernizing Asia.

Social Justice and Eco-justice in Neocolonial Regimes: "The Zemindar's Wife"

Well-intentioned national initiatives, however, are not the usual reason for subsistence economies to be torpedoed. The problem is often caused by the clash of tradition and modernity. As Ben Wisner et al. point out, modernity is often held in tension with discourses of vulnerability to risks in a rapidly globalizing world. In their book *At Risk: Natural Hazards, People's Vulnerability and Disaster*, they argue that it is important to show how risks from environmental disasters are connected to the vulnerabilities of everyday lives. Shahraz's "The Zemindar's Wife" is such a narrative that connects vulnerable villagers and a traditional wife to the hazards that surround Bauxite mining.

A conflict develops between a greedy feudal lord (zemindar) in a Pakistani village and the illiterate, naïve, and trusting villagers. The feudal lord wants to lease their lands to a mining corporation. The deep class and economic differences reveal the vulnerabilities of those whom Kevin Bale labels "disposable people":

> Sarfaraz Jahangir, a man of thirty-seven years, was sitting on his horse, on the outskirts of the village, inspecting the sugar-cane fields. Apart from a few plots, most of the land around the village belonged to him, and before that to his forefathers. He gained his income from the cash crops that the land produced. Most of the villagers worked for him. He paid them good salaries, but also profited from the crops. (268)

The complete dependence of the villagers on the goodwill of the zemindar reveals the uneven nature of modernity in Asia. The conflict, symptomatic of the clash between global modernity and local custom, is manifest at both societal and individual levels between traditional roles of leadership versus individualist initiatives. As Saurabh Dube identifies:

> In South Asia, a certain haziness regarding modernism and modernity derives not only from the manner in which they can be elided with each other, but the fact that they are both frequently filtered through the optics of modernization. At stake is the acute, albeit altering, importance of being modern—as a person, a nation, and a people . . . In this scenario, tacitly at least, different, often hierarchically ordered, peoples are seen as succeeding (or failing) to evolve from their traditional circumstance to arrive at a modernized order. ("Modern Subjects")

Dube's observation about the imperative to be "modern" and be co-opted into what is seen as "legitimate profiteering" in a modern global economy is what drives the zemindar's actions in this narrative. The zemindar's aspirations toward modernization, and the way this is at odds with traditional ethics of a feudal order and questions of eco-justice, is a central theme.

The son of Kaniz, a villager, is twenty-year-old Younis, a student at Lahore University and a Marxist. Younis is the only villager who is skeptical about the zemindar's intentions toward the villagers, and sees his various acts of goodwill as self-serving. But his is the sole voice that advances a deep reservation about the pitfalls of the feudal system. He refuses to participate in the periodic dinners hosted by the zemindar for the villagers. The zemindar's wife, the beautiful and initially haughty, city-bred girl Noor, is the first to discover a sinister reason that prompts the zemindar's generosity.

The zemindar has discovered large bauxite deposits in the village. Very conveniently for him the villagers have, for generations, followed the practice of placing their land deeds in the hands of their feudal master for safekeeping. Now all the land deeds are held by the current zemindar, who plans to lease all the village lands to a mining corporation. However, when Noor ferrets out the truth from her husband, she takes the initiative of hiding the deeds. The unfolding tale reveals her emotional maturation as she comes to understand the helplessness of the villagers and learns to empathize. She takes up the villagers' cause and boldly berates her husband: "Is that what the dinners were for? To psychologically blackmail the . . . families into signing those documents for you?" (274) Her intervention can be viewed as an agentic moment for the woman in the representational discourse of modern Asia to suggest that native subjects, particularly women, are not merely passive victims of a globalized modernity but often are its (uncertain) negotiators, challenging its practices, beliefs, and modes of being.

Here, Noor's questions to her husband also explicitly reveal her vulnerability and that of the villagers, holding these in tandem and tight tension. Noor's marriage, her individual security—both personal and economic—are at stake. Noor, putting aside her self-interest and simultaneously fighting for the environment and for the rights of the villagers, is an eco-warrior. The collective dangers that the community would face are dark and manifold. The perils surrounding mining natural bauxite ore that consists of aluminum hydroxide, iron oxide, titanium oxide, and reactive silica, are known to be very hazardous to human health and to affect ecosystems, causing irreversible damage. These extensive and widely recorded risks also lead to long-term neurological problems, including Alzheimer's and Parkinson's. The content of iron oxide, a heavy pollutant, causes air and water to turn red—all of which are examples of "slow violence" which is "not just attritional but exponential, operating as a major threat that multiplies" (Nixon, *Slow Violence* 3).

The central scenario unfolds as one that the greedy and ruthless zemindar is prepared to foist on the villagers: "'Well I would be paying them!' he blustered, cheeks reddening, going on the defensive . . . It would only be for three years. They could have their land back after that" (Shahraz 274). Noor retorts with: "[w]hat sort of land would they be getting back? It would be sour and no longer productive," pointing to soil acidification and potential desertification of the land. "How could you destroy so much of what your family has protected for generations?" (274) The responsibilities of feudal governance come into conflict with an individuated, solipsistic value system that cohabits securely with capitalism.

The pitfalls of feudalism are made manifest. But history's lessons are filtered through ideology and self-interest, as the zemindar's words reveal: "We could make a lot of money! We could choose to live somewhere else!" (Shahraz 274). The baneful influence of international capitalism and its effects on ancient feudal societies stands exposed. Noor believes that her husband holds the lands as a sacred covenant, an obligation that goes back generations, while the young zemindar sees the land as an exploitable resource. The zemindar's views may appear opportunistic but they are couched in a language of initiative and gain that has been rendered acceptable in the discourse of modernity. Noor appeals to his ethical side and points out how his breach of trust will lead to a subaltern tale of dispossession. The story could easily have devolved to one where simple binaries are promoted, with feudalism romanticized and the zemindar vilified. However, the narrative does not yield to this temptation. Rather, the zemindar's character is more complexly mediated. He becomes emblematic of a breed of Asian elite caught up in a web of desire, influenced by a tempting ideology of gain and consumption emanating from the global metropolis. This provides more scope for a thoughtful reflection on the bumpy ride to modernity that many traditional Asian societies have had to face, riding on the back of colonialist ideology that has always been firmly yoked to modernity and capitalism.

As these issues are being debated between the couple, Noor hears that Younis has been killed in a car accident and decides to take action in a hitherto unprecedented way, given the ingrained gender hierarchies in her society. During the Muslim festival of Eid, a time for giving, she gathers together the villagers and hands them their land deeds, much to the ire of her husband. Here her agency, and the personal risk she opens herself to, is overtly expressed:

> By her action, her *juruth*, she posed a direct threat to him as a man, a husband and a Zemindar. His head reeled . . . she wasn't the "decorative" wife he had chosen . . . she had trespassed into his space, nearly making him lose his face in front of the village women. (283)

But surprisingly, the text ends on a scene of reconciliation between the couple. The husband carefully calibrates his options and decides that forcing a quarrel will not benefit him since he has already lost the land deeds in a fait accompli enacted by his wife. So, when his wife makes a tentative reconciliatory move, he "graciously" accepts it. The story describes a feudal society threatened by a major environmental hazard. But it combines this with scenes of personal threat that the twice-colonized women face in courageously fighting for the collective rights of community and self. Overall, the narrative highlights ways in which environmental conservation cannot be disengaged from either personal or communal spaces.

Importantly, while these texts treat weighty themes related to colonial, neocolonial, and capitalist agendas on the one hand and questions regarding human rights, the voice of the subalterns, and subsistence economies on the other, they do not overlook the fact that the greatest victims of these overarching debates being fought out within national spaces, the ones most open to risk, are usually subalterns and, indeed, women. Therefore, I go on to discuss how these texts are sensitive to the plight of women in their diverse spaces within the nation.

Women, Subalterns, and the Environment in National Spaces

In both *A Different Sky* and *The River's Song*, the lyrical love stories of the protagonists end on a note of uncertain hope—that of finding solace in nature. For Howard and Mei Lan, this comes about during their last boat ride with Mei Lan's *amah* Ah Siew. While on board, Ah Siew's aged and confused mind conjures up a boat with her deceased "sisters" waving to her. She jumps overboard in joy and her frail body is tragically ripped apart by the ship's propellers. In contrast to the viciousness of this man-made gadgetry, as Mei Lan plunges to her rescue a few seconds later, it is nature—the sea—that envelopes her body to save it; and it is the sea and the sky that reach out to Mei Lan's tortured mind that had closed itself to love and life, teaching her the most valuable lesson of all:

> The salty wind blew against her face, her hair streamed out about her. Mei Lan spread her arms as if they were wings and knew with a surge of joy what it felt for a bird to fly. Both death and life flew in the wind beside her, and she knew in that instant that love itself was but a series of deaths and rebirths. She had run from life as she had run from death, ignoring the transformative power of each. Now, as she flew towards Ah Siew, she knew at last that death had released her; life claimed her again with all its palpitating power. (Chand 469)

Mei Lan, raped repeatedly in prison and traumatized by the world of culture, risking all, briefly gives herself up to nature and feels comforted by it. The therapeutic qualities of nature make this moment an affirmative one, healing her deep inner wounds. It is also the moment that returns her to her partner Howard. Similarly, for Ping and Weng in *The River's Song*, it is the delightful "natural" sight that they once witnessed together that leaves them filled with hope about themselves and their world that has been ripped apart: "I keep thinking of two solitary crabs Weng and I once saw. The crabs had climbed out of their mud holes at the river's low tide and touched claws. A rare and wonderful sight" (Lim 306).

Thus, in these narratives that rearticulate colonial histories, and narrate neocolonial wars and postcolonial hegemonies in South and Southeast Asia, women are centered. Their battles, both social and ecological, are shown as marking important moments in the journey from tradition to modernity, from local to global. However, their significant though qualified triumphs are their journeys from "ego" to "eco," for all of them ultimately fold into either the solace of nature or achieve a (limited) victory over an egotistical or militant patriarchy. Hence these narratives inhabit Bhabha's "Third Space" that describes "borderline conditions." But the Third Space is, importantly, "peculiar to itself, not simply the space between or the sum of different cultures, but a space where the enunciation of cultures is a transformative, emancipatory act" (*The Location of Culture* 56). These subdominant humans participate wholesomely in transformative projects.

Ping, Mei Lan, Noor, and Alice stand at the forefront of change in Asia. The roles they play within their national spaces and in their specific historic locations, nevertheless, resonate across all of Asia, signaling the emergence of a more emancipated, self-aware continent, both socially and ecologically.

Concluding Thoughts

It might be pertinent, at this juncture, to remember that colonialism in Asia can be identified as having laid the foundations for Beck's "second modernity" to emerge since aside from environmental management, colonialism was also crucial in engendering a "risk society" in Asia. For good or bad, colonialism initiated the creation of a pan-Asian consciousness with the introduction of a common language, and also blurred national boundaries through mass transportation of people and goods across its dominions. In Beck's formulation, the social transition from an industrial to a risk society coincides with a larger and more encompassing shift within modernity: a shift from first to second modernity. Colonialism facilitated this in Asia. We find that Nixon's idea of "slow violence" and Beck's idea of "risk society" feed into each other for in risk society, the identified risks may not be imminent or spectacular but marked by "slow violence."

The texts in this chapter record the impact of slow violence and the gradual transition of Asia to a risk society. The narratives discuss the playing out of several risk scenarios: the two world wars in Singapore that sparked an awareness in the populace of the dark side of globalization; a civil war in Sri Lanka, when global capital began preying on resources that were the staple of subsistence communities; feudalism and its problems in Pakistan, where soil acidification through mining threatens a community; and finally, hegemonic environmental management in Singapore that can erode human rights. These texts reveal that both the powerful and the powerless across nations in Asia *were* and *are* increasingly exposed to risk.

Power becomes an important marker, dividing rich and poor. For the former, there may be relatively more avenues for recourse from certain risks and thus, in Huggan's words, risk for them may merely be "a narcissistic form of existential grandstanding" ("Australian Literature" 100) while for the poor, risk becomes, perforce, a way of life that cannot be avoided, underlining their subaltern status. Hence these texts describe the diverse yet not dissimilar "environmentalism of the poor." The protagonists, whether Alice in Sri Lanka or Mei Lan or Ping in Singapore or Noor in Pakistan, "read" cultural risks well because they think from "the underside of history" and cognize the impact on natural ecologies. Slow violence and risk society are thus shown to have become entrenched in South and Southeast Asia.

In the next chapter, I examine an idea important to ecofeminism that offers a convincing explanation for the passive spaces Asian women have been pushed into. I explore the depictions of women, animals, and animality and their conceptual interconnections in South and Southeast Asia.

CHAPTER TWO

Women, Animals, and Animality

❧

The Laws of Animality Govern almost the Whole of History.
—Henri-Frédéric Amiel (Swiss writer)

If a man has to make a woman the centre of his love, why does he integrate animality into this sacred human emotion?
—Saadat Hasan Manto (Urdu writer)

Abstention from cruelty is the highest Religion. Abstention from cruelty is the greatest self-restraint. Abstention from cruelty is the highest gift. Abstention from cruelty is the highest penance. Abstention from cruelty is the highest sacrifice. Abstention from cruelty is the highest power. Abstention from cruelty is the greatest friend. Abstention from cruelty is the greatest happiness.
—Mahabharata, 116.38–39

Women and Animality

The animated fantasy film drama *The Red Turtle,* released in 2016 (directed by Dutch animator Michaël Dudok de Wit and produced by Toshio Suzuki from Japan), was nominated for the Academy Award in 2017, and won several international accolades. In this film, a red turtle turns into a woman and lives a full life with a man who is marooned on an island until his death, when once again the woman turns back into a turtle and swims away into the ocean. The film centers some universal themes. The initial animosity of the man toward the turtle and his attempts to kill it mirrors the predatory position that humans (and patriarchy, specifically) adopt toward nature in the Anthropocene era; the long imagined tacit connection between woman and nature is emulated in the turtle seamlessly changing into a woman in the man's eyes, as also the final merging of the woman back into nature. Finally, the woman and the turtle are constantly at risk of annihilation. All these instances speak of the status of women, animals, and nature under patriarchy. These ideas become central to this chapter that explores the theme of women, animals, and animality. In the previous chapter, I focused on "the environmentalism of the poor," nature and its related politics being the central concerns. This chapter continues this examination, extending it to gender politics, animals, and animality.

It is significant that *the real and symbolic spaces occupied by women and animals are cognized as both threatened and threatening spaces*. Historically, this ideology has played out consistently across civilizations with witch-hunting in Europe and America, sati in India, foot-binding in China, and female genital mutilation in parts of Africa, the Middle East, and Asia as outstanding examples. The variations in practice only underscore the entrenched, unifying, patriarchal sentiments behind these practices that combine misogyny and fear. As Andrea Dworkin reminds us, "the naming by decree gives power over and against those who are forbidden to name their own experience." This gave man the power "to exterminate nine million women as witches because he has named women evil" (17–18). It is this power that led to witch-hunting in Salem, and also gave the Nazis licence to exterminate 6 million Jews.

Closely linked to patriarchal ideologies that dictate such practices is the idea of "biopower," a term coined by Michel Foucault, which relates to the practice by modern nation-states to regulate their subjects through "an explosion of numerous and diverse techniques for achieving the subjugations of bodies and the control of populations" (*Discipline and Punish* 140). In *The Will to Knowledge: The History of Sexuality, Vol. 1*, Foucault refers to "biopower," which for him is "a technology of power" for managing humans in large collectives. This political technology refers to the control of human bodies through an anatomo-politics of the human body and the biopolitics of the population through disciplinary institutions such as schools, hospitals, prisons, and so forth.[1] By this, Foucault means that modern power becomes encoded into social practices as well as human behavior, as the human subject gradually complies with subtle regulations and the expectations of the social order. This compliance is necessary for the smooth working of the nation-state. This is what makes the emergence of the nation, as well as systems such as capitalism, possible.

Put simply, "biopower" is power over life that becomes politicized. The current battle in the United States over women's reproductive rights (abortion, birth control, etc.) is an example of biopolitics, and the force exerted by biopolitics over women's bodies is biopower. The underside of biopolitics is what Foucault terms "thanatopolitics" or the politics of death. Foucault observes that one of the greatest transformations that the political right underwent in the nineteenth century with the change from sovereignty to liberal democracies was that sovereignty's old right, "to take life or let live," changed to "make live and let die." S. J. Murray reaffirms that "operating through multiplex neoliberal networks, biopolitics today is the post-sovereign state power 'to make live and let die'" (718–19). As Jemima Repo phrases this:

> It is no longer sufficient to theorise the discrimination and oppression suffered by immigrants, ethnic minorities, refugees, and asylum seekers as merely unfortunate effects of prejudicial ignorance and scapegoating. Foucault's genealogy of race helps us grasp how the exclusionary operations of biopower are designed to uphold and enhance the survival and wellbeing of the population by normalizing, weeding out, or killing threatening others. (111)

Repo therefore emphasizes how, by implicitly formulating hierarchies of race, the political right of neoliberal politics endorses the death of certain people. Thanatopolitics is the underside of biopolitics for it challenges the fundamental ideologies of power central to biopolitics. Murray states that "[t]hanatopolitics would expose the fault-lines of biopolitical logics" (718). Murray points out that the suicide of American soldiers, dismissed by the Pentagon as the consequence of mental illness or substance abuse or the forced feeding of those on hunger strike in solitary confinement, raises questions about who has the right to live and who can be allowed to die. Thus, thanatopolitics becomes the powerful "politics of death" that interrogates racism, gender, and other classifications that determines who has the right to live and who is expendable.

An understanding of these ideas enables us to examine the texts in this chapter in productive ways. All of them engage with biopolitics differently. But they all also encourage a biocentric ethic: the view that all organisms, including humans, are part of a larger biotic web or network, whose welfare must constrain or direct human interest, failing which we as a species have to face dire consequences, thus rooting for the rights of all threatened organisms including women, subalterns, and animals. These Asian texts explicitly address the risks of ignoring a biocentric ethic by focusing on the endangered spaces that women and animals inhabit. Thanatopolitics is also a persistent theme that is identifiable. All four texts revolve around thanatopolitics that links in specific ways with the sociopolis. Therefore, a biocentric ethic and thanatopolitics compete for conceptual space in these texts.

In an interesting article titled "Literary Fiction Influences Attitudes Toward Animal Welfare," Wojciech Malecki et al. discuss how fiction has been "credited with considerable power to improve attitudes toward outgroups." In their view, fiction is "an important factor behind the global decline of violence against various minorities in the last centuries" and can "influence [human] attitudes toward other species." Such claims, if true, may further validate the significance of these narratives under study, where important questions about the "right to live" and the biopolitical power to "make live and let die" are raised within Asian spaces. An important aspect of biopolitics centered here is the right accorded or denied to the marginalized: women, animals, and subalterns.

Ecofeminism and Animal Rights

The discourse of ecofeminism has attempted to bridge the gaps that can be perceived in the works of both feminists and animal liberationists whose univocal focus, either on women's or animal rights issues, has failed to identify the often common and expansive nature of oppression that connects the two. However, in the last two decades, an increasing acknowledgment of the fact that within patriarchy, the categories of "woman" and "animal" serve the same symbolic function since they are both placed as the submissive "other" to masculine power, has led to a re-examination of a range of texts that highlight and connect women's issues with the sorry plight of the non-human. As Lori Gruen emphasizes, this connection between women and animals is "not to be understood as a 'natural' connection—one that suggests that women and animals are essentially similar—but rather a constructed connection that has been created by the patriarchy as a means of oppression" (61). In this chapter, I examine four texts by women writers from Malaysia, the Philippines, Vietnam, and Myanmar. In Beth Yahp's *The Crocodile Fury*, "Maharlika" by Irene Carolina A Sarmiento, Vo Thi Hao's "The Blood of Leaves," and "Heartless Forest" by Khin Mya Zin, the animal and the woman are entangled in interesting ways that shed light on the use and misuse of both. In all the stories, therianthropism—humans represented as animals—is a strong theme and is deployed with interesting variations. Furthermore, all four narratives bring a quintessentially Asian perspective to women/animal representations. These are diverse, localized, embedded in local beliefs, myths, and histories, and engage various Asian perspectives. *The Crocodile Fury* insists on the obliteration of "speciesism." However, the exercise of biopolitical power is evident in the actions of some characters though their perspectives do not flourish; "Maharlika" enacts biopolitical power that leads to its draconian end, "thanatopolitics"; "The Blood of Leaves" discusses the ways in which biopower can unfold in everyday life; and, finally, "The Heartless Forest" once again comes full circle to celebrate the biocentric fullness of life and the erasure of "speciesism."

Panchatantra and Some Asian Perspectives

One of the most ancient and quintessential of the texts that engage with animals and animality is the Sanskrit *Panchatantra* which is conservatively dated as the second century BCE. In this text, which is a precursor to the *Arabian Nights*, despite the fact that animals are anthropomorphized, their treatment sheds light on some ancient belief systems (Hindu/Buddhist/Jain) of Asia in relation to animals, beliefs that can be seen reflected either overtly or subtly in the texts I examine by contemporary writers. The *Panchatantra*'s avowed goal is to teach statesmanship and shrewd governance (*neeti*).

Chandra Rajan, editor of the Penguin edition of the text, clarifies that traditionally, the authorship of the *Panchatantra* is ascribed to Vishnu Sharma. His learned king, despairing of his three sons, who are "unlettered and therefore ignorant," invites this old and venerable pundit to teach them. Hence this five-volume book, filled with delightful animal stories, is not about animals but about teaching three young princes "to become able and competent rulers of powerful and justly governed kingdoms" (Rajan 5). However, despite this stated goal, what can be culled from the stories is also the prevailing attitudes to animals in ancient India, which wielded a lot of cultural influence over South and Southeast Asia across millennia. Indeed, Pradeep Kumar Gautam examines in detail how "the *Arthasashtra* and its variations such as the *Panchatantra* helped in the spread of Indian culture and concepts to both the east and the west" (65).

In the very first story in the first volume of the *Panchatantra* is a merchant setting out on a long journey with his two bulls. When one of the bulls falls ill, he tasks his two servants to stay with it until it either gets well enough to join him again or alternatively, in case it deteriorates, to stay until its soul passes on and then undertake the necessary rituals for its passing before they join him. This casts light on the fundamental belief, common to Dharmic religions, that the soul (*atman*) can take any form, animal or human, in its many incarnations, and should be treated with equal respect regardless of the body it is housed in. It is useful to be aware of these beliefs (despite the fact that they are very distanced from contemporary practices in Asia), as some central themes that emerge in the ensuing texts may be linked back to such ideas, especially from the point of view of "speciesism." Aside from the *Panchatantra*, where relevant I also look at other Asian traditions that clarify the women/animal and animality themes, such as *tawlar ratu*, the classical lyrical tradition of Myanmar, and the Bonbibi folktales that are popular across West Bengal in India, Bangladesh, and Myanmar.

Speciesism and Anti-speciesism in *The Crocodile Fury* and "Maharlika"

The first work, *The Crocodile Fury* by the Malaysian-Australian author Beth Yahp, was first published in Australia.[2] Grace Chin ("Angry Ghosts"; "Reading the Postcolonial Allegory in Beth Yahp's *The Crocodile Fury*"), Miriam Lo, and

Shanthini Pillai have analyzed the novel mainly from the postcolonial angle. Neither critics nor reviewers, however, have commented on the ecological connections that it invokes in a deliberate and sustained manner, nor its investment in biocentrism. This is perhaps due to the allegorical nature of the narrative and the postmodernist stylistics it adopts, both of which are rarely used for discussing ecological issues. But *The Crocodile Fury* manages to combine these to initiate a lyrical exploration of a world where potentially perilous divisions between species are dissolved to reveal the fundamental cohesion of all life-forms.

One of the remarkable aspects of the novel, which points to its biocentrism, is not just its lack of racial specificity, as pointed out by Chin ("Reading the Postcolonial Allegory" 96), but indeed its anti-speciesism. Speciesism, a term popularized by Peter Singer (*Animal Liberation*) who places it on par with other "isms" such as racism and sexism, is, however, not as universally acknowledged or upheld, especially in fiction, which is by nature deeply anthropocentric. However, *The Crocodile Fury* cannot be accused of centering humans. Rather remarkably, not just subaltern women but ghosts, animals—both reptilian and aquatic—and the animalistic, that is, humans who resemble animals or appear to be incarnations of various natural elements, thus elemental spirits—inhabit its pages. These slide into each other, never retaining specific identities, challenging the neat masculine/feminine or the human/non-human binaries that have dominated human/Western/colonial imaginings and have left an enduring impact on all those who fell on the *other* side of this polar divide. The text uses two kinds of nature metaphors, first, zoomorphic metaphors that compare humans to animals and second, anthomorphic[3] metaphors, which compare humans to larger elements like forests and oceans (Goldwyn 220). In the short story "Maharlika," too, ironically, humans are animalized but here it is based on class, power, and money. The poor are hunted by the rich such that their common species identity is discarded in favor of other divisive trajectories of identity such as the economic divide, thus forcefully invoking Foucault's idea of biopolitics that dictates who is to live ("give life") and whose lives are dispensable ("let die").

The Crocodile Fury is set in postcolonial Malaya and recounts the lives of three generations of women. All the characters carry only generic names and lack distinctive markers of identity. There is mention of a "rich man" and his "lover." The narrator is a convent girl who is a charity student, always accompanied by her inseparable companion, the local "bully," an orphan girl and also a charity case. The narrator's "grandmother" had been a servant to the rich man as a child but later in life became a renowned ghost-chaser. The narrator's mother has been adopted from the local brothel-keeper by the grandmother to serve as an apprentice in her ghost-chasing activities. But the mother turned Christian after seeing a beatific vision of the Madonna, thus eschewing the Oriental world of ghosts, and has now been inducted by the nuns to manage the convent's laundry. In the laundry is tethered, like an animal, a lizard boy, the son of the convent's caretaker, whose scaly, dry skin and reptilian features have scared people into tying him up.

The rich man's (imperial) racial identity is hinted at only through a passing description of him: that "[i]n sunlight the rich man looked as if he was dipped in gold" (Yahp 4). In early colonial times, he lived in a mansion atop a hill near a jungle that is alternately labeled "Mat Salleh" Hill or "Mad Sailor" Hill or even "Bandit Hill." This mansion was later renovated and converted into the convent's library. It is also the haunted mansion that gives sufficient scope for the grandmother to begin exercising her otherworldly talent. The grandmother, who discovers during her teenage years her "extra eye" that can see beyond the physical realm, becomes a revered professional "ghost-chaser" amongst the locals. Much of the narrative appears to be a jumbled attempt by the grandmother to impart her trade secrets to her granddaughter and revenge her past wrongs, even as she serves as the archetypal keeper and passer of ancient lore.

The very fact that the characters have universal (representational) labels rather than specific names and are more symbols than rounded characters, makes the narrative strongly allegorical. Filled with a wide range of sentient creatures—women, animals, and liminal, animalistic characters who seamlessly morph into other creatures—the text evidently rejoices in biocentric diversity. This serves as an ironic commentary on the rigid divisions that habitually segregate men from women and animals in the real world. Racial divisions too stand exposed. Thus, its themes are in direct contrast to "Maharlika."

The politics of death and normalization of murder become the central themes of "Maharlika." This normalization is made possible through therianthropism, with humans deliberately bestialized. This is a disturbing fantasy, set in the near future, where affluent humans pay to hunt the poor, termed "vermin," on safari vacations. In her introduction to her novel *The Left Hand of Darkness,* Ursula K. Le Guin observes that "[a]lmost anything carried to its logical extreme becomes depressing, if not carcinogenic" (1). This sentiment is realized in "Maharlika." The text intentionally invokes several tropes that make us reflect on the current human condition viewed through the ecocritical lens.

The title, which means "nobility" in Tegalu, could be a satirical reference to the Philippines President Ferdinand Marcos, in office from 1965–86, whose intention was to rename Manila as Maharlika, and could point to a certain sociopolitical elitism that marked the regime's ethos. The text is also a morality tale that presents the evil of capitalism carried to its extreme logical end. Jeff Sovern, discussing "The Risks of Unfettered Capitalism," declares: "[c]apitalism may be the best economic system ever devised [though this is debatable], but one of its drawbacks is that it provides financial incentives to harm and even kill people." Sovern is talking about how products that kill are sold worldwide for profit. But in "Maharlika" killing becomes even more direct. The people who kill and are killed are of the same species, even race. It is only money that separates them.

Foucault sees racial categorizing not as a social construct but as an apparatus of power, indispensable to liberal modernity ("Society Must Be Defended"). This concept is important to understand the ethos of both texts. The arcane ethos of *The Crocodile Fury* that consistently erases racial and speciesist identities is a statement against human predation. Its vision is opposed to Ulrich Beck's bleak picture of second modernity, which witnesses a reification of the categories of race, gender, and species. Likewise, eschewing patriarchal ideals that prize linearity and rationality, the narrative pushes for a rich, vibrant, sensuous conveying of experience, and an unrepentant, cyclical repetition of ideas that gradually adds details to the unfolding tale. These methods of narration negate hierarchies and the primacy of reason and logic, promoting more oblique modes. As Chin notes:

> *The Crocodile Fury* is deliberately made into a huge jigsaw puzzle whereby fragmented pieces of the stories must be fitted together. But unlike an actual puzzle, the novel will not yield a unified whole. There are still many unresolved voids left gaping in the novel; loose ends that are left open to questions, and thus frustrate our attempts at exegesis. ("Angry Ghosts")

The gaps, voids and thwarting of the readers' "attempts at exegesis" are deliberate and sustained throughout the narrative. They drill home the message that there are no neat, logical his/stories, where all the ends could be tied up and a clear lesson or two could be learned.

"Maharlika," however, is deeply invested in extracting a lesson that needs to be learnt urgently in Asia today, in nations that are divided deeply along economic lines with the chasm widening. The *ASEAN Post* reports, in an article titled "Southeast Asia's Widening inequalities":

> The richest one percent in Thailand controls 58 percent of the country's wealth and the top 10 percent earn 35 times more than the bottom 10 percent. The four richest men of Indonesia have more wealth than the poorest 100 million people, and about 50 percent of the country's wealth is in the hands of the top one percent. In Vietnam, 210 of the country's super-rich earn more than enough in a year to lift 3.2 million people out of poverty. The country's richest man earns more in a day than the poorest person earns in 10 years. In Malaysia, while only 0.6 percent of its 31 million people are living

below the poverty line, 34 percent of the country's indigenous people and seven percent of children in urban low-cost housing projects live in poverty. In the Philippines, the average annual family income of the top 10 percent is estimated at US$14,708 in 2015, nine times more than the lowest 10 percent at US$1,609.

"Maharlika" describes the extreme endpoint of this widening gap between the rich and the poor in Asia. This morality tale has a clear chronology, replicating the indisputable linear logic of capital.

In contrast, *The Crocodile Fury* admits several false starts, alerting readers to the artificiality of linear chronicling. "I've spent most of my life in a convent. That's the place to begin," declares the narrator firmly, only to reiterate this statement periodically (Yahp 1). "That's the place to begin. The convent on the hill when I spend most of my days and some of my nights . . ." (2) and a little further on, "That's the place to begin. The hill with the convent and the jungle called Mat Salleh Hill. It is a hill of many old sayings" (7). Toward the end of the book are parallel closing movements when, a good twenty pages before the novel ends, the narrator remarks: "That's the place to finish. The convent on the hill next to the jungle" (307). But a few pages later she admits: "Grandmother never wants anything finished. She never wants to get to the end" (317).

Also, there are no binaries in this a-logical world. The natural world and the human world persistently overlap in therianthropic descriptions. For example, the narrator imagines that she and her constant companion, the bully, "are underwater creatures, morsels curled in a shell . . . The bully's face is earth into which I dig my fingers. Her skin is tree bark, her elbows scabby . . ." (Yahp 60). The bully comes to be constructed in this passage as part mollusc and part human in a way that underscores the seamless connections between all creatures in the natural world. For the grandmother, the worlds of the living and dead routinely intermingle. She tells her granddaughter that "[m]en of these parts who cannot attract live women are famous for trying to catch spirit wives. They brave the seas at midnight, hang around jungle edges or at rivers where jungle spirits come to bathe" (76), emphasizing not only "anthomorphic" (Goldwyn 220) interconnections but, paradoxically, the embodiment of spirits, another persistent theme.

When the narrator and the bully question the grandmother about the "mad sailor," checking whether the sailor was a "he" or a "she" or if, in fact, s/he were "dead or alive," the narrator notes that her grandmother "burst out cackling" and replied "both" (Yahp 102). Thus, racial and gendered classifications seem unnecessary, even redundant, in a narrative where even the distinction between death and life is rendered superfluous. However, there is an important difference between the grandmother and the narrator. The grandmother, like her employer, the rich man, stands squarely opposed to the natural world.

The grandmother recounts how once, around the time the rich man returned from his voyage with a lover (a sea-spirit) of indeterminate identity, she began to have strange dreams. This was before the grandmother's extra eye opened, enabling her to see spirits and ghosts. She saw in her dreams the rich man, "braced on the prow" of a boat, "peering" down into the sea watching "strange shapes rising from the waters, teasing, slipping back" (Yahp 135). He then clambered over the prow and swam in the dark waters. Suddenly,

> His hand reached for a shape caught in a watery spiral downwards, a fish shape, smooth and fleeting. The rich man caught the shape mid-spiral, discerned arms and torso, a gown that tangled, a slippery skin [. . .] In the rich man's arms the shape bucked and struggled [. . .] In his arms the shape was turning, was a shape now suddenly long and scaly, now bloating, now ridged with spikes. Still the rich man gripped. (135)

It is not strange that the grandmother should have this vivid dream of the rich man's private life for, as a little girl, she too had been the rich man's pet. On his return home from his travels, he had always looked for her and petted and played with her, except once. She remembers that instance vividly:

> This time the rich man was at the end of the train, and he neither walked quickly, nor looked for my grandmother with red ribbons in her hair, stretching her body, waving both arms. The rich man walked alongside a closed litter draped with scarves of bright cottons and silks. Now and then the draperies shifted to hint at a reclining figure. Now dark strands of hair curled like seaweed through the crack. (109)

This is the entry of the lover into the rich man's life and house. The lover is kept locked in the rich man's quarters and he too rarely emerges from them. That the lover is unhappy and is pining away is evident from the fact that despite the cook preparing "a variety of different dishes every day" (110) the food is returned barely touched. Finally, however, when she is coaxed out of her bed, the lover's smile captivates everyone. "When she touched her cold hand to theirs, rich man or serving woman . . . was filled with an overwhelming kindliness, an immeasurable pleasure" (149). The description invokes a vision of all living beings bonded together and emphasizes the natural affinity, even the sense of enchantment, that exists between humans and other beings.

It is the lack of enchantment that has thrown the modern world into disarray. Alison Stone discusses how Friedrich Schlegel, the most influential theoretician of the early Romantic movement, approached nature:

> For Schlegel . . . humans "disenchant" (*entzaubern*) nature if they perceive it as not at all mysterious but completely intelligible by reason. Conversely, humans would "enchant" (*bezaubern*) nature by perceiving it as partly mysterious, not fully rationally comprehensible. (4)

The narrator's sensibilities strongly resonate to this sense of an enchanted and enchanting nature, but the grandmother stands apart. While other employees are charmed by the lover—the elusive sea-creature—only the grandmother "stood watching from the hidden corners of the rich man's mansion," filled with envy and suspicion (Yahp 140).

Just as the rich man wants to *possess* and *dominate* his lover, thwarting her attempts at escape and trying to cajole her out of her nostalgia for the sea by treating her like a household pet, the grandmother too wants to dominate and control the spirits that she espies with her extra eye. Therefore, from the biocentric perspective, the tale can be read as an allegory about the natural world (that unproblematically connects with the supernatural) being enslaved by predatory humans. This resonates with Foucault's "genealogy of race," which exposes the fact that the operations of biopower are designed to enhance the well-being of some of the populace by normalizing the neutralizing of "threatening others" (Repo 111). The grandmother becomes a facilitator with her knowledge of history. She is the storehouse of past knowledge and the keeper of memory, who binds the narrator to the weight of the past, so much so that she feels that young though she is, and only a schoolgirl,

> [e]very day I seem to get heavier. My walk to the convent is no longer as light as air, as crooked as a crab baby's; no longer a skip here and there [. . . .] Nowadays my convent walk is a pull against metal, a straight line, like tugging at the anchor of a ship. My chin is no longer lifted for whistling. My feet press further into the ground. (Yahp 241)

The narrator is methodically taught by her grandmother to take revenge on the lover, who displaced the grandmother from the rich man's affections. This predictably involves being tutored to adopt a hostile attitude toward the non-human other.

In contrast to the narrator, who resists this lesson, the bully is eager to adopt the grandmother's attitude wholesale. With her broken camera that she uses to photograph every random incident, the bully also stands for memory and an obsession with archiving. Since the rich man's lover, the sea-maiden, is one of grandmother's main antagonists on whom she funnels all her antipathy, it is a foregone conclusion that the bully, the grandmother's ardent follower, would be most enthusiastic about tracking the sea-spirit and destroying her. Also, the destruction of the sea-maiden is tied to the recovery of a treasure trove. The grandmother's and the bully's vengefulness is squarely allied to materialism and predatory biopolitics. In contrast, the narrator is shown to possess an affinity with the natural world. After searching far and wide in the jungle, armed with her grandmother's clues, she identifies the place where the sea-spirit is buried. In fact, both narrator and bully come upon the burial spot together. But being focused on the treasure, the bully misses the spot. The narrator remarks:

> The bully and I have walked and walked [in the jungle] and now we have found it. The lover's gown slips out of the earth as streaked as a precious metal. The bully and I have found it as grandmother told us, but the bully doesn't know. (Yahp 126)

Not seeing the treasure, the distraught, unseeing, and acutely disappointed bully "kneels at the graveside and weeps" (126). The bad-tempered bully "tugs at her frayed strap so hard it snaps and her camera smashes to the ground," this narrative moment signaling the break from the past. "'We have lost our spirit,' the bully says. 'How will we find treasure?'" (126) The bully's unhappiness is compounded by her camera breaking, her anchor to the materialistic and culpable world of history and gain. Conversely, on finding the grave of the sea-spirit, the narrator is instantaneously freed of the unfair antipathy that her grandmother had instilled in her. Standing over the sea-spirit's grave, she feels a stirring inside her which will not stop, and her response is the opposite of the bully's. She displays the untrammeled joy of connecting with nature:

> I am laughing. I am holding my sides with laughter, brushing the tears that spout from my eyes. In my hands the lover's gown is caught water, it slips and spills between my fingers so I have to keep snatching it back. I press my face to its shimmering folds, breathe the lover's salty smell . . . One deft turn and my arms are into its armholes, my shoulders shrugging to a perfect fit. (Yahp 126–27)

The sea-maiden's imbrication in the elemental ocean is underscored. Even her gown is "caught water." Not only does the narrator shed the antipathy nurtured by her grandmother's tales and admonitions but, most notably, the moment is also when she merges with the sea-spirit and thus, by implication, with the natural elements. This is a neat allegory that underscores the fact that it is humans' attitude that distances them from the natural world to which they are primordially linked.

> 'Something to do,' I say, my hair lifting on the sudden wind. My hair uncoils from grandmother's braid, it slithers untangled and free. The bully can't help staring. Suddenly I am the most beautiful woman she has ever seen. My gown glimmers so bright she can hardly bear to look. She stands with her mouth drooped open as I hold out my hand. 'Give it to me,' I say, and the bully doesn't want to, but she knows what I meant [. . .] obediently her hands drop her knife into my palm [. . .] the knife and the gown cleave together with a faint sound of the waves slapping, a memory of the toss and pull of the sea. (Yahp 128)

The narrator changing into the sea-spirit reinforces the sustained biocentric message of the novel that humans are elemental beings irrevocably linked to their natural world. The rich man, the bully, and the grandmother reinforce the hazards of being alienated from nature. These actions seamlessly dovetail into a material ecocritical outlook. Serenella Iovino and Serpil Oppermann, in "Theorizing Material Ecocriticism: A Diptych," examine how "the categories of humans, nonhumans, and things are inseparably distributed over biological spaces." They see this as an opportunity to examine "matter and meaning together." Furthermore, they highlight how:

> [t]he old conceptions of matter as stable, inert, and passive physical substance, and of the human agent as a separate observer always in control, are being replaced here by the new posthumanist models that effectively theorize matter's inherent vitality. In ecological postmodern terminology, we are witnessing a "re-enchantment" of nature, and material ecocriticism is a significant contributor to this new paradigm. (465)

This "re-enchantment of nature" enables the seamless transformation of the narrator from human to spirit; absorbing both human and non-human identities, she instinctually abhors her grandmother's antipathy to the natural world. We also find this composite identity entirely logical once we figure out that she is the daughter of the lizard boy who also, in an epiphanic moment that manifests as fury, turns into the crocodile. This is the moment on which the novel's title is based, underlining its significance.

Indeed, in direct contrast to grandmother's attitude, which is one of remembering the past to avenge its wrongs, the lizard boy's approach to life is one of forgetting. The lizard boy is introduced early in the narrative. His physical appearance is interesting:

> The boy's nickname was the Lizard Boy because his skin was cracked and scaly, his body thin and sinewy, his stomach bulging whenever he ate. His eyes were round and lizard-like, hardly ever blinking. Everyone could tell wherever he'd been by the trail of silver skinflakes he left. They watched fascinated and repulsed by the flicking of his tongue. (Yahp 83; uppercase in original)

The convent caretaker's son, the father of the narrator, and her mother's lover, the lizard boy is clearly "other" to the human norm. The biotic community with all living creatures seamlessly running one-into-another, and the biocentric ethic of the text, are made patent here. Also, the lizard boy's "subjective alterity" appears to be an unstable state and leads to metamorphoses (Chin, "Reading the Postcolonial Allegory" 95). He therefore mutates into a crocodile later in the narrative, invoking both pity and fear. But his unstable, ambivalent corporeality and reptilian physicality do not prohibit an inexhaustible thirst for knowledge, for he always carries a book scrunched into his back pocket. "The Lizard Boy wasn't choosy. One day he'd be reading a history book, next a five-cent novel [. . .] he read anything and everything" (84). The lizard boy appears to challenge the Cartesian mind/body dualism, wherein the ideal is the keen, enquiring mind housed in a fit body. Instead, he possesses a human, enquiring intellect in an ostensibly "repulsive," reptilian body. There is evidence of ambivalence here as well because, when we first encounter the lizard boy, he appears subnormal but later he seems to have evolved into a cerebral being.

The lizard boy is also the antithesis of the grandmother for he is not tied to history, rituals, or conventions and "[f]or hours each day he practiced forgetting" (Yahp 244). Also, he "secretly salvaged [books] from the stacks of damaged or unsuitable readings donated to the convent library, which the nuns set aside to be burnt" (244) and read anti-colonial literature and leaflets with loaded titles like "*Exploitation. Self-determination. United resistance. Necessary covert activity*" (245; italics in original) "He grew more and more excited, the more he read" (245). The lizard boy is poised for future action. He has freed himself from the shackles of the past and is able to disregard the weight of contemporary opinion. Secure in his selfhood, he is willing to be all things to all people. "They think they got a crocodile, fine! They got one. They think they got a human, they got one. All depends what they think" (246). As the lizard boy read more and more, barely touching his food, "[i]t seemed his bodily functions were winding down" (247). This is when he metamorphoses into a crocodile:

> His flesh shrank against his bones; his bones, flesh-shrunken, seemed to take on new proportions, limb bones shortening so his arms and legs became stubby, backbone lengthening so that from certain angles he looked as if he was growing a tail. His toe and fingernails grew curved and pointed, his face bones elongated, jutting out over his eyebrows, squeezing his cheeks into hollow pouches that sagged. The Lizard Boy's skin, stretching in places, in others wrinkling, was in some places steam smoothened, in others ridged leathery and cracked. His eyes acquired the startling fixity of black and radiant jewels. (247–48)

His insistence on erasing the past has energized the enervated lizard boy both physically and intellectually and turned him into a powerful crocodile to be feared and not pitied.

These moments of mutation in the narrative, when the lizard boy turns into a crocodile and the narrator (his daughter) turns into a sea-spirit, are significant because they signal that life patterns are being rearranged (Yahp 304). This epiphanic moment bears important messages. It brings about an instance of perfect clarity for the narrator when her illusions fade away. But it is also a frightening moment and she confesses that "[o]nly the press of the jungle earth against me, the leaves tickling my ears, hold me steady; hold me still" (302). Like her father—the lizard boy-turned-crocodile—she too emerges from under the weight of history and the past to savor the present—at long last, one with nature. "Unlike the jungle of my grandmother's stories, the one that presses against me is neither a jungle of jumps and shudders nor one to slide my sleeping eyes open for fear," she states, clearly spelling out the differences between false fears about nature and bonding with it (302–3). Now in touch with her senses and reality she realizes that "[t]he jungle earth is warm and silent. The jungle beasts are mere jungle beasts, no more, which scurry at my footfall" (303). With this realization comes liberation. The shackles that tie her to the cultural world of her grandmother with its weighted past dissolve, leaving her free to revel in her newfound kinship with nature in its autonomy and reality. She is released from the weight of history and its power, both inseparable. The narrative offers a counter-model to eco-localism (or ethnocentrism), promoting its alternatives–hybridity, creolization, *mestizaje* (miscegenation), borderlands, and liminality.

Foucault has persuaded us to think of power as not emanating from a person or collective but as a network or field of asymmetrical relations between individuals, and even between individuals and machines, all of which operate as nodes in a power field. However, Foucault later clarifies his ideas by arguing that major changes in this concept of power occurs when biological and policy sciences meet (Lemm and Vatter 40). When he first employed the term "biopolitics," Foucault identified a new kind of power adopted by dictatorships, which is negotiated through technologies and discourses of risk that made people their object. This played a central role in the emergence of modern racism and eugenics. However, he does not limit biopolitics to oppressive regimes but also traces it to the kind of political rationality characteristic of the liberal and neoliberal forms of government and governance that he terms "governmentality" (40). For Foucault, biopolitics can also refer to "technologies of self" where, as he mentions in *The Will to Knowledge*, "life itself may function as a source of critique and resistance to power formations" (143). It is interesting to identify the abundance of life (biodiversity) as resistant to power structures as an idea that emerges powerfully in *The Crocodile Fury*. The exuberance of life which, of course, co-opts nature, breaks free from under the mantle of power in all its avatars.

An informed reading of *The Crocodile Fury* would identify a narrative trajectory that presents the cultural world as weighted down by memory and history in the persons of both the grandmother, the local storehouse of folk knowledge and her burdensome rituals that distance nature, and the rich man, the emblem of imperialism, known for the way it systematically bound up, tamed, and othered nature. This reading would accede that in the end the natural world cannot be contained within culture; that its autonomy will reassert itself, stunting the humans who held it in thrall. The rich man and the grandmother, the two humans who manipulated the natural world, constantly attempting to subdue it to their cultural habits and habitats and undermining its autonomy, are both ultimately destroyed by the natural forces that regain power and vigor.

Such a neat ending is, however, also reductive in some ways. This is because *The Crocodile Fury* refuses to be contained by any one reading. Its narrative refuses to fix meaning. Thus, I would like to conclude this reading of *The Crocodile Fury* by proposing that perhaps it inadvertently fulfills Roland Barthes idea of text as para/doxical, that is, countering "doxa" or public opinion. As Barthes clarifies in "From Work to Text":

> [T]he Text tries to place itself very exactly *behind* the limit of the *doxa* [public opinion]. (Is not general opinion—constitutive of our democratic societies and powerfully aided by mass communications—defined by its limits, the energy with which it excludes, its *censorship*?) Taking the word literally, it may be said that the Text is always *para-doxical*. (157–58; italics in original)

If we unravel this, we realize that, to Barthes, the text functions as a paradoxical and subversive force, engaged in a movement which is a deferral, a dilation of meaning, a play of signification. *The Crocodile Fury* refuses to be defined by the limits of the doxa. As such, meaning is continuously disseminated and deferred, and is irreducibly plural. Submerged in a web of signification, it leads to an explosion of meaning, refusing to permit a single interpretation. With deferment comes a destruction of history and memory, and the emergence of a cautious hope for human and non-human interactions of the future.

Barthes' para/doxical text mirrors Foucault's notion of life in that both are shown to be resistant to censorship and formulations of power, respectively. This celebration of both textuality and life is accurately mirrored in *The Crocodile Fury*. A zest for life that is elemental and beyond the power of human cultural formulations overflow in its narrative. This reminds us that environmental risks, which might ultimately spell the end of our species, will hardly mean the end of the planet, which will continue to exist and resuscitate itself in multitudinous ways over millennia, long after the end of predacious humanity. The idea of thanatopolitics or the politics of death is therefore implied in *The Crocodile Fury*, as the flip side of exuberant life, the unspeakable end of the species that humanity risks by its actions. Thanatopolitics is another central concern of Foucault and also central to "Maharlika."

Extending his inquiry from Foucault's concept of biopolitics in his work *Homo Sacer: Sovereign Power and Bare Life*, the Italian philosopher Giorgio Agamben analyzes an obscure figure of Roman law, posing fundamental questions about the nature of law and power. Under Roman law, a man who committed a certain kind of crime was banned from society and all of his rights as a citizen were revoked. He thus became a *homo sacer* (sacred man). In consequence, and paradoxically, he could be killed by anybody while his life on the other hand was deemed "sacred," so he could not be sacrificed in a ritual ceremony. An interesting parallel can be drawn to the "vermin" in "Maharlika," where the poor can be said to have become equivalent to *homo sacer*. Their lives are open to "the kill" yet they are also the valued property of the state. In other words, the vermin are gradually bestialized and entrenched in nature. They become legitimized as "animals" to be hunted. Jody Emel equates the killing that takes place in hunting as motivated not only by the desire to master nature but, paradoxically, to separate the animal from the human, which arises out of fear. Fear that leads to the impulse to separate the "vermin" from "the human" is at the root of the enactment of the hunt in "Maharlika." Nature and culture stand clearly separated.

The near-future world where the safari begins is entirely artificial and its description underscores the "nature/culture" hierarchical dualism: "a crystalline river emptied into a megalithic concrete dam. The passengers fell silent a few minutes, mesmerized by the emerald glow of pure, chemically treated water" (Sarmiento 221). This is the world "after nature," to use W. G. Sebald's phrase. Marti Kheel's reflection is very pertinent in this sketch of the future. Kheel argues that in human history, the image of the "beast" has been used to achieve separation from nature.

> The Beast is conceived as a symbol for all that is not human, for that which is evil, irrational, and wild. Civilization is thus achieved by driving out or killing the Beast [. . .] The triumph over the Beast has been enacted through the conquest of wilderness, with its concomitant claim to the lives of millions of animals driven from their lands. (244–45)

The kill performed through the hunt becomes a means of entrenching human superiority over the animal. This enactment of the hunt is pivotal to "Maharlika" and drives the plot forward. An expatriate Filipino family—the parents and their two young sons—returns to the Philippines from the USA for a safari vacation. Even as we discover to our horror that the beasts to be hunted, the vermin, are actually "poor" humans, some fundamental questions about how capitalism works to divide the rich and the poor that are the legacies of the first to second modernity, are raised. Carlo, the twelve-year-old, asks inquisitively, "[a]re Filipino Vermin different somehow? . . . Mostly, we get to see just African Vermin and some from India, then only in pictures or on TV" (220). The children have internalized a process of "othering" of the poor.

In "Maharlika," the innocent observations of the two young boys, Carlo and Arch, is the end result of a process of indoctrination, resulting in the normalization of murder, similar to the ideology that led to slave trafficking in the seventeenth century. They also chillingly mirror the current Philippines President Rodrigo Duterte's sentiments about the extrajudicial killing of drug users and criminals.

> Carlo remembered his grandparents' stories of the demoralizing effect the Vermin had on Philippine society. They refused to stay . . . in the provinces but squatted on any vacant piece of city land. Vermin were amazingly resilient and could survive inside sewage culverts . . . Relocation efforts had been costly and futile. The Datu [President] used his constitutional emergency powers to issue decrees that resolved the Vermin problem. (Sarmiento 225)

As the endpoint of capitalism, in which development as a concept serves the needs of a growing technocracy that works in tandem with the economic and political interests of capital, the "vermin" are denied human status because they are deemed "a liability to Philippine progress" (225). Their negligible buying power as consumers also places them outside the interests of global capital. The poor are stripped of their individuality, indeed, humanity. Referring to them as a collective is a sure way of constructing them as the faceless other, bestializing them and likening their appearance to insects that can then be swatted away without guilt: "Vermin are pretty much the same, dirty, small heads, bug-eyes with spidery arms and legs" (220).

This society serves to illustrate, in Molly Wallace's words, the "thanatopolitical underside of the biopolitical triumph of modernity" (91). Biopolitics becomes a form of thanatopolitics pursuing a lopsided logic, where "defending" the "purity" and "health" of one "species" (human beings) over and against other (such) "species" calls forth not only state-imposed eugenic policies but also the "concentration" of these populations into camps and eventually their "extermination" as "life not worthy of being lived"—a process that the Nazi regime followed (Lemm and Vatter 43).

Language, as Ferdinand Saussure points out, is a system that *constructs* meaning rather than one that describes a prior reality.[4] As Daniel Chandler explains, in Sassure's theory, "[m]eaning is not 'transmitted' to us. We actively create it according to a complex interplay of codes and conventions of which we are largely unaware" (11). Thus, deconstructing the signs in a language system makes us realize whose realities are privileged and attain the status of "truths." Australia was declared terra nullius in the nineteenth century because the 250 or so language groups who had lived there for 40,000 years were rendered invisible as "non-subjects" as also the indigenous peoples of the Americas, and in Africa from the seventeenth to the twentieth centuries. In Asia, the Hindu caste system has deprived Dalits (so-called "untouchables") of their subjectivity for centuries. In fact, the reduction of poor humans to bestial status, and actively *licencing their hunting* is sadly even a part of Australian history. So, the narrative reenacts history in this hegemonic construct, where "truths" are fabricated and established by those in power. Cary Wolfe, citing Jacques Derrida and Georges Bataille, clarifies the process:

> The humanist concept of subjectivity is inseparable from the discourse and institution of a speciesism which relies on the tacit acceptance that the full transcendence to the human requires the sacrifice of the animal and the animalistic, which in turn makes possible a symbolic economy in which we engage in a "non-criminal putting to death" as Derrida phrases it, not only of animals but of humans as well by marking them as animal. (39)

The subjectivity of the human "vermin" is systematically eroded. The guide casually remarks that the hunt began when "[t]he nation's capital was already infested with Vermin since the upper and middle classes had moved abroad" (Sarmiento 225). Like natives in the colonial era, the vermin are imbued with despicable traits: "'I heard the Vermin eat their own dead,' Mom said softly; 'there's no telling what kinds of diseases they carry'" or "we'll run out of people before we run out of Vermin. All they do is multiply like bacteria" (222). The father's embarrassed recounting of an earlier hunt clinches this relentless othering:

> You see, fifteen years ago, the law was that you could hunt only free-range Vermin. And the pests were so damned fast! They'd even spit and throw shit into our jeep when they'd get close enough. So, on our first try, we made a few hits and probably no kills. Then I saw something moving in a dumpster, so I fired blindly [. . .] until it ran out and dropped dead. Turned out not to be Vermin at all, but a wild boar! [. . .] The accident got us into trouble with the conservationists. We ended up paying a fortune because the poor beast was on the endangered species list. (219)

The passage describes a paradoxical situation where endangered animals are valued above humans. This is not without precedent. Often, a pet can be valued higher than a "beggar." Even now, in many developing nations, "capital" in the form of crab-farm investments, for instance, involve vigilantes, who maim or kill humans who steal them for sustenance and survival. The issue of ecological justice comes full circle. Poor humans (slaves or trafficked girls) gain value as property but are otherwise dehumanized.

The safari begins and the family, wearing protective gear and armed with guns and daggers, enthusiastically commence their hunt. Before long, Carlo notes, "Pop was firing at a dark figure that frantically jaywalked through the maze of automobiles. It came to a sudden halt in the middle of the street. Without making a sound, it leaned against the hood of a luxury car and slid towards the asphalt, leaving a bright, red streak." It is worth noting how vermin are objectified by use of the neuter gender "it." "'Got one!' Pop exclaimed, turning to Carlo. 'Keep watch to your side'" (Sarmiento 230). For Carlo, at first the disappointment that he is not a good hunter is overwhelming. However, a strange moment of awareness, a tentative awakening of his conscience occurs, appositely, in a dilapidated church, where he sees infant "vermin." As he is about to shoot it, he is shocked into pausing when he hears "its mother enter and rush towards the infant, calling it 'Carlo.'" As his earphones announce that his time is almost ending with no kills, he takes a pot shot at the baby and kills it. The last words he hears are the mother's crooning with the dead baby in her arms: "*Carlo, anak ko...*" (my beloved) (235). As he joins his family, who are all showered after their bloodbath and are cheerily swapping tales of their success in exterminating large numbers of vermin, this final scene haunts the boy. His mother, mistaking his tears for chagrin at having killed only one vermin, hugs him and says "Don't cry, baby. It's okay. You'll kill more next time" (236).

The story reenacts all the problems that underlie the modern moral and ecological crises of Beck's risk society: human chauvinism, instrumentalism, hierarchy, parochialism, competitive individualism, and addiction to power (Birkeland 18). Carlo is disturbed because in an epiphanic moment his young mind unlocks to doubt his indoctrination. For the first time Carlo vaguely glimpses the depthless tragedy of operating on a premise that unremittingly scaffolds all relationships on the basis of power. It is of particular interest to the ecofeminist that the mother is not romanticized and is as proficient and ruthless a hunter as the father and as enthusiastic a participant. Carlo's powerful mother, who has completely bought into the androcentric ideology of hierarchical dualisms, is contrasted to the vermin mother crooning over her dead "baby Carlo." The division of predator and prey that emerges is made not along gendered lines but based on economic privilege. This is in line with the ideas of ecofeminists such as Carol Gilligan, Stephen R. Kellert, and Stephen R. Kellert and Joyce K. Berry, who suggest that differences in socialization are what account for gendered approaches to wildlife.

Aristotle believed that political life was what made humans transcend their animality. But Foucault argues that this animality itself has become the main concern of politics. Foucault contrasts the *general* idea of population—that refers to a group of individuals as abstract juridical persons, as bearers of legal rights and duties—to the *biopolitical* idea of population, in which individuals are specimens of a living species who need to be controlled *singulatim et omnis*, individually and as a totality (Lemm and Vatter 41). According to Foucault, biopolitics is that form of power which focuses on the:

> species body, the body imbued with the mechanics of life and serving as the basis of the biological process: propagation, births and mortality, the level of health, life, expectancy and longevity, with all the conditions that can cause these to vary. (*The Will to Knowledge* 139)

Biopolitical power is different to Foucault's notion of disciplinary power though both focus on the *bodies* of the individuals rather than on individuals as abstract juridical persons. They both operate through *norms* rather than law. This is significant since within the law one has the *choice* of breaking the law, of acting unlawfully. But with norms, the individual or collective has no choice. When one does not follow norms, one is not breaking them; one is simply showing dysfunctional or abnormal behavior. Once this is established, the human or the collective loses all legitimacy and rights. As Vanessa Lemm and Miguel Vatter identify, both disciplinary and biopower are "powers of normalization, but the meaning of the term is distinct in each." Foucault distinguishes between what he calls the "normation" of disciplinary power and the "normalisation" of biopower (*Discipline and Punish* 42). What is noteworthy is that in "Maharlika," we see both the "normation of disciplinary power" and the "normalisation of biopower" over the vermin that not only legitimizes their killing but makes it "normal" to do so.

In the ensuing text, "The Blood of Leaves," I show how the "normalization of biopower" operates in daily life and its impact on "abnormal" individuals, marking them as exterior to the norm.

"Ugliness" as Peril in "The Blood of Leaves"

The third text, "The Blood of Leaves" by Vietnamese writer Vo Thi Hao, explores the assumption that underlies all patriarchal societies to a greater or lesser degree: that women need to be "ornamental" in order to be valued. "Ugly" women are often undervalued or devalued.

Vo Thi Hao is both a journalist and a talented painter, which explains her crisp prose offset by vivid visual imagery.[5] "The Blood of Leaves" is featured in a collection of Vietnamese short stories edited by Charles Waugh, entitled *Family of Fallen Leaves: Stories of Agent Orange by Vietnamese Writers* and themed around stories involving Agent Orange (or a toxic dioxin), which was sprayed on flora, fauna, and people during the Vietnamese war. The stories in this collection emerge from experiences of extreme privation. Between August 10, 1961 and January 7, 1971, the United States military sprayed approximately 20 million gallons of chemical defoliants on roughly 6,000 square miles of Vietnam's jungles, croplands, and waterways, exposing millions of people to the defoliants' toxic by-product: "dioxin." It is no surprise that many of those sprayed directly were poor, rural people, ethnic minorities living in Vietnam's highlands or the Vietnamese soldiers and youth brigades operating in the Southern jungles and along supply routes from the North. Over and above rendering the visceral immediacy of the impact of the toxin on the Vietnamese, the narratives in the volume become rhetorically useful metaphors, where its specific historical, geopolitical, and toxicological discourses of risk can be extrapolated to a diseased planet. This is particularly because those sprayed included US soldiers and their allies. No one was spared. "After the war, when these soldiers had children, many of them unwittingly passed on the genetic damage the dioxin had wrought, increasing the disaster's effects to global, multigenerational proportions," thus raising levels of risk exponentially (C. Waugh 1).

All the stories pivot around environmental poisoning and every story in the collection includes a character or characters deeply affected by or dying from the toxic dioxin. Risk discourse, environmental justice, and "toxic discourse" (that Lawrence Buell coins to describe fictional and non-fictional works such as Rachel Carson's *Silent Spring* and Terry Tempest Williams's *Refuge*) get centered, drawing attention to the pervasiveness of risk ("Toxic Discourse").

Though several stories in the volume focus on dramatic events and the risks involved, "The Blood of Leaves" is more restrained. It demonstrates that risky ecologies can exist faraway from war zones and dramatic natural upheavals, insinuating their existence into everyday life. The story opens with the first-person narrator meeting his friend, Huan, a doctor, who is dying from Agent Orange. The narrator implicitly compares his condition to that of "the yellow leaves of the cycad suffering in its pot next to the bar. It was struggling to grow one small shoot" (Vo 134). The local fauna, like humans, has suffered cruelty. The text describes a dying nation, a "thanatopolis," the end point of "risk society." The dying Huan gives his friend an assignment: to write love letters to an "ugly" girl, Tam, a midget—born deformed because of the dioxin—the sister of Huan's friend, who was killed in combat.

The oppressions of man over man, over woman, and of man over nature that Ariel Salleh remarks are "triangulated like a Boromean knot" ("The Ecofeminism/Deep Ecology Debate" xi) are brought to the foreground early on in the narrative. The cruelty that "ugly" Tam suffers leads to a gradual erosion of her self-worth in her daily life that parallels the erosion of the planet through global warming, toxins, desertification, and deforestation—a slow death, or to use Rob Nixon's phrase, "long dyings" (Nixon, *Slow Violence* 29).

The narrative begins with a therianthropic representation, which as Greg Garrard reminds us "is the reverse of anthropomorphism and is often used in contexts of national or racial stereotyping, such as when the Nazis depicted the Jews as rats" (141). The mass murder during the Vietnam War is invoked through a graphic image: "A pulse of nausea rose in my throat each time I remembered the knots of green worms writhing in death from Agent Orange. Faced with such human cruelty, each of us was just like those worms" (Vo 134). Humans reduced to writhing green worms have no more subjectivity than plants and are deemed equally deserving of extinction. The bestializing of humans foregrounded in "Maharlika" and evoked in "The Blood of Leaves" reveals the gargantuan ego of the hegemonic class that is instrumental in objectifying humans and reducing them to animals or the animalistic.

True to John Berger's observation that "animals are always the observed" (14), "ugly" Tam becomes the focus of attention of all the main characters, including the narrator. Their observations lead to an "ever-extending knowledge" (14) about Tam, and her life and thoughts become the object of knowledge for three men. The first, her brother, decides that he needs to generate bogus love letters to assuage her need for love. When shot in the Vietnam War, he delegates this task to his friend Huan, who carries on the pretence with the help of the postal officer. Finally, the dying Huan requests the narrator to carry on the subterfuge. Tam's well-meaning friends do not realize that what they are practicing on her is the "normalisation of biopower" which, constructing her as abnormal by default, depletes her of human agency and exposes her to cruelty from her father and fellow citizens. When she finds out about the hoax that has been perpetrated by three well-meaning men, Tam refuses their patronage. She establishes her individuality and dignity when she remarks to the narrator, "[y]our world is endless but mine is tiny. I have to return to that world" (Vo 146). The story finally restores Tam's self-respect and agency.

Janis Birkeland discusses how the "historic association of women, nature and earth" is entrenched under patriarchy. This association automatically relegates both to subdominant positions as "man-servers." Both women and nature are valued to the extent that they are useful to Man, underwriting "instrumentalism" (24). Despite her possessing an excellent mind the girl in the story is deemed "useless" solely on the basis of her physical "unattractiveness" and disability.

In fact, the animosity that "ugliness" generates has been well documented, another stark instance of biopower. Recently Lizzie Velasquez—an American born with Marfan syndrome, a rare disease that gives her an aged appearance and makes it hard for the 63lb woman to gain weight—talks about how, when she was seventeen, someone posted a video of her online and strangers made awful comments, some even telling her to kill herself. Velasquez felt surrounded by hatred, even revulsion. But undaunted, she forged ahead to build her life and became a renowned motivational speaker.[6] Tam's case is similar in the way her "ugly" appearance makes her a target of cruelty for her own father and the community at large. Her self-excoriation is revealed in a letter:

> I earned good marks at school, high enough to enter university, but no university wanted such an ugly student [. . .] I burned incense often and prayed for an end to my life. How did God have the heart to put a good brain inside the head of someone like me, a girl he made by drunken mistake? (Vo 136–37)

The passage ironically underlines how human inhumanity to other humans is blamed on fate or God. The toxins sprayed during the Vietnam War are the reason for Tam's disfigurement. But she blames her destiny and God rather than history or man. The man-induced risk is made transcendental. This is "the normalization of biopower" that Foucault describes.

Tam's death wish, brought on entirely due to her "ugliness," emphasizes the instrumental value accorded to women under patriarchy. One of the projects of feminism since its inception has been to write women back into history: women who have been deliberately, purposefully erased from it. Tam is such a woman. At one point, Huan describes the land withered by war: "The earth all around had turned blackish brown. The trees had completely lost their foliage, leaving the black branches wavering and clutching at everything like ghosts" (Vo 135). The narrative draws implicit comparisons between this dead land and the young girl destroyed by the cruelty of the humans around her.

Ideas about risk in second modernity have undergone spectacular revisions. As Wallace points out, human annihilation is no longer envisioned as occurring amidst the drama of nuclear explosion but more as a slow switching off through an incidence of mercury poisoning here or a toxic spill elsewhere. Global risk is now measured in cumulative terms, in "long dyings" (Nixon, *Slow Violence* 29). Tam's gradual bodily decline through Agent Orange and the death of her brother and his friend then become symbolic of a dying humanity through human cruelty and avarice. What is enormously useful about "The Blood of Leaves" is how, in a volume that is focused mainly on the evils of war, no doubt a grave and important subject, Vo manages to raise awareness about other cruelties that are inflicted on women, the vulnerable inhabitants of risk society. Tam may have been disfigured by Agent Orange but the discrimination and cruelty she faces occur on a daily basis. The narrator's deliberate statement reveals her intention—"The street bubbled with hostility . . . War's not the only place to find it"—to expose the cruelty that women are regularly subjected to (Vo 144). For the so-called "ugly" girls like Tam and Lizzie the social world becomes a war field, and their everyday lives an ongoing battle. The "rhetoric of animality," as Steve Baker points out, is as functional in descriptions of human, social, and political relations as it is in describing actual animals (cited in Garrard 140). "The Blood of Leaves" serves as a poignant reminder that some deaths, like Tam's, like humanity's, can be gradual and painful. It is an ongoing saga. As Wallace points out, "in the twisting and open-ended narrative of risk society, both beginnings and endings are elusive" (162).

The Heart in "Heartless Forest"

The final text that is interesting from the point of view of women, animals, and animality is the titular story from *Heartless Forest*—published in 2013—by

Myanmar writer Khin Mya Zin. In 2012 her short-story collection *Clouds in the Sky and Other Stories* won the Myanmar National Literary Award. *Heartless Forest: An Anthology of Burmese Women Writers* is edited by Mon Mon Myat and Nance Cunningham. Khin's narrative draws attention, among other things, to the dangers of forest fires but is calm, even tranquil, in tone and mood. Like the earlier texts in this chapter, this too emphasizes a biocentric perspective, underscoring biodiversity and showing how it is the unconsciousness of "man" and his imperviousness to his embedment in nature that is the greatest cause of environmental destruction. The theme is important in the context of South and Southeast Asia.

On the *Climate Change Reality* website, an upload (on May 24, 2017) discusses how an increase in average annual temperature creates conditions that dramatically elevate the risk and severity of forest fires.[7] On March 19, 2007, the Moderate Resolution Imaging Spectroradiometer (MODIS) on NASA's Aqua satellite showed fire activity across eastern India, Myanmar, Thailand, and Laos. This is a continuing phenomenon. In Southeast Asia, fires are common and widespread throughout the dry season. People set fires to clear crop stubble and brush and prepare grazing land for a new flush of growth when the rainy season arrives. These intentional fires can give rise to accidental fires that invade nearby woodlands. Depending on the weather, the thick haze that fires produce lingers or disperses. The subsequent haze that is widespread in many Southeast Asian countries produces the side effect of making the air unbreathable and causes sudden spikes in asthma and bronchitis, sometimes leading to fatalities, especially amongst the aged in poor rural areas of the ASEAN.

This important theme runs through the narrative of "Heartless Forest" and culminates in a forest fire. The text mediates the issue of this pervasive environmental hazard with a lyrical, strangely haunting chronicle about Nyein, who is dead and roams the forests as a spirit, following the movements of her husband who is alive and unconscious of her presence, *unlike* the animals who sense her ghostly form. Thus, like in *The Crocodile Fury*, a seamless connection between customarily entrenched binaries such as life/death and human/animal is established. Also, the central theme of women, animals, and animality is foregrounded. The entire narrative unfolds from the focal point of the dead Nyein and thanatopolitics once again takes center stage over questions of *why* she died, *how* she died, and queries regarding her "*dispensability*." Moreover, the spirit Nyein's insistent embedment in a biotic community paradoxically speaks for a biocentric ethic, which rejoices in abundance of "life"(!)-forms.

The story can be said to unfold within the tradition of Myanmar classical poetry. LéLé Wynn of the University of Yangon, discussed in a lecture the different genres that present their close affinity to Nature:

tawlar-ratus (တောလားရတု) and seasonal verses (ရာသီဖွဲ့) such as *moetaw-ratu* (မိုးတောရတု), *moephwé* (မိုးဖွဲ့), *nwayphwé* (နွေးဖွဲ့), and so forth are the best examples to understand that the Myanmar [*sic*] feel a close affinity with Nature and that they appreciate the beauties of Nature and its seasonal changes. The romantic expressions of natural phenomena in Myanmar poetic literature can be found in compositions of *tawlar-ratu* since the Innwa period (1364–1526 AD). The literal meaning of the term *tawlar* is a journey through the forest. The sights and scenes along the journey are spiritualized and described in poetic language. (3)[8]

As in *tawlar ratu*, here the spirit Nyein roams through the forest, delighting in its many sights and sounds. The unusually lyrical language and poetic passages show a direct link to the *tawlar-ratu* tradition. As in *tawlar ratu*, the human spirit is not separated from plants and animals. Most importantly, in this tradition, nature is not silenced.

Christopher Manes argues that it is easier to exploit a "silent nature." Therefore, an agentic nature, one endowed with the capacity for *vāc* or speech and, equally importantly, the capacity to "observe," cannot be disregarded. The *tawlar-ratu* vision accords with the position held by material ecocritics that Iovino and Opperman sketch, when they assert that "matter is filled with agency." This is in direct opposition to the traditional view, which claims that agency is "connected with intentionality and therefore to human (or divine) intelligence" (453). Nyein's embedment in nature as spirit removes her from the realm of human agency. But it also means that she is as much the observed as the observer. Invisible to her husband, she is relentlessly *watched by the animals*. This is also in keeping with the quintessential Asian genre of Bonbibi stories, popular throughout Bangla and Myanmar cultures, in which animals are imbued with agency.

Bonbibi is the lady of the forest, a guardian spirit or nature goddess, an incarnation of *prakṛti* (nature) who is venerated by both Muslims and Hindus in the Sundarbans region of Bengal. She protects her devotees from man-eaters. Popular legend identifies these tigers as Dakshin Rai, a demon in disguise, who marks humans with his sharp eyes. The gaze exchanged between humans and non-humans becomes significant as it *complicates* the unequivocal power equations between predator and prey. The unusual narrative thus challenges the idea of animals as always "the observed." As Berger points out, the idea that they too can observe us has lost all significance. The animals are categorized as objects (14). "What we know about them is an index of our power, and thus an index of what separates us from them. The more we know, the further away they are" (Garrard 139). This text qualifies such universal assumptions in interesting ways.

When one realizes the remarkable similarity in the description of Nyein to the forest goddess Aranyani,[9] a logical way of approaching this text appears to be through the Bonbibi tales that are premised on the ancient *Sāṃkhya* philosophy and in the practices of Shakta cults that venerate nature as goddess incarnate. If we approach "Heartless Forest" from this perspective then the central protagonist, Nyein, the woman wandering the forest "spirit," becomes the spiritual guru of the living man. Thus, as described in the Introduction, the roles of *prakṛti* and *puruṣa* can be seen as enacted by Nyein and her husband. Nyein as *prakṛti* (here embedded in nature) is depicted as "all-seeing." At the end of the narrative, man has been taught the truth of his oneness with the universe (equivalent to nirvana or *mokṣa* in Buddhist/Hindu cosmology) and once again, *prakṛti* or nature has triumphed.

In fact, the "act of observing" is central to the unfolding narrative. The dead Nyein stalks her husband, enters his dreams at will, and wanders into his hut in the middle of the forest. In turn the animals—the domesticated dog and the wild panther—stalk Nyein and keep her under surveillance. The animals sense her presence when the man does not. We are told:

> Dogs are not like him
> They have sharp eyes and ears.
> They seem to know that she is there.
> They would get up to bark and howl in the dark of the night. (Khin 48)

The act of seeing is posited as a primordial activity, antecedent to words. As Berger points out, "[i]t is seeing which establishes our place in the surrounding world" (1). Here, the surveillance reveals a watchfulness that attends anxieties. Clearly, all parties involved assume danger from others and are vigilant in order to safeguard themselves. The man "fixes his [unseeing] eyes" where Nyein's spirit-being stands while the dog "barks as though she has seen Nyein"; Nyein "stares" at her husband (42–43). Also, Nyein's surveillance does not stop with her husband. At other times, "Nyein has followed the panther, spying on it, but it slipped away into a thicket. Before disappearing, it looked at where Nyein was with its piercing eyes" (43). The author completes the circle, setting up a connective link through these acts of surveillance a network and reciprocity between humans, the spirit, and animals. This *mutual inspection* undermines the hierarchy that prevails in the always one-sided human observation of animals (Fudge 4). When Nyein comes across her husband in his "worn-out blue jeans and his old brown coat" (41):

> Nyein does not try to go up to him.
> But he fixes his eyes on the place where she is.
> The dog following him barks as though she has seen

> Nyein, and dashes off through the leaves to stop at another tree.
> He walks towards the tree where Nyein is.
> He stands under the tree.
> In the thick darkness, leaning against the strong tree trunk, Nyein
>   stares at him. (42)

Ironically, only the human male appears supremely unaware of this unfolding tension that surrounds him, even though at times he is shown to nebulously sense a (Nyein's) presence. This seems to be an ironic reflection of humanity's obliviousness (blindness) to the impact of its exploitation of the environment. This is all the more ironic since both the man in the forest and humanity on earth do not sense their imminent extinction. The slow temporality of climate change that camouflages the great risks of ecological catastrophes waiting to occur ("long dying") is mirrored in the text by the deceptively lyrical style of the narrative that masks the dramatic end of Man that is about to occur. The forest to soon go down in flames is like Planet Earth: beautiful but teetering at the edge of extinction in geological terms. Thus, beauty hides danger and all life on earth (humans and non-humans) would end like man's.

Notably, "Heartless Forest" undermines the moral and legal distinctions between humans and animals (and spirits). While her humanity and capacity for emotion is conveyed, as a spirit-being Nyein appears closer to the flora and fauna than to her husband, from whom she was distanced even while alive. The sustained interest of the ecocritic in the subjectivity of the non-human and the problems of the troubled boundaries between the human and other creatures can be identified in the narrative. Interestingly, however, the binary that is usually drawn between domestic and wild animals along gendered lines that mark the former as female in contrast to the male as wild and is common across wilderness narratives, is obfuscated (Nelson).

> Nyein hides again, among the milkwood flowers.
> Nyein looks to see if the animal moving among the crops is the
>   panther.
> It is his dog.
> The dog, looking at the milkwood tree, howls long and loud. (Khin 44)

Here, panther and dog appear to be interchangeable and kindred. It is the man who stands alone and apart.

Nyein's animosity toward her husband follows the classic pattern of man against woman and nature. We are told that while she was alive, "Nyein's favorite dog was killed in the snare set up to catch the boar. He did not see that Nyein was desperate from that time on." While alive, "[o]n a page of the book, Nyein wrote with her small handwriting, 'I hate him most of all'" (Khin 44). Nyein's estrangement from her husband, that signals the distance between the man and the natural world, is set in contrast to descriptions of her ease and embedment in nature, which abounds: "She hid in the dark bamboo clumps all day. Sometimes, bamboo-cutters came, and then Nyein jumped from top of one bamboo cane to another" (47). In contrast to Nyein's attunement with nature, the male is shown as merely residing in the forest, relating to it only instrumentally:

> At night she heard whispers in the wind, and thought it was the sound of spirits talking.
> She thought the dark branches shaking were the hands of ghosts who would catch her.
> Her whole body shook at the howling of dogs.
> Why did he not see these things? (45)

The man's obtuseness (entirely comprehensible if we see him as symbolizing *puruṣa* within *Sāṃkhya*) is a cause of their estrangement. They also differ in their attitude to animals and land. While his tending to them is pragmatic and functional, hers is born out of love, ratifying Kellert and Berry's conclusion that "gender is among the most important demographic influences on attitudes toward animals in our society" (365). He sets traps to kill animals that destroy his fields, but she cannot accept this. The divide is ideological and categorical: "Nyein did not like the killing of animals. They did not speak to each other" (Khin 46). Their relationship disintegrates from then on. When Nyein becomes ill and later recovers, she turns inward:

> She began talking to her dead dog.
> He thought she was just play-acting.
> He gave her stern looks. She responded to his glares with fear. She vanished from the cabin.
> Nyein's body was found down by the stream, at the water's edge. (46)

Nyein seeks a symbiosis with nature that is outside the male's comprehension. Nyein, both alive and in spirit, seeks to find union in the biotic forest community, her likeness to Aranyani being most arresting.

> On moonless nights, Nyein walked throughout the forest. . . . On such nights, she would drive away the wild dogs that stalked the sweet rabbits . . .

> Nyein, sometimes coiling on the ground like a boa constrictor,
> stared down wild boars.
> When she heard the sound of woodpeckers tapping on the bark, she
> would go and guard the baby birds in their nests. She scared off
> the wildcats that hunted the little birds.
> She sometimes rocked the nests of baya weavers . . . (47–48)

Nyein seamlessly blends in with nature and is also at home in the world of culture. Like the goddess *Prakṛti*, who is both goddess of *vāc* or speech and the cultivated arts as well as of nature and the wilderness, such binaries are irrelevant to her. "Some nights, Nyein hid between the pages of her book of poems. She would play with the words moving them around. For example, she would move the word *hate* from here to there" (48). The end to this lyrical medley of verse and prose is brought about by the forest fire.

> One night, she catches the smell of fire, and sees the rabbits dashing
> headlong out of the farm.
> Then the deer
> wild boar
> panther
> The panther looks long at Nyein, as though it were observing her.
> Then it turns and runs.
> [. . .]
> The fire spreads to the vines and the yellow grass at the edge of the
> rocks.
> [. . .]
> Nyein runs for his cabin as fast as she can.
> [. . .]
> Nyein looks for him.
> [. . .]
> The fire swallows the hut. (48–49)

Nyein, searching in vain, cannot locate the man: "Where is he? [. . .] The woods he loves escapes the fire . . . The fire passes on, leaving only ashes and coals" (50). The narrative ends with a passage that bespeaks calm after the ravages of the fire.

> There is a crescent moon.
> A shadow moves under a tree.
> It's the panther.
> The panther watches Nyein.

> When she approaches him, he does not turn away as before.
> In the dark, the panther's eye glint green
> The green eyes sparkle like electric bulbs in the darkness of night.
> (50)

This is nature *after* man. The "Heartless Forest" becomes symbolic of Planet Earth—deforested, "burning up" with carbon emissions. Humanity's ever-expanding footprint on the natural world that will lead eventually to ecological collapse and mass extinction is enacted on a smaller scale here. The text points the way to the inevitable end of an orgy of overconsumption and self-absorption. The narrative ends as it began, with watchfulness, with a sense of threat and its resulting vigilance. And while the spirit of humans may roam the earth, embodied humans have sought their own demise.

Concluding Thoughts

All four texts in this chapter make critical connections between women and animals, expanding on the ecofeminist discourse around interconnectedness, speciesism, empathy, violence, trauma, and instituting and sustaining change. Interestingly, as allegories, postmodern fragmented texts, fantasy, lyrical eulogies to nature, and realistic depictions of haunting trauma, they go beyond their local contexts to speak to the global about the collective human predicament. Even as they speak from their distinctive cultural contexts, their content and goal seek to transcend the local to reach out to the global. They passionately expose the pervasive speciesism of humans and *draw nuanced connections between sexism and speciesism*. They identify many underlying causes of the modern environmental crisis such as chauvinism and human disconnection from the animal world. All the texts in this chapter underscore what Timothy Morton labels "the fragility and inadequacy of old distinctions between the natural and the cultural." In line with material ecocritics, these Asian authors contend through their plots and themes that "the ecological and the political cannot be fully separated from each other" (Morton 112). Their narratives do justice to the fact that "[a]ll things connect and cannot escape into separation" (Mentz 209). As mentioned earlier, this matrix of connectivity is also not at odds with the concept of dharma, where all of nature follows its defined, natural (and thus dharmic) course.

Finally, the narratives emerge as complex aesthetic pronouncements on risk and serve as reminders of Beck's thesis that risk society does not emerge suddenly "in the manner predicted in the picture books of social theory; rather the transition occurs on the tiptoes of normality, via the backstairs of side-effects" (*Risk Society* 11). The texts also interconnect in investigating biopolitics and consistently underscore the link between biopower and its dark underside, thanatopolitics. In keeping with the maxim that "fact is stranger than fiction," all these texts enact scenarios, which although fictional, speak to and about our planet in danger—a global reality that envelops our existence. These fictions remind us about events in human history since every barbarity they speak of—whether it is "human hunting," cruelty to the downtrodden and to animals, deforestation, punishing women, namely, biopower in diverse forms—has been enacted in our past and continues. Since the spaces occupied by women and subalterns are cognized as threatening spaces, they are also constantly under threat.

I briefly mentioned the idea of "enchantment" with nature in this chapter. This theme is further explored in the ensuing one that centers rivers, which are presented both in metaphorical and real terms. If women are linked to animals and animality, their connections to rivers in these Asian texts become equally significant and demand scrutiny.

CHAPTER THREE

Feminized Rivers, History, and Enchantment

❧

O Mother Earth! You are the world for us and we are your children; let us speak in one accord, let us come together so that we live in peace and harmony, and let us be cordial and gracious in our relationship with other human beings.
—"Prithvi Sukta," verse 16 from *Atharva Veda*, 1200–1000 BCE

The increasing rationalization and intellectualization . . . means that principally there are no mysterious incalculable forces that come into play, but rather that one can in principle, master all things by calculation. This means that the world is disenchanted.
—Max Weber, "Science as a Vocation"

In a 1917 lecture, Max Weber discussed the idea that (Western) modernity is disenchanted. He claimed that the loss of animistic connections and spiritual beliefs that characterized "traditional" societies had been lost, an idea that he also expresses in the epigraph above. Similarly, Alison Stone observes that Friedrich Schlegel's early writings presuppose that the specific form of rationality—which he calls "the understanding"—that he sees as a characteristic of modernity, encourages a disenchanted view of nature. Because "the understanding" analyses natural phenomena into their component parts, it makes the operations and interactions of those parts transparently intelligible, depriving them of the mystery and inexplicable agency they previously appeared to possess (7). These thinkers therefore have inexorably linked modernity with disenchantment. Enchantment is a theme that I examined with regard to women, animals, and animality in the previous chapter. Here, I extend it to the conceptualization of rivers.

The texts by women writers from South and Southeast Asia that I examine in this chapter counter the deeply entrenched view of modernity as disenchanted. In their texts, nature, even in the midst of often chaotic and corrupt sociopolitics, is imbued with enchantment. This feeling of enchantment is ancient in Asian traditions, acknowledged and conveyed in the epigraph from the *Atharva Veda*. In these contemporary ecofictions, too, rivers are depicted as mysterious and resistant to intelligibility, ideal and enchanted realms beyond rational apprehension. In two of them, the rivers are feminized. It would be apt to assert that the depiction of rivers by these Asian authors fit Diana Coole and Samantha Frost's affirmation of matter "as possessing its own modes of self-transformation, self-organization, and directedness, and thus no longer simply passive or inert" (10).

Ironically, however, the contrast between these metaphorical/enchanted rivers of Asia and the reality—rivers polluted, many beyond repair—is stark. Between 1980 and 2013, rivers across Asia, from India to the Philippines, have been steadily becoming polluted due to industrial effluence. The headline of a *Times of India* report reads: "The Lifeline of Madhya Pradesh: Narmada River Battles for Survival." The report describes how huge quantities of waste from cities and villages situated along the river, and effluents from industries, have already pushed the quality of water down to the "B" category, according to the Bureau of Indian Standard norms.[1]

Again, out of more than 100 million Filipinos, 9 million rely on unsafe water supply. In fact, water pollution in the Philippines and a lack of proper sewage kills fifty-five people every day. Katrina Ebora, working for the UNICEF's Water Sanitation and Hygiene program in the Philippines, notes that access to adequate sanitation facilities is a problem for more than 30 million Filipinos.[2] Reuters reports that the once mighty Buriganga river, which flows by Dhaka, is now one of the most polluted rivers in Asia because of rampant dumping of industrial and human waste. "Much of the Buriganga is now gone, having fallen to ever insatiable land grabbers and industries dumping untreated effluents into the river," says Ainun Nishat, a leading environmental expert from Bangladesh.[3] Furthermore, throughout Asia, future increase in flood frequency and severity due to climate change is anticipated.

It is against this background that I examine fictions from the Philippines, Bangladesh, and India respectively, all of which focus on a river as a central topographical feature though they treat it in magical and metaphorical terms. For some time now, the aesthetic value of enchantment has come to be gradually acknowledged and assessed in ecocritical studies. Celebrated American author Rachel Carson states unequivocally that a sense of wonder is important because it dictates ethical behavior toward nature. In her 1952 acceptance speech for the John Burroughs Medal, she elaborated clearly on this sentiment:

> It seems reasonable to believe—and I do believe—that the more clearly we can focus our attention on the wonders and realities of the universe about us the less taste we shall have for the destruction of our

race. Wonder and humility are wholesome emotions, and they do not exist side by side with a lust for destruction. (94)

Carson stresses the importance of enchantment and believes it inculcates humility. In *The Sense of Wonder*, she observes: "It is a wholesome and necessary thing for us to turn again to the earth and in the contemplation of her beauties to know the sense of wonder and humility" (44).

The idea of humility and knowing the place of the human within the vast scope of nature emerges as important. The epigraph from the "Prithvi Sukta" in the *Atharva Veda* enjoins a graciousness toward both non-human and human relationships, thereby implicating the culture/nature interconnection. It is chastening to admit that this civility to non-human nature that is recommended through the ages and underscored by numerous conservationists like Carson, is not a lesson that humanity appears to have mastered.

Nevertheless, these ideas clue us into the value of these fictions by Asian women to environmental humanists, who are committed to the preservation of riverscapes and endangered flora and fauna. I argue that these writings, while they appear to disregard realities about pollution in Asia are, in fact, deeply committed to highlighting political, social, and environmental problems, which are shown to be entangled. They also foreground the plight of women and subalterns, whose fate is closely tied to the river. As ecofeminists repeatedly assert, it is difficult to separate environmental problems from social problems. The "logic of domination," as Karen J. Warren points out, is responsible for the domination of nature, subjugation of women, and suppression of [non-white] races ("Introduction," *Ecological Feminism* 1). Therefore ecofeminists find that separating environmental problems from social ones becomes nearly impossible.

Littoral Literature

The texts chosen for study here clearly display a commitment to both social and environmental problems. Since they all center a river, they can be labeled littoral literatures. The *Cambridge English Dictionary* defines the littoral zone as "the part of a river, lake, or sea close to the land." For Michael N. Pearson, the littoral is a transitive, threshold site characterized by "permeability" (356). Greg Dening emphasizes the "endless ambiguity" and "ambivalence" of the littoral, which is often conceived of as a transitional, magical zone of possibilities (149, 158). *Fish-Hair Woman*, a novel by Filipino-Australian writer Merlinda Bobis, is based on the "Total War" in the Philippines; "Immersion" by Bangladeshi writer Dilara Hashem is about a "special" child fixated on a river; and *A River Sutra* by Indian-American writer Gita Mehta is constructed of several subordinate stories held together by a frame narrative. The stories are very different in content, tone, and form but they all make a river, which is localized—either imaginary, representative or real—the focal point of their narrative. Even where the river, as in *A River Sutra*, is real, namely, the Narmada, it is treated in equally metaphorical and mythic terms as the Iraya river in the Philippines, which is representative (deliberately distanced from the river that flows through Estancia and mythologized as Iraya [Bobis "A Conversation," 310]) or the unnamed, imaginary river in Bangladesh.

Another important feature that links these fictions is a self-consciousness about form. *Fish-Hair Woman* adopts an elaborately parodic metafictional form which is at odds with the unfolding plot that conveys angst, and the subversive tone that prompts a self-reflective attitude about the corrupt political ethos. The Iraya river is treated in mythic and metaphoric terms while the historical fallouts of political corruption are played out on its banks. In "The Immersion," repeated references to an unnamed river form a refrain, such that although it is never geographically present for much of the story, it becomes the primary referent and signals to an idyllic yet elusive geographical feature that is intensely desired and desirable. It is ironic, therefore, and entirely fitting for a short story that centers both social and environmental concerns, that in the twist at the end, this longed for imaginary river proves to be deadly in literal and material terms.

The textual form of *A River Sutra* is appropriate in that the earliest known frame narrative that precedes better known ones such as Giovanni Boccaccio's *The Decameron* or Geoffrey Chaucer's *The Canterbury Tales* can be traced to India. The *Panchatantra*, that dates back to earlier than third century BCE, is universally accepted as the precursor to *The Arabian Nights* and other well-known frame narratives. The introduction to the Penguin Classics edition of Vishnu Sharma's *The Panchatantra* details the "triumphal progress" of this text over the globe (Rajan xvi-xviii). The form of *The River Sutra* thus links the river with a cultural ethos indigenous to India. It also plays a pivotal role in the narrative since every subordinate tale is connected to the Narmada, the central Indian river which forms the traditional boundary between North and South India and flows westward over a length of 1,312 kilometers before joining the Arabian Sea at the Gulf of Cambey. But the Narmada of *The River Sutra* is not merely a physical feature. It is a liminal Third Space of quest and seeking, yielding answers to mystical questions. In fact, one could argue that the rivers in all three texts occupy the Third Space.

The idea of the Third Space, discussed in the Introduction, becomes important to my argument here as well. As Edward Soja, borrowing from Henri Lefebvre's spatial thinking, understands it:

> [b]y introducing a third dimension, Lefebvre made it possible to escape the prison of the Firstspace—Secondspace dualism. This dimen-

sion, a third possibility or moment that partakes of the original pairing, . . . can be understood as critical thirding-as-Othering. It . . . [transforms] the categorical and closed logic of either/or to the dialectically open logic of both/and also. Two terms are never enough: *Il y a toujours l'Autre*. There is always the Other, a third term that disrupts, disorders, and begins to reconstitute the conventional binary opposition into an-Other that comprehends but is more than just the sum of two parts. ("Third Space" 52)

Soja emphasizes that the Third Space breaks up the hierarchical dualism of the self/other. The rivers in the texts discussed break up the hierarchical dualism of the real/imaginary, history/myth, and culture/nature by focusing on rivers that cannot be bound to either side of the binary. They are thus *both* real (or representative) and imaginary, tied to both history and myth, and to nature and culture.

Homi K. Bhabha adds his view to this discussion of the Third Space by negotiating Michel Foucault's notion of governmentality. Bhabha examines its archaic, prejudicial, and discriminatory forms that normalize and discipline cultural groups, calcifying and imprisoning people within authoritarian structures of representation. He argues that cultural identity is, in fact, often ambivalent and displaced, formulated in the interstices of supposed differences. This interstitial space is liminal and transformative. It is subversive and "initiates new signs of identity, and innovative sites of collaboration and contestation" (*The Location of Culture* 1). Bhabha calls this "the realm of the beyond" (1). He describes "the beyond" as a contested space, "the borderline of the 'present'"(7), seeing this as the moment of transit, where space and time cross to produce complex figures of difference and identity, past and present, inside and outside, inclusion and exclusion (2).

I claim that, in these three texts, the rivers become these "realms of the beyond." The narratives present them as transitional, liminal, and transformative spaces. These spaces allow them to explore taboo social issues, probe grim historical eras, and tactically comment on corrupt politics and/or the failed role of religion, tying all of these to environmental problems. I argue then that their presentation of rivers in metaphorical terms is not an abdication of responsibility but a reiteration of it.

Semiotician Algirdas Julien Greimas, while discussing the actantial model in his book *Structural Semantics: An Attempt at a Method*, elaborates on the structural roles that are integral to storytelling such as the hero, the villain, the object (of quest), the helper (of the hero), and the sender (who initiates the quest). He argues that each of these roles fulfills an essential component of the story and is indispensable to it. Hence an "actant" is, in fact, more than a character; it is an integral structural element, the pivot around which the narrative revolves. I contend that the rivers in question are geographical entities that morph into actants in these fictions. Their imaginative construction imbues meaning(s) that goes beyond the limits of geography, making them "characters" with the power to affect plot. They thus blur the divide between agentic humans and passive nature: evidence of their transformative potential. In so doing, the very nature of Asian modernities is calibrated by these authors in ways that differ from the dominant imaginings of Western modernity.

Rivers, Texts, and Politics

The idea of using rivers or water bodies to nail home hard-hitting facts about either environment or sociopolitics is not new to Asian writers. In her Booker Prize-winning novel *The God of Small Things*, Arundhati Roy brings her activist scorn to her description of the Meenachal river in small-town Ayemenem located in Kerala, India. The polluted river that "smelled of shit and pesticides bought with World Bank loans" stands as both material and metaphorical witness to political corruption that has damaged the environment. We are told that "most of the fish had died. The ones that survived suffered from fin-rot and had broken out in boils" (14). Roy exposes political corruption and how it pollutes the river.

Amitav Ghosh—in *The Hungry Tide*, a distinctly different kind of novel but with perhaps overlapping intentions about conserving the environment and raising awareness about the related problems of corruption—writes about the Sundarbans and a young researcher's pursuit of the Irrawady dolphin to be found in sporadic subpopulations near the coast, and in estuaries and rivers in parts of the Bay of Bengal. In both texts, the littoral becomes a transitional zone that stands at the interstices of cultural differences and class. One could place the narratives I examine here as aligned with Roy's and Ghosh's intentions in calling out, equally, sociopolitical corruption and environmental pollution through their writing. Despite this common thematic that runs through the texts, however, these three works display discrete styles, objectives, and settings. Therefore, it is necessary to examine them separately in order to carefully preserve their distinctive features, before proceeding to analyze their common sociopolitical explorations.

Postmodern Stylistics and Postcolonial Angst in *Fish-Hair Woman*

I begin with Merlinda Bobis' *Fish-Hair Woman* that is set in a village called Iraya. The word could mean "upstream" in the Visayan dialect and so the village and the river become representational, losing their specificity and standing for *any* village in the Philippines that a river flows through. Bobis herself says that "Iraya" is a directional reference to place: it means "toward the water." She remarks that "[w]riting *FHW* [*sic*] was a return to water, to the wellspring of story, the 'true' destination" (311). "Iraya" may also refer to an indigenous tribe and therefore could reinforce notions about co-opting marginality. Also, in the Irayan language of the Mindoran-Iraya tribe, the word is a term for an adult or man. So, in this sense, "Iraya" could become a reference to "every woman or man" who are pawns in the hands of corrupt politicians, in the Philippines and elsewhere.

The narrative spans three eras a decade apart: 1977, 1987, and 1997 which cover the beginning, the duration, and the aftermath of the Total War. This was the civil unrest where government soldiers fought communist insurgents (or the historical New People's Army) under President Ferdinand Marcos, a kleptocrat, who ran a regime that aligned him closely to American interests.

The novel comprises two narratives of Stella or Estrella entitled "Beloved" and "Iraya," 'the longest love letter' to the Australian, Tony McIntyre, who, it appears, was loved by two sisters—Estrella and her foster sister, Pilar, the "kumander" of the insurgents and an object of Tony's admiration. But it is not Estrella who is the narrator/author because at the end of the segment titled "Iraya," Estrella instructs Luke, Tony's son—who has arrived in the Philippines at the behest of the corrupt Governor Kiko, believing it was his father who had beckoned him—to finish the story, which Luke does. In "A Conversation," appended at the end of the Filipino edition of the novel, the author, Bobis, refers to the "unease" felt by the erstwhile "colonized" readers about the significance accorded to a white Australian character. Bobis categorically states: "It's my strategy to implicate the white man in this war . . . in the global politics authored by the West" (311).

Inside these global chronicles of war are subsumed other tales: the stories of Mamay Dulce, Estrella's foster mother and the birth mother of Pilar and Bolodoy; Pay Inyo, the gravedigger in love with Mamay Dulce, and who adores her children; Governor Kiko, Estrella's corrupt and illegitimate father who had raped her mother when she was a maid in his house; Brother Ibay, one of Pilar's soldiers, later to become a Catholic priest; Matt Baker, an Australian searching for the truth behind the disappearance of his missing compatriot Tony; and Professor Inez, Estrella's estranged schoolfriend, who is bitter at having lost her husband at the corrupt hands of Governor Kiko. These stories overlap with, intersect with, revise, and contest each other so that, while a central story emerges, it does so only in fits and starts and is repetitive, with clear disruptions to linear time and chronology. Furthermore, the narrative deliberately misdirects the reader. Thus, Estrella in the segment labeled "Beloved" claims Tony as her lover. It is only later that Professor Inez queries the "truth" of Estrella's narrative to both Luke and Matt. "She has written herself into our history from which she abdicated long ago. But of course, you don't know these things, Mr Baker," she says (Bobis 224).

The form, content, even authorship of the two narratives "Beloved" and "Iraya" appear confused and open to dispute. Luke's aunt and uncle quarrel over these and other aspects of these narratives: *"Fish-Hair Woman.* Sub-title: *Beloved.* So, a novel in progress, or a love letter . . . Your father wrote it. No, your father's lover wrote it. . . . It's fiction. No, a love letter. A literary letter then . . ." (107). The characters in the story appear equally elusive: "[. . .] Tony and Estrella: lovers. No. Tony is Estrella, and Tony's staging one of his love stories. No. Estrella is searching for Tony. With her hair—ha-ha!" (107–8). The mocking reference to the hair refers to the magic realism that the book incorporates. Estrella begins her work "Beloved" with these lines: "I am a Filipina, tiny and dark as a coconut husk, but what red fires glint on my head. In 1987, in my twenty-eighth year, the village told tales about my hair" (Bobis 4). It describes how she uses her twelve-meter-long hair to retrieve corpses from the river during the civil war. While the woman described is the stuff of Filipino mythic lore, like a *duyung* (mermaid), the corpses are a literal reference to the innocent civilians killed by soldiers during the Total War and ex-judiciary killings during Marcos' regime. But figuratively, *they signify the death of innocence (wonder and enchantment) and the taint to purity, simplicity, truth, and faith, and the end of a nebulous but pristine hope.*

The story is recounted from multiple points of view with first- and third-person, and omniscient narrators. Inserted in between are realistic simulations of newspaper clippings from the fictitious *Philippine Daily News*. The style appears playful and parodic. There are stories within stories and the novel employs the techniques of narrative disruption, layering, and misdirection. The beginning, middle, and end are confused such that it is only midway through the book that the setting of the novel is clarified, in an off-handed manner, through Estrella/Stella's school essay, which states:

> [s]omewhere in the south of Luzon, in the Philippine archipelago, is my beautiful, peaceful home. It is called Iraya. . . . It has a very long river with many shrimps, fishes and also eels. I swim in it, wash clothes in it with my sister Pilar and catch fish from it with my brother. (Bobis 150; italics in original)

The postmodernist dimension of *Fish-Hair Woman* appears to endorse a postmodernist ethic, refuting an overarching moral dimension, and unwilling to classify or clarify who the heroes and the villains are. From this angle, everything appears relative: Pilar is a heroine to Tony and Brother Ibay; but to the villagers, she is the woman who killed her own brother, Bolodoy, who was part of Governor Kiko's army and hence "corrupt" in her eyes. Again, to Luke, Tony is the father who deserted him and his mother, which led to his mother's suicide but in Pay Inyo's opinion, "he good, he fool . . . he love too much. Truly-truly" (291). The narrative appears to support the idea that life is complicated and the comforts born out of simple convictions can never last long. Toward the end, even simpletons like Pay Inyo lose their faith in the idea of undisputed truths:

> But who is the hero in this story? Pay Inyo is not sure anymore, nor is he sure about what the story is in the first place. There are too many stories weaving into each other, only to unweave themselves at each telling, so that each story can claim prominence. Stories are such jealous things. The past and the present, ay, what wayward strands. (259)

Comments like these, which deliberate over the unfolding story, underscore its metafictionality. Inez's perspective, which contrasts with Estrella's, which contradicts Pilar's and Bolodoy's, all appear to point to its relativism and seem to be a sophisticated attempt at demonstrating that the chaos is insurmountable; the artist is impotent, and the only alternative to "ruin" is to play within the chaos.

This parodic façade, however, is belied by the tone of the narrative. It is possible to identify an all-encompassing rage, a relentless, pervasive emotion that hangs over the narrative, at odds with its postmodern parody and playfulness. This is borne out by one of the speakers participating in the postscript, "A Conversation," where he confesses that he "had to put the book down several times to rest my mind from painful memories and fear that it brings back even after all these years" (307). In fact, the text fits Ann Heilmann and Mark Llewellyn's observation about how:

> [. . .] in the last decades of the twentieth century and into the new millennium, historical fiction, particularly that written by women authors, has been transformed from an essentially escapist form of literature with a predominant interest in the romantic into a genre at the cutting edge of postmodern conceptualizations of the past and of contemporary worlds. (1)

I submit that despite its use of postmodernist modes in fashioning the narrative, at heart *Fish-Hair Woman* is deeply postcolonial in its thrust and intention, namely, to critique the Marcos regime using metaphor and myth, to mine all the problems that women and the subdominants faced during the Total War. Hence it combines postcolonial resistance and fervor with postmodernist stylistics that confuse (but also shield) the reader from trauma, thwarting any simple attempt at meaning-making. Myth and fantasy are nimbly combined with historical facts.

Characters and the storyline place the narrative in the Third Space between fact and fiction. Governor Kiko is a fictional reference to real-life President Marcos.

Like Kiko, Marcos occupied a position of power that the United States vacated, ruling in his own self-interest at the expense of the Filipino people, even going so far as to enforce "[the people's] gratitude at each election ... to express confidence in their God-Mayor and soon to be governor, on illegal ballots" (155). Therefore, the text works hard to ensure that fiction and fact are not easily identifiable or, indeed, distinguishable. For instance, the "news item" inserted between the first and second chapters, with the headlines "Justice Delayed is Justice Denied," reports that "forty-six bodies had been found in the river since the seventies" (250). Although the report is made up and the daily does not exist, the contents it reports are real and correspond to actual events.

Moreover, the Irayan river is treated in both real and metaphorical terms. It is tainted such that fireflies do not fly near it anymore. The corpses thrown into the river have robbed it of its sweet lemongrass scent which would attract the fireflies. But the day before the soldiers arrived, the simple gravedigger, Pay Inyo, is excited by these natural phenomena that he spots in the river, which symbolizes its purity both materially and sociopolitically:

> Lemon grass and fireflies, Estrella, you better believe it. Strange but beautiful, perhaps a sudden miracle, ay, our chance for salvation, perhaps shards of the light of Damascus, sent to pierce the hearts of the soldiers, truly-truly. (15)

The fragrant river lit with fireflies is magical. However, with the arrival of the soldiers, the river gets polluted in real terms and is a river of death in more ways than one. Facts about pollution and political murders in Marcos' regime mingle with fiction and magic.

Dee Ayroso reports in *Bulat Lat*, the online "Journalism of the People," how, aside from culpability for the massive human-rights violations committed under the dictatorship, the Marcos regime "left an environmental legacy of 'dirty energy' projects and laws." Ayroso is convinced that these continue to serve as "the base for many of today's flawed laws and projects" that have adversely affected farmers and indigenous peoples, and polluted "agricultural and forest lands," water resources and even air.[4]

Through its fusion of history and metaphor, the text challenges the notion of coherence in an attempt perhaps to mirror the political chaos and its fallout, both social and ecological. The postmodern dimension is manifest in the way the text conveys through its several repetitions and metafictional features how some experiences resist representation, even language.

Mark Currie defines metafiction as the "assimilation of critical perspective within fictional narrative, a self-consciousness about the artificiality of its constructions and a fixation with the relationship between language and the world" (2). These are intrinsic to the text. As Bobis herself remarks on the novel: "As metafiction, the novel is self-reflexive. I construct story while I interrogate its construction. Addressing the reader, I want her/him to interrogate it with me, because I am my own unreliable narrator" (308).

The fish-hair woman, a magic-realist figure "who trawls the river for dead bodies" (4), becomes myth and metaphor. Her amphibious denomination marks her liminality. She is many things in the novel. Bobis asserts that "the only way to make this core image work was to write it as both magical and real" (308). This amphibious woman becomes an iconic figure of myth but also a feminine, even maternal, refuge from the violence that rocks the village. Her hair also becomes a metaphor for memory, resonating to Currie's claim about a "fixation with the relationship between language and the world." The text literalizes this metaphor. Estrella queries, "Hair. How was it linked with the heart? I'll tell you—it had something to do with memory. Every time I remembered anything that unsettled my heart, my hair grew one handspan" (3). Bobis believes that this kind of mythologizing is not just exaggeration but essential in traumatic times. Magic-realist features augment the metafictionality of the text, systematically drawing attention to its status as an artifact. In doing so, the writer is posing questions about the relationship between reality and fiction and querying the ability of fiction to convey reality to the reader. Patricia Waugh takes this perspective one step further when she asserts that:

> In providing a critique of their own methods of construction, such [metafictional] writings not only examine the fundamental structures of narrative fiction, they also explore the possible fictionality of the world outside the literary fictional text. (40)

Waugh's idea of the "fictionality of the world" is not far-fetched since the text dismantles and questions the *truth* of history. Even as the (simulated) "newspaper clippings" insist on the "authenticity" of the narrated events, the magic realism in the narrative undermines this gesture made toward realism. Thus the history that is narrated becomes symptomatic of trauma, rendering it resistant to narrative structures and linear timelines. As trauma theorist Cathy Caruth explains: "The traumatized, we might say, carry an impossible history within them, or they become themselves the symptom of a history that they cannot entirely possess (5). Trauma and history are both centered on the river that is mythicized. "A river sweet with lemon grass and breathing fireflies" (209) becomes a living river. The river informs and shapes what the characters do and is intertwined with their ultimate destinies. But its physicality is as important as its mythic dimensions, for the river is part of the history. The simulated report from the *Phillipine Daily News*, dated July 20, 1997, refers to "[. . .] the river murders in Iraya in 1987 and in the 70s. . . . He said the government did its best to find the truth about 'those bodies in the river" (opposite Prologue inlay).

The river is powerfully affected by the dead bodies that are submerged in it. The fish-hair woman wonders if:

> [t]he disappeared could be retrieved for a decent burial and perhaps the river would be restored to its old taste, sweetened again by the hills. Then we could drink it again, we could fish there again, we could gather the river fern and taro leaves again. We could have our river back. Always the village cried, ay, Estrella, have mercy on us. (14)

Estrella, the fish-hair woman, was Iraya's merciful mother. Associated with the river, she was also their nurturer.

While discussing how, in Western societies, a scientific perspective has superseded an organic vision of nature, Carolyn Merchant clarifies that for most traditional cultures, the image of the earth as a living organism and nurturing mother meant that "Earth Mother" was in the image of a woman and digging into her "entrails and her womb" was considered unethical behavior (10–11). These organic images are widely assimilated into the descriptions of the river: "The river's womb is pitch-dark at night. So how to search the riverbed for you, my lemon grass lover" (Bobis 45). The reverse is also true. For "another river swells on desperate nights like this, flowing in the pelvis" (15) when the woman's orgasm, during lovemaking, mimics the river's swell. The human body's embedment in nature is further reinforced by the imagery that emphasizes a seamless flow between the human and the non-human, connecting the two.

> Each night . . . my *tapis* betrayed me, reweaving its flowers into fishes, which grew as luminous as the moon on the river then swam to my breasts, biting behind the nipples. His [The Australian, Luke's] blue fingers reached for them, coaxing the fishes to leap out. (15)

These metaphors link female sexuality with flowers and the fish in the river. Human memories are shown to be hopelessly entangled with the natural elements and the two are inextricable: "How to draw you out of the water with my memories, when they can only rise as dead fishes with scales that peel then float like a beautiful, silver alphabet" (45). Equally, however, the river, in and out of time, is closely linked to the idea of salvation, a concept central to the Total War in this Catholic country. The narrator intones: "What hopeful word, the sibilants a gentle hush:

salvacion. The soldiers and rebels spoke of this same cause, even as they remained in opposite camps, and our village festered in between (38). Though both sides in the raging civil war long for salvation, the word takes on meanings that are sinister. The narrator instructs us on these dangerous dimensions.

> Consider their intent: to salvage a village. Consider the word: 'salvage'. From the Latin salvare: 'rescue', retrieve, preserve from loss or destruction. But in Iraya, we whispered salvage with a weight in the tongue sinking the word like a body thrown into the river. Liquidated, made liquid, made to disappear. Such was our definition of the word. Salvage: summarily execute. (38–39)

The narrator recounts the central tragedy: "our beloved village disappeared in the bid for salvation by the rebels and the military" (39). The word "salvage," as the narrator explains, from the Latin *salvare* means "to save" and is related to the word "salvation." However, ironically, as in Margaret Atwood's dystopian novel *The Handmaid's Tale*, where the word "salvage" refers to public executions, here too the word, tossed between hope and despair, takes on ominous overtones. It is also closely associated with the river and other natural elements. Wading through this mythic and metaphorical recounting of brutal history, the *clear binary between* the vicious, misogynistic space of *culture* and the benign space of *nature*, which connects woman, river, and indeed "benediction," appears muddled.

Their distinctive attitude to the river is a means of establishing the difference between the villagers of Iraya and the military personnel. To the villagers, the river is a living presence, shrouded in myth which is part of their lives:

> The old folks said that if the river spirit Onglo makes you itch, you should seek the help of a woman with long hair . . . the unseen water-dweller could curse you if you stepped on him by mistake. You'd break out in rashes and itch for days. If this happened, you must ask Carmen to whip you with her long hair, in time with this incantation: *Hale, hale,* Onglo. Away, away, Onglo! (43)

But for the soldiers these myths are nonsense. To them, the river is a dumping ground for corpses. In keeping with the plea of material ecofeminists like Stacy Alaimo and Susan Hekman (145), *Fish-Hair Woman* reconceptualizes nature—the river—as agentic, a mythic force to be reckoned with. When corpses float in the river, its constituents change. The river smells of brine, signaling the taint to its clear waters, a tacit acknowledgment of its pollution. Nature is intricately connected and responsive to the brutal actions of humans, a geological force in themselves, as Dipesh Chakrabarty (206) and Naomi Oreskes (2009: 73, 74) have pointed out. The text iterates the impossibility of disentangling corrupt politics from pollution to the environment.

Finally, the river is both material and metaphoric. The narrative posits the material as not just reconceptualized in human terms but as an elemental other in what Catriona Sandilands discusses as "a radical democratic project that would make space for nature in politics, not as a positive human-constructed presence, but as an enigmatic, active Other" (181). Thus understood, the river in the novel is rarely a passive, silent resource for human exploitation. On the contrary, it is an active signifying force, agentic and interactive.

The Real and the Ideal in "The Immersion"

The second text, "The Immersion" by Dilara Hashem, also uses an unnamed river as an enigmatic, active other. Suspended between the "imagined and the real," "the desired and the feared," and the "pristine and the polluted," the river in "The Immersion" occupies a liminal Third Space which, in Robert J. C. Young's words, is:

> a site in the sense of a situation, and, for the subject, a site's other sense too, that is, of care or sorrow, grief and trouble: to make site is to lament or mourn. For the third space is above all a site of production, the production of anxiety, an untimely place of loss, of fading, of appearance and disappearance. ("The Void of Misgiving," 82)

The Third Space, as Young interprets it, is associated with emotions. In "The Immersion," this signals the mindscape of Badal, a mentally deficient teenager, who appears to inhabit this Third Space. The material and the imaginary are completely indistinguishable to Badal, and he is never able to understand why his words and actions cause anguish to his family. Like the natural man Caliban who is opposed to Prospero, Badal's "naturalness" is opposed to his family's cultivated responses and he is bewildered by their sorrow at his actions. Exultantly, Badal shows off to his mother, "See, Ma—how big I have become."

> As the animated shadow of his penis spread from his fists on to the wall and became bigger and bigger, Badal, in his new untasted ecstasy, stood and trembled with mirth. His mother covered her welling tears with her sari and rushed out, closing the door behind her, mumbling, "Allah, Allah! Give my child some peace, O Lord." (111)

The narrator meaningfully intones that Badal could never understand why everyone was so concerned about his peace. "He knew where peace was. Peace reigned only in himself" (Hashem 111). The narrator desires to present, through Badal, the delights of an unfettered, liberated temperament that can respond to life and beauty without being "cabined, cribbed and confined" by society. Thus enchantment becomes an active component in the story. It goes beyond "the aesthetic" to become a plot device.

In *Reading for Wonder: Ecology, Ethics, Enchantment*, Glenn Willmot believes that "irrational wonder is awash in feeling and in aesthetic apprehension. To be wonder struck is to arrest thought, to yield oneself, a kind of immersion" (6). It is this kind of immersion that is the essence of Badal's being. Badal, whose name means "cloud" in Bengali, is nature's child, responding delightedly to its various aspects. Badal appears an embodiment of Rachel Carson's "ideal child." In her work *The Sense of Wonder*, Carson states:

> A child's world is fresh and new and beautiful, full or wonder and excitement. It is our misfortune that for most of us that clear-eyed vision, that true instinct for what is beautiful and awe-inspiring, is dimmed and even lost before we reach adulthood. (44)

Badal is awestruck and enchanted by everything around him. Rivers in particular hold a fascination for him. He is mesmerized by them.

> As a child, Badal had lived by a river. The memory of the golden stretch of the river would sparkle in his breast, and whenever he strained his ears to hear the splashing laughter of the river, Badal too, without any reason, would burst out in merriment. (111)

Unconstrained by social proscription, Badal often likes to be free of his shirt, lungi, or trousers. But the sorrow of his family would weigh him down: "suddenly—Badal would become aware of their presence, a solemn presence that overwhelmed him with grief. Agitated, he would stare vacantly, the laughter would come to an abrupt halt, as Badal became absolutely silent" (111). His mother strains to comprehend his instinctual behavior and knows some ways to calm him, such as giving him a can of marbles to play with. Overriding the local physician's instructions, she desists from rubbing the smelly medicinal oil into Badal's hair, instead stroking it with cooling *mehendi* or henna paste. Random natural elements like herbs and pebbles calm Badal. Resting in his mother's lap, he dreams about the river, the active other, the natural element that captivates him.

> He could never see the banks of the river—the river was too wide, an extraordinarily large expanse of water. Badal would see himself drifting on the crest of the waves as the beams of the sun transformed the water into molten gold. Badal felt like a king astride the throne of the golden waves as he sailed into the far horizons. (115)

Like a pastoral hero in a state of innocence, a prelapsarian youth, Badal rolls to the tune of nature, out of kilter with the demands of culture. The omniscient narrator exclaims, "They did not understand that it was the colours of happiness that sparkled in Badal's soul" (111). This appears to be a stricture on the rigid, inflexible social practices that stifle individuality and agency in her society. The narrator transgresses the niceties of appropriate storytelling by illustrating with examples that would be considered offensive. For instance, Badal would often etch his favorite river with charcoal on the floor of his room. But since the "river he had drawn had no water. It only twisted and turned in dark lines." He would use his logic to fill it. He would:

> "drabble urine over it and be overcome with joy." He watched his pee winding its way, like waves of the river, rolling across the floor. Truly it seemed that the golden river had found its flow. Badal "clapped his hands and danced with joy." (112)

Badal's golden, gliding river, which he creates for his pleasure, is a matter of deep embarrassment to the family. Badal exists at the simplest level of sensual pleasure and pain, intractable to being schooled into appropriate conduct. To all except his mother, who stumblingly attempts to understand him, Badal stands opposed to propriety, decorum, and reason. Consequently, as the family gears up for his sister's wedding, Badal is restrained in his room so that he does not disturb the laughing girls who are gathered in the bridal chamber. But since he finds ways of escaping his prison, the father finally sends him to his relative in a village for the duration of the wedding ceremonies. In the calm village with a beautiful river, Badal finds peace but also a newfound unexplained excitement in a young girl, Moina, who lives there. One day, giving in to his impulses, "he crushed Moina against him" (132) and when she shook herself free and ran away, Badal, his whole body on fire in its budding sexuality, raced out, finally reaching the banks of the river.

> He flung himself into the waters of the river. And finally, as he had always dreamed, Badal was floating and drifting on the waves. His *lungi* ballooned like the sails of a ship. He tried to grasp the wind with

his excited hands . . . Badal surrendered the desires and yearnings of his youth to the depths of his beloved river. (122)

When his uncle and father arrive the following day to fetch him back home, they find him "attired in peace, in quietness—finally at rest" (123).

Using the leitmotif of the river, the narrator shines the light on many taboo social issues. Several difficult problems such as proscriptions on speaking out about sexuality, and the silence around the treatment meted out to "intellectually challenged" children, are exposed. As Rashed Al Mahmud Titumir and Jakir Hossain point out in their comprehensive study *Disability in Bangladesh: Prevalence, Knowledge, Attitudes and Practices*, the taboo and ignorance surrounding disability, despite kindly intentions, is patent all over the country.

Bhabha heralds the indeterminate spaces between subject positions as the points of disruption and displacement of hegemonic narratives of cultural structures and practices (*The Location of Culture*). He proposes hybridity as such a form of liminal or in-between space, where the "cutting edge of translation and negotiation" (38) occurs and this he terms the Third Space. "The Immersion" becomes one such *point of disruption of fixed cultural hegemonic narratives*. It introduces subject positions that thwart ideas of propriety and "the norm." By further aligning this Third Space with "enchantment," the narrative makes the challenge to "the accepted norm" a *desirable* alternative.

But the metaphorical river also makes a pronouncement on the differences between the ideal and the real. Badal's imagined river signals to an idyllic yet elusive geographical feature that is intensely desired and desirable. This untainted, "pure" river, it is shown, can only be the stuff of dreams. The reality is vastly different. This longed-for imaginary river ultimately proves to be deadly in literal and material terms. "The Immersion" then utilizes metaphor to draw attention to *the contrasts that operate between what ought to be and what is*. One could speculate that by centering the river, at one level, the story also extrapolates to ironize the contrast between the political rhetoric of conservation and the realities on the ground.

An Agentic and Feminine River in *A River Sutra*

The final text, *A River Sutra*, is written around the pilgrimage tradition of circumambulating the Narmada river. The novel is constructed by six different tales of passion, enchantment, love, and loss, held together by a frame narrative that centers on an unnamed senior bureaucrat, the manager of a guest house along the Narmada river. It is in the vicinity of this guest house that the bureaucrat meets the various characters who inhabit the subordinate tales, marking the river itself as a flowing theme, with every story rising from and ebbing into the Narmada. The word "sutra"[5] in the title, which in Sanskrit means a thread or line that holds things together, is derived from the verbal root *siv*, meaning "to sew." The text thus sews together tales along the river Narmada, making it *A River Sutra*.

Of a contemplative turn of mind that has persuaded him to downgrade his career goals, the bureaucrat is predictably the audience for the six tales that bead the narrative. Interestingly, too, the frame narrative is interspersed with comments by the bureaucrat and his friends, all of whom are male. Thus, we hear the views of Tariq Mia, the mullah from the neighboring village; Dr Mitra, the local physician; Mr Chagla, the bureaucrat's faithful assistant; and even the local constable, Sashi. The Narmada gets objectified as a feminine presence open to the androcentric gaze of these males. The narrative underscores this perspective by recounting the myth of the Narmada's "birth" in magical and erotic terms:

> It is said that Shiva, Creator and Destroyer of Worlds, was in an ascetic trance so strenuous that rivulets of perspiration began flowing from his body down the hills. The stream took on the form of a woman—the most dangerous of her kind: a beautiful virgin innocently tempting even ascetics to pursue her, inflaming their lust by appearing at one moment as a lightly dancing girl, at another as a romantic dreamer, at yet another as a seductress loose-limbed with the lassitude of desire. Her inventive variations so amused Shiva that he named her Narmada, the Delightful one, blessing her with the words, "You shall be forever holy, forever inexhaustible." Then he gave her in marriage to the ocean, Lord of Rivers, most lustrous of all her suitors. (Mehta 8–9)

This mythic, erotic description of the river is sustained throughout the novel in the frame narrative. The bureaucrat imagines that he can hear the feminized river's "heartbeat pulsing under the ground" (5), and cognizes the river as female in many other instances as well: "Dawn lightened the sky and I was able to see the Narmada . . . refracting the first rays of sun into arcs of color as if the river were a woman adorning herself with jewels (139). And again, "I . . . imagined the river as a woman painting her palms and the soles of her feet with vermillion as she prepared to meet her lover" (139). The Narmada becomes "everywoman," described as virgin, seductress, bride, courtesan, and mother (as the protector of the pilgrims who come to her banks to worship her) all rolled into one. It is thus both sacred and erotic. It is the holy river, where:

> [i]n the silence [the bureaucrat] . . . can hear waves lapping at the riverbanks and . . . think of the ascetics meditating by the holy pool

at Amarkantak, seeking through their meditations to liberate themselves from the cycle or rebirth and death.(42)

Therefore, to re-invoke Schlegel, the text "points to what is higher, the infinite, [it offers] a hieroglyph of the . . . holy fullness of life of creative nature [*Bildenden Natur*]" (334/Tr. 106–7).

Not entirely unexpectedly, such musings that link nature to a "holy fullness of life" are not alien to Hindu philosophical thought either, where the concept of nature as active and dynamic, as *prakṛti*, is deeply inscribed. As discussed in the earlier chapters, in *Sāṃkhya philosophy, prakṛti* or nature is the feminine principle which is active while *puruṣa*, the individual aspect of cosmic consciousness, is the masculine principle which is passive or spiritually dormant. *Prakṛti* needs to be agentic for *puruṣa* to evolve, though *prakṛti* by itself is stable and only a catalyst. *A River Sutra* can be seen as reworking the principles of *Sāṃkhya* philosophy. Interestingly, the bureaucrat falls within the Hindu archetype of the *jñānamārgi*—the Hindu spiritual aspirant who follows the intellectual path of spiritual enquiry to attain salvation—(*jnana* = intellect; *margam* = path) as different to the *bhakthimārgi and karmamārgi*, who embrace the paths of devotion and duty, respectively. In this view, the bureaucrat could become representational of *puruṣa* while the Narmada river could be *prakṛti*, representational of nature through whose influence he struggles to spiritually evolve.

Furthermore, the yoga system within Hinduism is based, by and large, on *Sāṃkhya* tenets and stresses the perfect balance brought about by the union of masculine and feminine principles. This philosophical equilibrium is echoed in the textual form of *The River Sutra* where the characters who pepper the frame narrative are all male whilst their teacher is the objectified Narmada river, which stands for manifest nature or *prakṛti*, the feminine principle. Also, of the six subordinate stories, three are narrated by men and the other three by women. This yoking of opposites where the masculine and feminine principles are held in equipoise can be traced as a pattern that also emerges at the thematic level. The bureaucrat, who gives importance to masculine qualities, is repeatedly brought up short and made to realize the importance of balance. His perspective is inexorably revealed as hackneyed and caught up in binary modes of thought that need to be transcended.

Indeed, the narrative consistently underlines the importance of transcending binaries. The Narmada emerges simultaneously as both subject and object. "She" is the primary subject of the narrative, the divine mother or *prakṛti*, but also the ultimate, objectified "other"—"mythicized" by the worshipers, "deified" by the tribals, and "feminized" by the bureaucrat, who imagines the river "flowing to meet her bridegroom in all those variations that delighted the Ascetic [Lord

Shiva]" (Mehta 9). The Narmada is balanced between nurturance and eroticism, between the sacred and the profane.

Even the medical man, Dr Mitra, grasps the significance of this remit. When he shocks the bureaucrat with the remark "[d]id you know Narmada also means 'whore' in Sanskrit?" (150), it shows that *he has already absorbed the idea that binaries such as sacred and profane, virgin and whore, discipline and excess, science and mysticism, and reason and enchantment are not opposites but only different dimensions of the great drama of life* and hence different attributes of the great feminine principle of *prakṛti*, which stands for the fullness of life. The river is a facet of *prakṛti*—both material and symbolic—a geographical entity but also larger; a value-laden cultural symbol, emerging as an ecotone; a littoral zone filled with potential and inhabiting the Third Space of possibilities.

Thus, the reductive nature of the bureaucrat's cerebral attempts to apprehend the "Absolute" is shown up. He insists on dealing in abstractions, not taking in "life," *prakṛti*, nature, the material universe. The mullah says, "[d]rink your tea, little brother. How can you say you have given up the world when you know so little of it?" (50) Hence, the bureaucrat can be read as the personification of the hapless *puruṣa*, who refuses to heed the clues planted throughout "his" life to teach him about the futility of man-made dualisms. The Narmada, as *prakṛti*, ceaselessly strives to teach him the importance of transcending these man-made boundaries, especially the reductive "nature-culture" binary, in order to initiate his evolution.

Equally, all the subordinate stories challenge binaries. The first of the stories is narrated by Ashok, a Jain monk whom the bureaucrat meets on the banks of the Narmada. The son of a fabulously wealthy diamond merchant, he renounces his life of luxury to lead a life of extreme poverty as a Jain mendicant. His narrative falls squarely within the genre of a *vita* ("life" in Latin; refers to a brief biography, often that of a saint) within the broader category of hagiography. However, unlike typical hagiographies, which are predominantly narratives of praise, emphasizing the progress of the spirit and prizing cerebral male values such as austerity and discipline, here the first-person narration by the monk registers an ambivalence to his renunciation and indeed his panic at the moment of renunciation.

In the ensuing subordinate stories, we encounter an austere executive, a hitherto beer-swigging, macho man, Nitin Bose, who arrives in Rudra calling himself Rima, with made-up eyes. He appears now to be a transgender. We hear that Bose retreated to a remote estate located in what was once believed to be *naga* (serpent) land—that, significantly, is on the boundary between the so-called Aryan land of reason and the Dravidian zone of myth—to escape from the sleazy, depraved lifestyle of his urban colleagues. This subordinate story infers a judgement on the impact of industrialization and urbanization on humans, enabling an eco-spiritual perspective to emerge. Here, Bose resists the lure of a local women but ultimately became enchanted by her and reaches this transgendered state, a holistic state that is a rebuke for his refusing the woman's passion.

The Calcutta that Bose inhabits has air-conditioned cars and subways, and dates the Pakistan–Bangladesh war to "twenty years earlier" and "the partition of India fifty years earlier" (110), thus placing the narrative in the late twentieth century. Yet, if you fly out of this eminently contemporary Calcutta and make "the eight hour drive from the small airport to the tea garden" (114) to where Bose is bound, you have not merely moved out of an urban to a rural setting but have seemingly moved out of a modern world to a mythic landscape where legends of "[a] world devoted to pleasure and learning, its serenity guarded by hooded serpents with great gems flashing from their hoods" (120) and "of magic performed during the eclipse of the moon when a man's soul could be captured inside the two halves of a coconut" (127) become lived realities. The story blends urban and rural, contemporary with timeless, reason with magic such that they all coexist. The epicene and mythic landscape that Bose inhabits, like the Narmada, is timeless and yet as contemporaneous as myth, constantly evolving and ancient but relevant. The story works to achieve an equipoise between masculine and feminine principles. As the bureaucrat's assistant, the simple Mr Chagla, explains hesitantly:

> It is not a woman who has taken possession of Mr Bose's soul, sir. How can such a thing can [sic] ever happen? . . . Sir. Really, sir . . . The goddess is just the principle of life. She is every illusion that is inspiring love. . . . she is what a mother is feeling for a child. A man for a woman. A starving man for food . . . And Mr Bose did not show her respect so he is being punished. (142)

Mr Chagla unequivocally links the Narmada, worshiped as a goddess, with a fundamental principle of life, *prakṛti*:

> [D]esire is the origin of life. For thousands of years our tribals have worshipped it as the goddess. You have heard the pilgrims praying, 'Save us from the serpent's venom'. Well, sir, the meaning of the prayer is as follows. The serpent in question is desire. Its venom is the harm a man does when he is ignoring the power of desire. (143)

Chagla's blundering simplicity that counters the austere intellection of the bureaucrat points to the wisdom of not attempting to subordinate human desire—a natural aspect of being human—but to embrace it. Bose is finally cured only when the tribals lead him to Narmada the goddess, and teach him to embrace emotion along with cerebration, passion along with austerity. Each of the subordinate stories challenges entrenched binaries like spontaneous desire versus groomed sophistication and science versus mysticism, as when renowned archaeologist Dr V. V. Shankar turns out to also be a "Naga baba," naked and covered in ashes from the graveyard.

One of the primary eco-political messages that *A River Sutra* advances is about the profound futility of pursuing binary modes of thought that patriarchal discourse has constructed to privilege the male and the human over the female and the non-human. Life on the banks of the Narmada is certainly not so neatly compartmentalized. As Amir Rumi's poem explicates and the wise, old mullah realizes, even so pure an emotion as "love" can, paradoxically, destroy: "Do not turn in loathing from me./O Beloved, can you not see/Only Love disfigures me?" (71) Like the outward-bound astronaut pulling away from Planet Earth gradually gets a more holistic picture of Gaia, the reader, pulling back from the subordinate stories to the frame narrative and beyond realizes that the bureaucrat himself is symbolic of the human subject. The most important lesson that the human subject (as *puruṣa*) needs to learn is equilibrium. *Prakṛti, as nature, has imbued ecological systems with natural balance. It is puruṣa*, the blundering human subject, who has undermined, damaged, and polluted this exquisitely balanced ecosystem.

Interestingly, the contrast between the bureaucrat's attitude to the Narmada and that of the protagonists in the subordinate tales—in whose lives the river plays an active and dynamic role, changing their destinies in salient ways—prompts a reflection on the differences between an idealistic and a realistic approach to the river.

In deliberately invoking the Hindu ethos in presenting the Narmada river, Mehta's text poses some significant questions about the role of religion in preserving nature or in its failure thereof. It also provokes thought on how idealizing nature often impedes its material conservation: a lesson that is particularly relevant to contemporary India where, sometimes, conservative religious ideologies appear to overrule reason or even common sense. At such moments, it is worthwhile to step back and consider the virtues of a concept such as dharma. As mentioned in the Introduction, Troy Wilson Organ discusses this "impossible to translate" (211) term:

> Dharma is both reality and ideality. The dharma act may be chiefly prescriptive, i.e., a chosen act intended to preserve a value, or it may be chiefly descriptive, i.e., an act flowing from the nature of a thing. In either case it is related to *ṛta*, the ancient conception of the orderliness of the world. (211)

In the littoral literatures that I have discussed here, it becomes interesting to observe that when human conduct is against dharma (*adharmic*), it upsets cosmic balance. The polluted river, the corrupt society, the Narmada river that is forced to absorb human excesses, the instinctual man who should have his "own place" in the cosmos but is scorned and driven out, finally finding a haven only in the river, are all illustrative of cosmic imbalance.

While a dharmic surveillance reveals the entanglements between the human and the non-human that result in social and ecological violence, other views enable an examination of the use of metaphors in these texts to challenge corruption and ecological pollution.

Rivers, Metaphors, and Social and Environmental Politics: Some Thoughts

It is noteworthy that *The River Sutra* was published in 1993, soon after the Babri Masjid violence, when the far-right Hindutva movement in India was gathering force. The Archeological Survey of India (ASI) states that the Babri Masjid mosque was built on land where a non-Islamic structure had previously existed. On the strength of this assertion, in the 1980s the Vishva Hindu Parishad (VHP) began a campaign for the construction of a temple dedicated to Rama at the site, claiming that this was the site of Ayodhya, Rama's legendary kingdom. With the Bharatiya Janata Party (BJP) as its political voice, several rallies and marches were held as a part of this movement, including the Ram Rath Yatra.

On December 6, 1992, the VHP and the BJP organized a rally at the site of the mosque that involved around 150,000 *kar sevak*s or volunteers. The rally turned violent, the security forces were overwhelmed, and the rioting crowds tore down the mosque. This led to widespread Hindu–Muslim rioting in India. Placed against this background and given the sociopolitical context of the time, *A River Sutra* and its theme that is centered on Hinduism—especially with Tariq Mia, the mullah from the neighboring village shown as patently wiser than the Hindu spiritual aspirant—makes it a particularly radical and volatile text.

What is particularly compelling about the book is the insidious way in which it challenges the dominant ideologies of the Hindutva movement while ostensibly subscribing to a Hindu ethos. It is noteworthy, first, that it is the bureaucrat, a government official (significantly unnamed hence representative), who imagines himself the spiritual aspirant but whose ignorance is constantly pointed out by his friends, and is always the butt of their jokes. Second, it is the unassuming mullah, Tariq Mia, who is the wiser man, and educates the Hindu bureaucrat about the "meaning of life." Third, and very significantly, hierarchical dualism, with its entrenched self/other binary mode of thought, is torpedoed in the text by invoking the Third Space of hybridity and inclusivity, where Muslim and Hindu, male and female, the sacred and the profane cohabit joyously.

Indeed, in the three texts examined, rivers become metaphors that enable a thoughtful reflection on the social and political problems that confront a rapidly evolving Asia. The river as a focal point is poised between the ideal and the real in these texts. The ideal exists as a myth, dream, or philosophical concept. The contrapuntal real is pushed forward either subtly or overtly in all its contradictions, corruption, and pollution. The question remains as to why these writers adopt oblique, metaphoric images to address concrete problems such as political corruption, social taboos, and, indeed, environmental pollution.

One could perhaps argue that such writing is symptomatic of works written under censorship, even self-censorship, for fear of social and political repercussions. In "A Conversation," it is most telling that in responding to a question about why it took her seventeen years to write this novel, Bobis confesses that "[o]bsession and survival" sustained its writing. She admits "while researching the Total War, I 'found' the bodies of the violated and the dead. I shuttled between insomnia and nightmares" (309). For her, writing becomes an act of endurance. "To write is to survive, Survival is also about the *survival of story* (309; italics in original). She remarks that in the writer's attempt to "*recapture* 'as it happened', . . . we embellish and mythologise . . . especially in remembering war . . ." (308; italics in original).

Again, contravening social taboos in conservative societies like Bangladesh is not tolerated as, for example, multiple fatwas have been enacted on writers like Taslima Nasrin, who dared to be different. In India, increasingly, certain Hindu sects have turned intolerant of critical opinions voiced against Hinduism. All this could have persuaded these writers to adopt an indirect, euphemistic approach in discussing complex problems that probe the corrupt sociopolitics and the related environmental problems they either help generate or ignore.

Ultimately, however, it is difficult to hold this view when one scrutinizes the backgrounds and contexts of these texts. First, Bangladeshi writer Dilara Hashem is renowned for her works and for her writing as a journalist. She was sensitized to the pressures of history and politics that led to repeated personal uprooting, relocation, and emigration in her life. Hashem translated these experiences into contemporary novels of the most varied subject and settings, from contemporary Pakistan—the epic *Chandragrohan* (Lunar Eclipse, 2002)—to recent New York—the "novel in dialogue" *Sesh Rater Songlap* (Twin Towers, 2003).[6] Besides literature, Hashem has made time for a professional career as a newsreader and international broadcaster with Radio Pakistan (where she was a national newsreader), Radio Bangladesh, the BBC London and, since emigrating to the USA in 1972, the Voice of America. She has also debated on environmental pollution.[7] So, reality is no stranger to her.

Similarly, Gita Mehta is the daughter of Biju Patnaik, an Indian independence activist and, later, the chief minister of the post-independence state of Odisha, then known as Orissa. She and her family are no strangers to conflict and controversy. The year of publication of *A River Sutra*, 1993, was not only in the immediate aftermath of the Babri Masjid violence but also at the height of the controversy over the building of the Sardar Sarovar Dam over the Narmada river. Agitated and angry activists, including Arundhati Roy, were at the forefront of the protests. The World Bank withdrew its funding for the dam in 1994.

Finally, the Marcos regime was in power thrice, from 1965–67, 1969–72, and 1972–81. During this time, martial law was proclaimed in the Philippines. Bobis' novel was in the making for thirteen years, which means that she began writing it in 1999. By this time, there were many hard-hitting accounts of the regime, including those that discuss the impact of the regime on the environment.

These authors surely would not have been that afraid of being controversial, living overseas as they were, away from their native countries. We have to conclude that all these writers, who in other ways have not hesitated to challenge authority, deliberately chose to present these works through metaphorical images invoking "enchantment." Perhaps they chose not to be another voice that was dismissed as "taking a side" amid the cacophony of voices in such divisive issues. Or, in the ultimate analysis, perhaps they understood the value, indeed, the power and efficacy of metaphors.

As German philosopher Hans Blumberg has observed, metaphors are anything but seamless similarities. They are disturbances. They can be disruptive and suggest new analytic spaces and new associations even as they seem smoothly to line up with that to which they refer. Metaphors can be political actors when they stretch our visions to new domains. Blumberg reminds us that metaphors are never precise. In this gap lies their traction (3). *Metaphors have the potential to imbue enchantment to the mundane and the real.*

In all the three texts, each of the rivers is treated metaphorically, but also exists as an indispensable narrative element and elemental force of nature; nevertheless, it also has a material impact on the characters. As a geographical entity that has a cultural impact, it transcends the binaries of nature/culture. Also, in all three texts, the river becomes an actant because without the active role that it plays in the plot, the story would not progress.

Concluding Thoughts

The rivers in these ecofictions are specific and/or representative geographical locations. They are also mythic and metaphorical narrative elements. But, most of all, they are carriers of human history and affected by the consequences of human actions. They expose, question, and challenge exploitative attitudes and/or cerebral, impractical approaches to nature. The narratives prompt a radical revaluation of human relationships with the environment.

It is interesting to note that these contemporary authors—dynamic women whose lives also reveal a strong social conscience—have chosen to present their complex ideas on sociopolitics and the environment by using the trope of enchantment. This leads us to cogitate on whether Weber's ideas on modernity and disenchantment can be applied to Asia. *It would appear that the strong secular trend that was a post-enlightenment legacy in the West does not apply in the same measure in Asia, where traditional attitudes to a "mystical nature" are not really discredited despite the influx of "modernity" and "globalization."*

In these texts, the strong *rejection* of anthropocentrism is connected to: The Catholic idea of salvation; the Muslim child's ecstatic reaction to nature as an elemental source of joy and wonder; and the Hindu philosophical view of nature as *prakṛti*. These writers who hail from, and tie their narratives to, their respective Catholic and Islamic and Hindu traditions, position their imaginings as counter to contemporary world's factual/secular approach to nature. Enchanted nature, they seem to declare, has value since it has a hold on human imagination. Hence, they hark back to their disparate Asian traditions to reconstruct such enchantment.

The next chapter deals with the idea of the apocalypse, which is often conceptually placed in direct opposition to enchantment.

CHAPTER FOUR

Women, Pasts, and the Apocalypse

❧

Aham Bramahsmi! I am Brahman
I (*aham*) [or the individual soul (*atman*)] am Brahman (Universal
   Consciousness)
—*Brihadaranyaka* Upanishad 1.4.10 of the *Yajur Veda*

My friend from Asia has powers and magic, he plucks a blue leaf from
   the young blue-gum
And gazing upon it, gathering and quieting
The God in his mind, creates an ocean more real than the ocean, the
   salt, the actual
Appalling presence, the power of the waters.
He believes that nothing is real except as we make it. I humbler have
   found in my blood
Bred west of Caucasus a harder mysticism.
Multitude stands in my mind but I think that the ocean in the bone
   vault is only
The bone vault's ocean: out there is the ocean's;
The water is the water, the cliff is the rock, come shocks and flashes of
   reality. The mind
Passes, the eye closes, the spirit is a passage;
The beauty of things was born before eyes and sufficient to itself; the
   heartbreaking beauty
Will remain when there is no heart to break for it.
—Robinson Jeffers

The Apocalypse in Literature

In the last chapter, I showed that cultural ideologies that affirm an "enchanted nature" have value since they influence human behavior toward nature. In this chapter, however, the subject is brought up again in an inverted form, interrogating the impact of nature on humans, which demands answers. The texts I examine here attempt to explore this problem.

The second epigraph above, Robinson Jeffers' poem "Credo," charts a clear divide between the mysticism of Asia (as reflected in the first epigraph from the *Yajur Veda*) and the consciousness of the unrelenting material reality of nature in those "bred west of Caucasus." For the latter, "the water is the water, the cliff is the rock" and there is a deep conviction that "the heartbreaking beauty will remain where there is no heart to break for it." Jeffers' poem foregrounds two ideas, both of which are central to the discussion in this chapter. The first is an awareness of the supposed differences in the approach to nature between two civilizations, broadly and often inaccurately defined as West and East. The second is the awareness of the apocalypse—the extinction of the human species—that is inbuilt into this consciousness.

The apocalypse narrative, with its portrayal of our planet on the brink of an ecological collapse and human population on the edge of extinction, has been one of the most popular genres espoused by cinema, pop fiction, and climate fiction. As Ursula Heise points out, the apocalypse has often been held in opposition to the pastoral (*Sense of Place* 123). There is a diametrical contrast, even a modal friction, between the apocalyptic and pastoral modes. As Terry Gifford insists, it is important to differentiate between the pastoral *genre* (for example, Milton's *Lycidas*) and the *mode*, which is defined by "theme rather than form" (19). I would add that risk provides a third point for a triangulated vision. While the apocalypse envisages a dramatic ending, the pastoral presents serene living, and risk is about a prolonged crisis. Thus the (in)congruence between the apocalyptic and the pastoral, which makes for interesting interventions with risk, is useful to explore as it unfolds in Asian women's fiction.

Apocalyptic imagery has proliferated in the imagination of the human race since ancient times and is not exclusive to the West. In fact, most religious texts paint a version of the end of time. In the Bible is the "great flood" brought on by God's wrath, with Noah's ark and its inhabitants surviving the disaster. There is also the concept of the Armageddon. In Hindu mythology is *Pralayaa* (or dissolution of the world) and the coming of Kalki Avatar as a parallel. There are also two major points of Buddhist eschatology, namely, the appearance of Maitreya and the "Sermon of the Seven Suns." In the Mayan calendar, the year 2012 was widely proclaimed as the year of dissolution. It is no wonder then, as Gary Baines has recognized, that "apocalypse might well be embedded in our collective consciousness" (21).

In secular Western literature, too, beginning with the "Epic of Gilgamesh" dated around 1000 BCE to the twenty-first century, are texts proclaiming the end of time. Mary Shelley in *The Last Man* and Bram Stoker in *Dracula* construct doomsday scenarios in Victorian times. This was in response to growing imperial fears about the end of civilization brought on by a series of factors, including guilt over the excesses of colonial rule and fears centered on Darwinism with its theory of the survival of the fittest. These fears were linked to anxieties about the growing effeteness and perceived weaknesses of the European races and the "robust native hordes" taking over. The twentieth century, with its two world wars, was equally prolific in doomsday narratives, many of which form part of the science-fiction or fantasy genre. The most famous of these is H. G. Wells' *War of the Worlds* which he first began serializing in 1897, prior to the world wars. The culmination of World War II, with the atomic bombing of Hiroshima and Nagasaki, demonstrated humanity's capacity for self-destruction. This inevitably led to a lot of introspection, giving rise to a plethora of books that came to be labeled as "apocalyptic fiction." Pat Frank's *Alas Babylon*, Stephen King's *The Stand*, and Cormac McCarthy's *The Road* are a few examples of this genre of fiction that captured the popular imagination. The aftermath of World War II with decisive Asian involvement through both colonial and Japanese intervention, gave rise to several Asian apocalyptic movies and fan fiction, though mostly in Asian languages.[1] *Dusk* and *When Yesterday is Gone* are some popular Asian blogs in English that have a following.[2] *Severance* by Chinese-American author Ling Ma is one of the few Asian apocalyptic novels in English.

These instances point to the fact that most apocalyptic narratives, whether of the science-fiction or fantasy genre, articulate visions that are heavily based on existing social and ecological problems.[3] Thus, although they all reflect some apprehension about a contemporary predicament, often political or ecological, the fictional texts at least are almost always speculative and project their plots into the near or distant future. Hence apocalyptic fiction habitually deals in fantasy and envisions future events. The important tension in the genre appears to arise from imagining the future but also simultaneously reflecting the present.

Apocalyptic Narratives by Asian Women

I explore five apocalyptic narratives by Asian women, chosen for their perspectives that emerge from the margins, from countries that have historically been placed on the "other side" of liberalism, democracy, and indeed, progress. Short stories and novels from Laos (which was part of the topography of the "American

War" through the Ho Chi Minh trail), Pakistan, Indonesia, Sri Lanka, and India, countries which have been labeled either as generators of terrorism (Pakistan and Sri Lanka) or as "hotspots of violence" (India and Indonesia) demonstrate eco-variations in that they hold ecological perspectives that are often overlooked or remain marginal.

The tension between present and future in apocalyptic narratives, as mentioned earlier, can also be witnessed in these Asian apocalyptic narratives but with a difference. The perspectives they present are often generated from the first-person point of view and are more centered on the past than on the future. These texts recount traumatic incidents in their communities brought about by either extreme weather or war that has had a lasting impact on the local ecology. The first text analyzed, "The Roar of a Distant War" by Viliya Ketavong, is a flashback by an adult who recalls her childhood in Laos during the American War. She tells the "other side" of the story, which is different to the accounts played out through Hollywood films and American war-hero narratives. This story of a terror-filled childhood features a seven-year-old Laotian girl as its protagonist. The story reveals how her trauma surfaces at unguarded moments. The second narrative, *Rani in Search of a Rainbow: A Natural Disaster Tale* by Shaila Abdullah, has a young Pakistani girl as the protagonist. Rani loses her home due to torrential rain and flooding and, along with her family, is taken to a refugee camp. The story is about her initial loss and (non-material) gains in the refugee camp. The third story, *Wave: A Memoir of Life after the Tsunami* by Sonali Deraniyagala, is about how the protagonist, a young mother, loses her children and indeed her entire family, to the tsunami in Sri Lanka. The final two texts, the Indonesian Lily Yulianti Farid's "Lake" and Chitra Divakaruni Banerjee's *One Amazing Thing*, contend with scalar effects as they connect global ecological events to individual histories.

At least four out of five of these texts are based on true incidents. Thus, again, fact and fiction coexist in the Third space. All the narrators are young girls or women who are empowered to voice their views. It is noteworthy that the young narrators are depicted as having a special relationship with their grandmothers. They pepper their narratives with these elder women's wisdom and truisms, creating a space where they receive validation. In all the narratives, the harshness of the perils experienced are, at least partially, ameliorated by the sharing of myths and folklore, as well as through the act of narration itself, which is prioritized.

The Apocalypse: Future and Past

The general perception about apocalyptic fiction is that it is tied to the future. Therefore, having identified these five texts that are tied to the past necessitates discussion, that is helped by Frederick Jameson's perceptions in his essay "Progress Versus Utopia; Or, Can We Imagine the Future?" In this essay, Jameson raises some pertinent questions with regard to science/futuristic fiction. He argues that current theories pertaining to ideology enable us to view abstract ideas like "progress" as revealing a certain type of orientation to history that includes the *past* as well as the *future*. Just as Georg Lukács argues that historical fiction reflected the ethos of the nineteenth-century bourgeois class, Jameson believes that science fiction defines our *current* historical moment despite it appearing to be concerned with depicting the future.

Reviewing Stanley Kubrick's film *Barry Lyndon*, with its reconstruction of a whole vanished eighteenth-century past, Jameson observes that this historic reconstruction raises issues that relate to our relationship with the past, demonstrating that "any other moment of the past would have done just as well" (150). Thus, the sense that "this determinate moment of history is, of organic necessity, a precursor to the present," Jameson says, has vanished into "the pluralism of the 'Imaginary Museum', the wealth and endless variety of culturally or temporally distinct forms, all of which are now rigorously equivalent" (150). He ties this to Lukács's classical study *The Historical Novel*, where Lukács registers a difficult perception, namely, the genre's "increasing incapacity to register its content; the way in which Gustave Flaubert's *Salammbô* (1862) becomes emptied of its vitality and survives as a dead form, a museum piece, as 'archaeological' as its own raw materials, yet resplendent with technical virtuosity" (149). Jameson ties the decline of historical fiction to the rise of science fiction:

> The moment of Flaubert, which Lukács saw as the beginning of this process, and the moment in which the historical novel as a genre ceases to be functional, is also the moment of the emergence of SF, with the first novels of Jules Verne. We are therefore entitled to complete Lukács' account of the historical novel with the counterpanel of its opposite number, the emergence of the new genre of SF as a form which now registers some nascent sense of the future, and does so in the space on which a sense of the past had once been inscribed. (150)

From this perspective, historical and futuristic fictions merge in the symbolic realm, for the most characteristic speculative or apocalyptic fiction does not earnestly attempt to imagine the "real" future of our social system. Rather, in Jameson's view, "its multiple mock futures serve the quite different function of transforming our own present into the determinate past of something yet to come" (151). Jameson thus sees futuristic (read apocalyptic) fiction as enacting and enabling "a structurally unique 'method' for apprehending the present as history, and this is so, irrespective of the 'pessimism' or 'optimism' of the imaginary future world which is the pretext for that defamiliarization" (151).

Jameson's idea that the relationship of science fiction to its ostensible content—the future—is complex in that it has concealed a "temporal structure," one that defamiliarizes and restructures our experience of the present (152), is particularly pertinent to Asian apocalyptic fictions. These Asian narratives by women angled to the past serve, as Jameson theorizes, the same function as those set in the future, namely, they *offer an opportunity to review our present*. Therefore, these fictional biographies, though apocalyptic in tone, offer an opportunity to understand our current predicament(s) through the lens of the "future-past" that would hone our appreciation of the varied versions of the present that emerge from these alter-perceptions. Analepsis and prolepsis are used interchangeably in these fictions while this present, defined as it is by risk, is one where, as Ulrich Beck asserts, the myriad promises for the utopian future presupposed by scientific advances and technological leaps of the past decade or more, has turned into a dystopian nightmare (*Risk Society*). Thus, these apocalyptic fictions emerge more as soul-searching narratives that grapple with the idea of what it is to be humans-at-risk in the midst of a failing ecosystem, unspeakable communal calamities, and personal traumas.

Most of the selected fictions are based on definitive and distinct historical moments from the past. They all register moments of great catastrophic risk, both communal and personal. Damien Thompson's description of apocalyptic fiction as "underground literature, the consolation of the persecuted" (14) certainly fits these texts. However, they also place a premium on resilience, especially female resilience. As in *The Salt Eaters* by Toni Cade Bambara, here too are explicit links to race: "Whose community do you think they ship radioactive waste through, or dig up waste burial grounds near? Who do you think they hire for the dangerous dirty work at those plants?" (242) These links are presented either overtly or subtly. Thus this chapter makes space for formal and textual mediations that co-opt issues of race and the powerlessness of subdominant groups to show how, in times of apocalypse, risk and race are interconnected.

Apocalypse from the Other Side in "The Roar of a Distant War" and *Rani in Search of a Rainbow*

Communicative ethicist Sharon D. Welch, in *A Feminist Ethic of Risk*, reviews Afro-American literature and Womanist (Black feminist) literature from a white liberal perspective to identify values such as "finitude, interdependence, change and particularity" to form a new ethic of our times. She believes that an "ethics of risk" formed out of "solidarity and community" *will* and *should* counter "ethics of control" practiced by the white bourgeoisie. Welch advocates for "the creation of a matrix" that is grounded in community and focuses on the possibility of limited strategic actions. Unlike the "ethics of control" premised on an omnipotent, powerful God which drives "White middle-class ambitions for total power and control," Welch believes that women of color, the most vulnerable group, have devised this "ethics of risk" that is readjusted to strategic risk-taking with community support (1–27). One could argue that our ensuing texts are centered primarily on this "ethics of risk," wherein courageous women have faced and overcome great perils in both their natural and cultural ecology.

Viliya Ketavong, a Laotian-American currently residing in the USA, works to educate people from around the world about Laotian culture and history. "The Roar of a Distant War" is, unlike customary apocalyptic fictions, analeptic and not proleptic. Nevertheless, the picture it paints, its mode, and the narratorial vision are indisputably apocalyptic since the narrative vein is akin to "end-of-time" chronicles permeated by gloom and predictions of doom. Second, unlike most such narratives that are vested in sketching out a collective human destiny, making only occasional inroads into the personal, this story is built entirely on the personal history of one family with only occasional references to the larger collective of the nation. But one great similarity connects it to many other apocalyptic narratives in that the climactic moment in the story, ending the apocalyptic past, is indeterminate, poised between despair and promise.

The same is true of *Rani in Search of a Rainbow: A Natural Disaster Survival Tale* by Shaila Abdullah, an award-winning Pakistani-American writer.[4] This novel revolves around the 2010 floods in Pakistan that affected 20 million people, nearly 8.6 million of whom were children. The author wrote the book to raise awareness about the great privations that adults and children routinely face in developing countries. The story is about Rani, a young Pakistani girl who, along with her family, becomes a climate refugee. Displaced by the torrential rain, the whole village is evacuated to a refugee camp. Both texts depict the extreme vulnerability of marginal communities and their lack of immunity against risks in culture and nature, emphasizing also the uneven impact of "global" risk.

In both these texts, the focalizers are young girls who are close to their grandmothers, who are a storehouse of wisdom and stand for traditional knowledge. They are instrumental in passing on their wisdom to their granddaughters, creating a matrilineal line of knowledge that bypasses patriarchal hierarchies. These poor, old women are marginalized figures in patriarchy. However, they are given prominence and power in these tales that not only reveal the impact of extreme environments on families and communities, but also *stress an alternative set of values that counters "progress through competition" with "survival through cooperation."* Most importantly, their values introduce a sense of pastoral harmony, self-reliance, and agency to an otherwise risk-filled, hopeless world.

Both texts begin on a light-hearted note. The Laotian girl, Nanda, and her family are celebrating the fourth of July in Southern California with a picnic in the nearby park, while Rani, the Pakistani girl, is playing with friends in the rain. But in both cases, fun turns to terror. For Nanda, the Independence Day fireworks display unexpectedly brings on a panic attack that her rational mind attempts to soothe her out of: "BOOM! BOOM! BOOM! BOOM! *Nothing to be afraid of. The dark night sky was aglitter with harsh explosions of light. Nothing to be afraid of. I am just watching fireworks in the loving presence of my family*" (Ketavong 96; italics and upper case in original). This contrapuntal dialogue that alternates between instinctual terror versus reasoned calm culminates with instinct taking over. Despite her rational mind repeating the phrase *"Nothing to be afraid of"* like a chant, her scarred, subconscious self fearfully queries *". . . or is there?"* (97). Nanda's childhood fears surface and she admits, "I dropped to the ground" [to cower in fear] since "I was a child of war" (97). The innocuous picnic becomes the catalyst that catapults her into the past, to her childhood in Laos. The moment becomes the entry portal to a past trauma.

For Rani, too, childish play turns into trauma. "A few weeks ago, the rain had started innocently in their village in Pakistan. Pitter patter, dancing droplets were a signal to the young children that it was time to celebrate by dancing. And dance they did" (Abdullah, *Rani in Search of a Rainbow* Loc. 26). But "the rain did not stop. And in a few days, the bright blues of the rain turned to murky brown and stayed still on the ground" (Loc. 28). The villagers find that their "[r]ivers and creeks overflowed." But the rain continues relentlessly. "Rain, the adults warned, was not a friend anymore. That is when the dancing stopped" (Loc. 28). As the families in the villages are rescued by helicopters, her home looks like a floundering boat to young Rani. The families, only permitted to carry the most minimum of necessities, leave all their precious belongings behind. Ramadan goes unmarked. Rani "looked down at her worn-out clothes that had once been bright blue but were now darkened by dust" (Loc. 90).

In both texts, while the dire problems faced by the dispossessed community is centered, the emphasis is on demonstrating an alternative set of values. Welch's belief that the "ethics of risk" is grounded in community is demonstrated in these texts. Rani's sense of adventure and feeling of joy, unmarred by circumstances that might be traumatic to the adults, reveals that the potential for joy is not dependent on possessions or even situations. The idea that ownership and consumerism are core to happiness is challenged. Rani leaves home with the barest of necessities. She feels sad that the beautiful red dress that her Daadi (grandmother) had stitched for her for Eid has been left behind in her drowning house. But like Nanda, Rani always seeks out her grandmother as she makes her smile. At the refugee camp, the sense of community and reciprocity is emphasized.

Rani's mother, who is well-versed in midwifery, assists in the birth of Beeni's baby. Rani's grandmother helps with cooking for the multitude of refugees while her father helps with carrying the supplies that are brought by helicopter to the camp. Through her interactions with her grandmother, her family, and others in the community, Rani gradually realizes a basic truth: that human communities can only survive through mutual help and selfless acts of service, an important message for the inhabitants of risk society. The narrative speaks directly to Al Gore's sentiments: "Human civilization is now so complex and diverse, so sprawling and massive, that it is difficult to see how we can respond in a coordinated, collective way to the global environmental crisis. But circumstances are forcing just such a response" (385). The dire impact of these crises indelibly scars the poor. Cathy Caruth's observation that traumatic experience "suggests a certain paradox that the most direct seeing of a violent event may occur as an absolute inability to see it; that immediacy, paradoxically, may take the form of belatedness" (91). This is palpable as Nanda's adult picnic is one instance of such "belated seeing." The lingering and delayed effects of trauma, as described by Caruth, are experienced by the adult Nanda—a belated outcome of her childhood experience of war. While Rani deals with the catastrophes of climate change, Nanda deals with the dire consequences of war.

Nanda's narrative emphasizes the ubiquitous nature of war that engages people in developing countries and ways in which even children get irrevocably embroiled in it. Nanda recalls, "[a]t the very moment I was born, Laos was erupting into a terrible civil war. Gunfire cracked, bombs thundered, and bursting shells roared every second to welcome my birth" (97). The twisted parallels set up in the narrative between the fourth-of-July fireworks and the bombs that killed thousands, clearly registers the stark differences that demarcate privileged lives from those of the subdominant. The unevenness of global risk is exposed in Nanda's unvarnished recital: "From 1964 to 1973, Laos was the most bombed country in the world and my province of Savanaketh was the most bombed province in Laos. Villagers perished by the thousands from the bombing. Tons and tons of bombs changed the face of Laos into a cratered surface like the moon" (97). The passage is a brutal reminder that war between superpowers—here between the USA and the USSR—is rarely played out in their own backyards. It is the "remoter," poorer countries of the world that get embroiled in the power struggles and suffer the devastation that follows. Ironically, despite the heavy American involvement, I cognize the fact that no American child or indeed from any developed nation would have been placed in a position to make this observation: "All through my childhood, I lived about 100 kilometres away from the atrocity of the war. It escalated as American T-28s and B-52s unloaded bombs in Laos along the Ho Chi Minh trail. Although only the trail was targeted, along the way people, animals, villages and fields were not spared" (97). The passage renders visceral the helpless entrapment of the disenfranchised.

This idea of the clear binaries that exist between mighty and impoverished nations is brought to the foreground by the story's title, "The Roar of a Distant War," which is an echo of the eighteenth-century British nature poet, William Cowper's lines from the poem "The World at a Distance." In this poem, Cowper ruminates, from his sitting room, on the distant war and repeats just such sentiments as are implied in the story.[5] His reflections on peeping at the "Babel" through his "loopholes of retreat"; his comfort in merely "sighing but never needing to tremble at the sound of war"—displaying his transcendent position above the tumult—is an unknown luxury to the residents in these blighted nations. Cowper's lines demonstrate this difference: "I behold the tumult, and am still. The sound of war [h]as lost its terrors ere it reaches me; grieves, but alarms me not." Unlike the landscapes of Laos, Cowper's "Nature" is unsullied by war. Some visible differences emerge between the positioning of the West and the rest. They make us ponder over the historical reasons which have enabled a "harder mysticism" that Jeffers insists as being "bred west of Caucasus" to emerge ("Credo"), no doubt in the relative solitude and peace that admits an appreciation of an untroubled nature. In contrast, the title of Ketavong's story, with its ironic insistence on the adjective "distant" in relation to war that begs the question distant to whom, already points to the relative *situatedness* of the powerful and the powerless, a harking back to Beck's observation on the unevenness of risk.

Whether the risks are war-induced or through climate change, the effect on the landscape is catastrophic. Nanda recalls that "bombs rained down at a rate of twenty to three hundred loads per day" (97). She remembers the "unholy brightness of the night sky and the shimmering whiteness of the trees" that reminded her of the hell she had heard so many times being described in her grandmother's stories. "The raining fire, the heat, the shaking earth, the howling of the dogs, the mooing of the cows, *everyone and everything was in agony*," she declares passionately (97–98; emphasis added).

Here again, Nanda's words are an echo of the Buddha's *Fire Sermon*. In the *Ādittapariyāya Sutta* (Pali, the "Fire Sermon Discourse"), the Buddha preaches about achieving liberation from suffering through detachment from the five senses and the mind: "Bhikkus, all is burning . . . with sorrow, with lamentation, with pain, grief and despair it is burning" ("Fire Sermon"). The burning attests to the agony suffered by all of humanity. Ketavong's textual echoes of this foundational Buddhist text—which T. S. Eliot, in a footnote to *The Waste Land*, equates to the "Sermon on the Mount" for Christians—are not surprising since this would be central to Laotian Buddhists. It is also noteworthy that all three texts—"The Fire Sermon," "The Roar of a Distant War," and *The Waste Land*—are apocalyptic in their tone and content and can be said to emanate from allied locations, which is a remarkable illustration of how apocalyptic visions haunt humanity across time and space. All three texts display the awareness of the relentless "turbulence of life" and the very real possibility of the *death of hope*.

"What are the roots that clutch, what branches grow/Out of this stony rubbish? Son of man,/You cannot say, or guess, for you know only/A heap of broken images, where the sun beats,/And the dead tree gives no shelter, the cricket no relief,/And the dry stone no sound of water" (Eliot 19–24). These words could well have been uttered by Nanda. In the "Fire Sermon," the Buddha describes the sense bases and their resultant mental phenomena or states as "burning" with passion, aversion, delusion, and suffering. Even here the tone is apocalyptic and speaks to a Buddhist soteriology.

It is pertinent to note that the passage also reinforces Martha F. Lee's claim that apocalypse is at least peripherally concerned with the environment and that one cannot be dealt with without encountering the other (ix). "The Roar of a Distant War" signals, through its title, the complex web of associations that exist between privilege, politics, and war but equally links the (auditory) senses to human passion and violence. The narrative takes this further to emphasize the close interconnectedness between *earth*, *humans*, and the *environment*. All of these images are collectively invoked through the several textual echoes. Nanda avers: "To my young mind . . . [t]he shaking earth and the booming sounds pierced my heart and soul . . . The coldness chilled my bones. I shivered, my soul left my body. But I still felt Mother Earth beneath the house shaking and rattling" (98). The shivering is more than symbolic. The bombs, as the young Nanda records, cause a climactic upheaval in the tropical country. It is no surprise therefore that within a decade of the Cold War ending, climate-change issues would be gradually acknowledged and addressed as part of the global political agenda, at first at the World Conference on the Changing Atmosphere in Toronto in 1988 and subsequently at various other world forums. The story thus underlines the sociopolitical dimensions of apocalyptic narratives. As Jonathan Coward observes:

> [E]nvironmental literatures . . . can be seen to have traditionally served the two primary functions of criticism: diagnostic, and remedial. The inclusion of an apocalyptic tone adds a third aspect, oriented to the future. Put simply, this teleological-critical function says implicitly or explicitly: Either the status quo must change, or humanity and nature will end. Second, in uncovering this desire or need to change, the implementation of the apocalyptic narrative in environmental literature is political. It is employed both to increase

the saliency of environmental issues in the minds of the public and to encourage change on an individual or collective level. (5)

When Coward's expressed sentiments about apocalypse as "oriented to the future" are linked with Jameson's thesis that was discussed earlier in this chapter, a case can be made for Ketavong deliberately attempting to create a link between a distinct historical moment in her past with her present. Coward argues that apocalyptic rhetoric has a counter-effect as well, making people more skeptical about the alarmist scenarios that are presented. In Matthew Feinberg and Robb Willer's study, it was observed that individuals who were informed of the "just-world hypothesis,"[6] followed by exposure to dire messages of the severity of global warming, reported higher levels of climate-change skepticism (36). These participants, it was found, were less likely to change their lifestyle to reduce their carbon footprint.

Accounts such as Ketavong's and Abdullah's, however, as stories of personal fear and loss, the blighting and recovery of hope, and the unpredictability of life, can have a more powerful impact. Their apocalyptic vision is complemented by a code of resilience, especially by the womenfolk. Despite leading hard lives in a refugee camp, the women go about their day with equanimity and good cheer. Rani finds the women "chanting a little tune, inviting the sunshine to stay forever" (*Rani in Search of a Rainbow* Loc. 103). Rani's Daadi too always has time for her. On Eid, when Rani and her friend Juju go looking for her, they find her helping the women at the camp make *haleem*, a delicious meat and lentil stew. "Daadi was in a corner grinding spice on a stone. 'Rani, Juju, come over here,' she called. 'Sit by me and tell me what you have been doing today' [. . .] Daadi kissed both children on their cheeks and wished them happy Eid" (Loc. 109). The women bring happiness and comfort to the children in the midst of chaos.

In Laos, as their village is bombed, Nanda listens to her mother "whispering to grandmother." She realizes that "[t]hey were sitting next to each other planning our escape from hell on earth" (98). Despite the war closing in on them from all sides, Grandma admonishes the seven-year-old Nanda, "[r]emember to put a smile on your face, Nanda [. . . .] It will help us keep calm and ward off all evils" (100). Grandmother's tales with their optimism inspire Nanda: "A princess can do anything and overcome any obstacles [. . .] She [. . .] sniffed the air from my cheek, a Lao version of a kiss. Then she gave the inevitable moral of every story. 'Remember, Princess Nanda, a princess will always overcome any obstacle'" (101). Such moments that turn risk into enchantment are culturally validating and shore up Rani's and Nanda's self-confidence, that is vital to their growth and determination to survive. They also reinforce Heise's idea that the apocalyptic and the idyllic pastoral can move closer (*Sense of Place* 142). But reality cannot be wished away. Rani and her friends continue to suffer the privations of camp life. Also, by midmorning of a day, when Nanda and her family trudge a few kilometres outside their village, Nanda recalls witnessing a strange spectacle: "Airplanes were buzzing and giving birth to mushroom-like objects—scattering, dangling, and slowly descending, from the sky. Each night I saw more and more of the horrific balls of fire, falling out of the dark sky" (100). As they struggle through the war, constantly on the run with villages burning around them, they are very aware of their father, who, fighting against the communists on the American side, was a "wanted" man. With the disbanding of the Royalists' army, he would have gone into hiding. Nanda's infant brother dies of an undiagnosed and untreated infection. The ailing grandmother wants to return to the village and Nanda's younger sister, Salee, is assigned to lead her back. They finally hear from their father who instructs them to come to the bank of the Mekong river.

Through the month-long journey and escalation of risk, Nanda realizes her embedment in nature—that her family is part of an ecology at risk. They live hidden for days in "a rat-hole" like rodents (101); at night she realizes that her "eyes adjusted to the darkness like an animal's" (107). Also, when it comes to death, there is little that marks the humans, for "the mutilated and bloody dead bodies of humans and animals exposed on Mother Earth or half-buried" are indistinguishable from each other because, "the green leaves turned red instantly upon the scorching liquid from the exploded lifeless beings" (110). All these incidents bring home to her that war, with all its advanced technology, ironically only reemphasizes their inescapable connection to "Mother Earth."

The passage exemplifies Martin Heidegger's notion of "dwelling." Heidegger speaks of the fourfold primal order. In this order, the sky, earth, the divine realm, and mortals unite in a primordial unit. According to Heidegger, it is the acknowledgement of the fourfold oneness and our role as mortals within it that establishes "dwelling" ("Building, Dwelling, Thinking" 346). Heise understands this phrase as "an awareness that certain limits in the exploitation of nature have already been exceeded, that past warnings were not heeded, and that slowly evolving risk scenarios surround them on a daily basis" (*Sense of Place* 141–42) and Greg Garrard identifies "dwelling" as one of the central tropes of ecocriticism. Frederick Buell's use of the phrase "dwelling in crisis" (*From Apocalypse to Way of Life*) aptly sums up Nanda's predicament. Heise differentiates between an "apocalyptic perspective" in which "utter destruction lies ahead but can be averted and replaced by an alternative future society," and a "risk perspective" in which "crises are already under way all around, and while their consequences can be mitigated, a future without their impact has become impossible to envision" (Heise 142 cited in Huggan, "Australian Literature" 88). Ironically, in both Rani's and Nanda's narratives, it is difficult to disentangle an apocalyptic vision from a risk perspective. The two feed into each other.

At the end of the narrative, an adult Nanda, safely restored to the family, is now living with her parents, brother, and sister Salee, and is still haunted by the past, although now it seems to be a different world: "It seems so long ago that I lived in constant danger, in the midst of the crashing and booming catastrophic nightmare of bombs and bullets . . . the flashing brightness in the night sky, the executions [. . .]" (110). The strange juxtaposition of the family's innate reverence for earth, their relationship to it and to the flora and fauna, which appears to be emotional and inclusive, when contrasted with the stark images of the "rain of fire that befell Mother Earth" (107) also becomes a consciousness-raising exercise, more effective than any future-based alarmist speculation can be. The overall message that is conveyed points to humanity's deteriorating relationship with nature. It highlights the differing relationship to risk between the powerful and the powerless.

This consciousness pervades *Rani in Search of a Rainbow* for, although it is an environmental catastrophe, the greatest *impact* it has is on the economically vulnerable. The text works to reinforce what Heise calls the "sense of planet" (Heise *Sense of Place*), since these refugees cannot afford to claim a "sense of place." The refugee camp becomes a microcosm of Planet Earth. The simple story underscores the themes of resilience and self-help where individuals act responsibly and selflessly. But most of all, it underscores Welch's philosophy: that in this global risk scenario, we can never hope for control. We can only hope to "manage the risk" through strategizing in limited ways and through cooperation (12).

I have argued that both Ketavong's and Abdullah's narratives, while articulated from within a discursive and historical formulation that has shifted and may be seen to belong more to the genre of historical fiction emerging from the post-World War II and Cold War-era nuclear narrative, and cli-fi genres, are distinctly apocalyptic in tone and mood and function as end-of-time narratives. They help rearticulate our present time and the perceived future in ways that reflect the current ecological predicament as concomitant and also a defining historical moment. *The narratives bring the future and the past together in the present.* In doing so, they qualify the common view that risk and apocalyptic perspectives raise different sets of aesthetic as well as ethical questions: that the former is more likely to emphasize "indeterminacy, and the possibility of a variety of [crisis] outcomes," while the latter may hold up "ideals of naturally self-regenerating ecosystems and holistic communities in harmony with their surroundings as a countermodel to the visions of [environmental] exploitation and devastation they describe" (Heise, *Sense of Place* 142). Here, Nanda's and Rani's apocalyptic narratives that emerge out of their past, repudiate this optimism. The texts' aesthetics synthesize the ethical vision of *both* apocalypse and risk to generate a profoundly pessimistic vision of the future, where our only hope lies in human communality and selflessness.

Self and Beyond: Apocalypse in Wave

It is hard to reconcile the pastoral and the apocalyptic in *Wave: A Memoir of Life After the Tsunami* by Sri Lankan writer Sonali Deraniyagala, an academic based in the United Kingdom. In the blurb, Michael Ondaatje describes the book as the "most powerful and haunting book I have read in years," is autobiographical and so, like the previous two texts, is rooted in the past and in (personal) history rather than futuristic speculation. The narrative is a painful recounting of the immense loss the author suffered when, on the morning of December 26, 2004, her husband and two young sons as well as her parents were swept away by the tsunami while she miraculously survived.

The narrative begins on a pastoral note: a calm sea, a happy family, an idyllic holiday, only to be immediately followed by apocalyptic images of the dreadful tsunami of 2004, the deadliest in recorded history, when around a quarter of a million people died. Deraniyagala's family was obliterated by its fury while holidaying in Yala, a national park on the southeastern coast of Sri Lanka. The memoir begins with her words: "I thought nothing of it at first. The ocean looked a little closer to our hotel than usual. That was all. A white foamy wave had climbed all the way up to the rim of sand where the beach fell abruptly down to the sea. You never saw water on that stretch of sand" (3). Her desultory curiosity combined with her recollection of her friend Orlantha's words about her family: "What you guys have is a dream" (4), display her feeling of insulation, even invincibility, against nature, indeed against life's afflictions. The elite academic, with her anthropocentric perception of a nature tamed and contained by culture, is representative of privilege, revealed by her offhand remarks such as her referring to her seven-year-old son Vikram's fascination with a family of white-bellied sea eagles, "They always turned up, as reliable as the tooth fairy" (3). Her words are tragically replete with irony when, minutes later, the unreliability of nature and unpredictability of risk are forcefully brought home through the disastrous tsunami.

> The foam turned into waves. Waves leaping over the ridge where the beach ended. This was not normal. The sea never came this far in. Waves not receding or dissolving. Closer now. Brown and grey. Waves rushing past the conifers and coming closer to our room. All these waves now, charging, churning. Suddenly furious. Suddenly menacing. (5)

Shouting out to her husband, Steve, she recounts: "I grabbed Vik and Malli, and we all ran out the front door. I was ahead of Steve. I held the boys each by the hand. 'Give me one of them . . .' Steve shouted, reaching out. But I didn't. That would have slowed us down. We had no time" (5). Not even stopping to warn her parents who are staying adjacent to their room at the resort, the young family dash toward the road, where a passing jeep stops to pick them up. For a short while everything seems under control, only for the jeep to be suddenly deluged by water.

> Suddenly, all this water inside the jeep. Water sloshing over our knees . . . I didn't see those waves get to us. . . . What *is* happening? The jeep moved forward slowly. I could hear its engine straining, snarling. We can drive through this water, I thought . . . Then I saw Steve's face . . . A sudden look of terror, eyes wide open, mouth agape. He saw something behind me that I couldn't see. I didn't have time to turn around and look. (7–8)

At last, when she comes to, she sees "billowing brown water, way into the distance" as far as the eye could see. She feels herself being swept along at tremendous speed, tasting salt. "Water battered my face, it went up my nose, it burned my brain" (10). A while later, when the pain seems bearable, she opens her eyes to gaze on "[a] blue spotless sky. A flock of storks were flying above me, in formation, necks stretched out. These birds were flying in the same direction that the water was taking me" (10). The image of the cerulean sky and the beautiful storks after the calamitous tsunami is once again ironically, pastoral, and runs in tandem with the biologist Daniel B. Botkin's discussion of dynamic and unstable ecosystems in *Discordant Harmonies: A New Ecology for the Twenty-first Century*, where he counters placid views that congeal nature in unchanging stasis. Instead, he argues that natural ecological systems are constantly fluctuating. This narrative moment is akin to a caesura, a deep holding of one's breath, the calm before the storm. Scott Slovic's discussion of Robinson Jeffers' poem "Oh Lovely Rock" (1937), where he suggests that meditating on the rock proffers humans the ability to think of mutability and contrasts their ephemeral existence to the permanence of nature (85), is particularly apt. But the narrative, with distinctly apocalyptic imagery, moves relentlessly forward to replace this pastoral image with a graphic one of a violent nature: "I saw then the toppled trees everywhere [. . .] trees on the ground with their roots sticking up [. . .] I was in an immense bog-land. Everything was one color; brown, reaching far [. . .] What is this knocked-down world? The end of time?" (Slovic, "Introduction" 11). To paraphrase James Lovelock, Gaia has wreaked her vengeance on humans, and Deraniyagala's family is one of several thousands the sea swept away in its wake. After weeks of refusing to leave her dark room, on the first day her friend parts the curtain and lets in light, Deraniyagala resents being reconnected to nature and therefore to life. Her first view is again ironically pastoral: "There was the first time I saw a paradise flycatcher." But the pastoral is inappropriate to her extreme grief. "Now look what's happened, I thought. I've seen a bird. I've seen a flycatcher, when all the birds in the world should be dead" (40). The pastoral has no place in this extreme, dystopic world with no lingering hope: Dante's Hell.

This glimpse of a pastoral nature threatens to stir her to a sense of the reality of her (continued) existence in the face of her unspeakable loss and she rejects it categorically. Being suicidal, Deraniyagala is vigilantly guarded by her aunts and cousins, who nurse her back to health and a semblance of normalcy. But her return to everyday lucidity does not occur overnight. Nature in the form of the tsunami that had destroyed her family and life as she knew and understood it, continues to overwhelm her mind in unaccountable ways. Nevertheless, despite her anger at it, nature seems to be the only aspect of life that she *can* connect with, albeit in more negative than positive ways. She walks for miles on a dark, deserted beach one night to search for the place "where turtles came ashore to lay their eggs"; finally, coming upon "a green turtle, her soft eggs dropped into the huge pit she'd dug up in the sand" helps her find a measure of her place in the larger world where she doesn't feel she needs to belong (49). Returning months later to the hotel in Yala, the scene of the calamity, Deraniyagala witnesses the ravage on the landscape in the aftermath of the tsunami. "Dust, rubble, shards of glass. This was the hotel. It had been flattened. There were no walls standing, it was as though they'd been sliced off the floors [. . .] Fallen trees were everywhere, the surrounding forest had flown apart. As if there'd been a wildfire, all the trees were charred (61). As she wanders the desolate land, she is sensitized to aspects of nature that had never before impacted her:

> The wind was fierce that day we went back, it flung sand into our faces. A strangely quiet wind, though, bereft of the rustling and shaking of trees. It was midday, and no shelter from the seething sun. The sea eagles that had thrilled Vik, they were still there. Bold in this desolation, they sailed low, sudden shadows striking the bare ground. Eagles without Vik. I didn't look up. (61)

The details of the landscape, while scrupulously observed, are anthropocentrically qualified by human loss and emotion. The eagles favored by her son bring no joy in his absence. "I couldn't make this real. This wasteland," she exclaims tellingly (61).

Kali Tal defines trauma as "a life-threatening event that displaces preconceived notions about the world" (15). This displacement, essentially a disjunction from reality with feelings of being severed from it, often overcomes Deraniyagala. What she experiences is, as psychologist Elizabeth Waites observes, "an injury to mind or body that requires structural repair." Waites clarifies that "a main effect of trauma is disorganisation" which could, she insists, cause "fragmentation of self, shattering of social relationships" (22, 92). But what is noteworthy is that, in this state of "disorganization," Deraniyagala compulsively turns to nature. Viewing the land ravaged by the sea, she feels some kinship: "Nothing was normal here, and that I liked [. . .] My surroundings were as deformed as I was. I belonged here" (64).

The ravaged land seems more a part of her than the cultural world. Nature, however, also persists as an enemy. She cannot grasp nor forgive its continued existence in the face of her family's extinction. Furthermore, nature's awesome powers have to be recollected repeatedly for its proportions to enter her mind and be acknowledged as reality. She needs to relearn and come to terms with the sheer dispassion and indifference of nature to human predicament. Nature's power, never truly cognized before, has to be recalibrated. Repeating the statistics about the tsunami is a useful tool to tutor her about nature's power and to anchor her to the facts of her calamitous, unreal loss. "The wave was more than thirty feet high here. It moved through the land at twenty-five miles an hour. It charged inland for more than two miles, then went back into the ocean. All that I saw around me had been submerged. I told myself this over and over. Understanding nothing" (62). In the awe-inspiring statistics of the tsunami, she seeks an understanding of her immense loss—the death of everyone who had shaped the contours of her everyday life. But her loss and disorientation continue: "I was directionless. Where do I go? What did I come here to see? Then I remembered the rock. There was a large rock here on the bank of the lagoon that is to the side of the hotel. A black, peaceful rock that we'd often sit on at dusk . . . with that rock I found my bearings" (62). This thought of Deraniyagala's on locating the rock and finding it reassuring is by no means unique. Slovic refers to the deepest urge in any environmental writing as the "quest for contact with external reality" ("Oh, Lovely Slab" 83), a quest that now gets centered in Deraniyagala's life. As Slovic affirms, "[w]hen we say 'environment', we seem to mean what's 'out there', what's hard and fast and externally verifiable [. . .]" (82–83). It is this quest for some certainty in the midst of her loss, through which she can acquire a grip over her life again, that leads Deraniyagala obsessively to search for these external "chthonic" certainties of nature. She finds, however, that nature appears to mislead her time and again for her confused mind misreads the signs, cocooning her in false images of comfort. "It was the light that did it. It was the angle of the sun at five o'clock on a Sunday evening in early March on a country road somewhere in Shropshire [. . .] This light that is so familiar unexpectedly makes me forget" (79). Although Deraniyagala is a Sinhalese Buddhist, religion never intrudes in her narrative except in very veiled and unobtrusive ways as when she recalls visiting the Buddhist temple with her grandmother. Nevertheless, it is worthwhile to pause here to probe her experience and link it back to my initial thesis that began with the idea of an irrefutable materiality versus a notion of Eastern mysticism. In his "Sermon of The Not-self Characteristic" (*Anatta-lakkhana-sutta*), the Buddha declares:

> [B]hikkhus, any kind of form whatever, whether past, future or presently arisen, whether gross or subtle, whether in oneself or external, whether inferior or superior, whether far or near, must, with right understanding of how it is, be regarded thus: 'This is not mine, this is not I, this is not myself.
> Any kind of feeling whatever [. . .]
> Any kind of perception whatever [. . .]
> Any kind of determination whatever [. . .]
> Any kind of consciousness whatever, whether past, future or presently arisen, whether gross or subtle, whether in oneself or external, whether inferior or superior, whether far or near must, with right understanding how it is, be regarded thus: 'This is not mine, this is not I, this is not myself. (Buddha's *The Fire Sermon*)

The Buddha's distinction between the higher consciousness, leading to dispassion, and state of enlightenment or nirvana as opposed to the overt attachment to earthly or material things that bring suffering, appears to reinforce the contrast between the worldly and the mystical attitudes that Jeffers mentions. In the face of the extreme anguish of Deraniyagala's predicament, the Buddha's words appear distant, unworldly, and ungraspable. We are all sucked into her trauma, where we stand poised in the consciousness of the overwhelming dominance of nature while attempting to grapple with the unreality that grips her after the trauma. Hence it is doubly ironic that in her state of post-traumatic stress disorder (PTSD), many of her utterances appear to echo the Buddha's spiritual insights in a gross parody of spiritualism. Her extreme anguish seems to put her in a state which mimics and indeed mocks the idea of nirvana. What appears to be immediate and central is the overwhelming *presence* of the material world, whether it is the sight of turtle eggs or a setting sun.

Over many years, as she struggles to come to terms with her irrecoverable loss, nature, which had, first and foremost, been her enemy, the irreducible, indifferent "other" which had robbed her of all that she held dear, now gradually and insidiously becomes her (sole) source of solace. Deraniyagala re-establishes a relationship with the land and seascape, in other words with the "place of trauma," despite or *because* of her loss. The unreality of her extreme circumstances, which are at odds with the commonplace routine of her everyday life, drive her to re-establish her relationship to the event, and to the land and sea that caused it. She develops a reluctant bond with the land that had thwarted her life of meaning. Terry

Tempest Williams labels this compulsive bond with land the "erotics of place." Williams says: "I am interested in a participatory relationship with the land. I want to reclaim the word erotic at its root, meaning 'of or pertaining to the passion of love; concerned with or treating of love; amatory'" (*An Unspoken Hunger* 16). An "erotics of place" encompasses a "relationship with the natural world that includes many aspects of an intimate relationship with another person: love, risk, surrender, vulnerability, connection, trust, and merging" (cited in Cory 2012). Deraniyagala gradually moves from feelings of anger, mistrust, and hatred toward the place of her loss to an obsessive focus on it. The land and sea are indelibly etched in her memory and she compulsively revisits the place, giving truth to the stark title of her book—*Wave*. All it took was one gargantuan tidal wave, a mere grain of an incident in the vast spectrum of time, but it spelt the end of all that was meaningful in her life.

Wave demonstrates a central paradox that Timothy Clark identifies as "scale framing [. . .] a strategy for representing complex issues in ways that make them more amenable to thought or overview" (*Criticism on the Edge* 74). Clark discusses the patent incongruities that can emerge in representing the scale of a global phenomenon of risk from the perspective of the local or, indeed, the individual. *Wave* reveals the futility, indeed the impossibility, for an individual devastated by a natural phenomenon to impersonally grasp the magnitude and significance of the climate crisis, demonstrating its inability to grapple with scale-framing.

Such gradations chart the gap between the span and value of a human life against the vast span of evolutionary time. Gradually, "time," which itself is an aspect of nature, causes Deraniyagala to come to terms with the cause of her loss and make it the source of her solace. The "two sea-eagles" that she always comes back to watch (61, 160); the blue-whales "who keep their hugeness hidden" (185), and the "vast isolated landscapes" allow her moments of clarity when she realizes that her loss has not robbed her sense of identity as her sons' mother, the central truth of her transient life. In that moment of Deraniyagala's reconciliation, the Buddha's sermon provides a meaningful framework for our lives as readers, journeying with her and searching for a meaning to this unbelievable tragedy. It conveys a quiet, calm wisdom, a reprieve in the face of human vulnerability and helplessness. These moments of clarity allow her (and her readers) to gain a sense of perspective. Nature, the perpetrator of her great misfortune, also becomes her companion:

> Sometimes vast isolated landscapes allow me this. Recently [. . .] in sub-Arctic Sweden, on the deserted shores of a lake of ice, surrounded by naked birches sheathed in frozen fog, each branch glowing like a stag's antlers in velvet in that mellow light. Immersed in that

endless white, I knew I was their mother, my horror dormant, or not that relevant even. (116)

It appears that the wheel has turned a full circle. Her journey away from nature ends with her coming back to it. To return to Jameson and the apocalypse, on leaving this tortured narrative we could legitimately echo his words that "its deepest vocation is over and over again to demonstrate and to dramatize our incapacity to imagine the future [. . .]" (152). The untold hazards in nature and culture appear inextricable and unpredictable. The pastoral, which had lingered on then was ousted by the apocalyptic, returns limping, only to be overwhelmed by the unimaginable scale of the apocalypse. Once again history, here an autobiography, and the apocalypse join hands to point an accusing finger at the present, validating Jameson's perspective.

The final two texts, Lily Yulianti Farid's "Lake" and Chitra Banerjee Divakaruni's *One Amazing Thing*, grapple with scalar effects as they attempt to link global ecological perils with individual destinies. They implicitly or explicitly foreground the efficacy of narrative as the bridge between the local and the global.

Environment, Risk, and Anti-pastoral Selves in *One Amazing Thing* and "Lake"

The unpredictable connections between the environment, culture, and risk are found prominently in the foreground in the final two texts that link the art of narration to apocalyptic moments. "Lake" by Indonesian writer Lily Yulianti Farid, popularly known as Ly,[7] and *One Amazing Thing* by Chitra Banerjee Divakaruni[8] set up a dialogue between apocalyptic moments in culture and nature and, by default, between "a sense of place and a sense of planet" (Heise, *Sense of Place*). In both, a young Asian woman is the primary focalizer.[9] Once again, the triangulation between risk, apocalypse, and the pastoral is interesting to examine.

One Amazing Thing opens in the basement of an office building in an unnamed American city, which serves as the Indian high commission. There are two officers dispensing visas for travel to India while customers from widely differing racial and ethnic backgrounds wait in queue. Toward the evening, after their appointment slots have long since expired, seven frustrated, long-suffering customers still remain: Lily, a young Chinese-American teenager with an "attitude" toward Asian conservatism and in possession of great musical talent, who has accompanied her grandmother to procure an Indian visa for the latter; Mr and Mrs Pritchett, a Caucasian couple with unvoiced, unresolved marital problems who wish to tour India; Tariq, a young Muslim-American affected by the pervasive anti-Islamic sentiment in the USA, who is about to visit his recently widowed mother who has relocated to India; Uma, a graduate student of Bengali extraction who is embarking on a visit to her parents in Calcutta; Cameron, an African-American ex-soldier, whose efficiency ensures the group's survival but who also hides his lost and seeking soul behind his self-contained exterior; and, finally, Jiang, Lily's grandmother, whose secret past in India is beckoning her there again. They have all visited the Indian high commission to apply for a visa to undertake their journey to India for different reasons. Along with them are the two consul officials, Mangalam, the Indian high commissioner from South India with an unhappy marriage behind him, and Malathi, his assistant, who are both on the brink of an adulterous affair. All are caught unaware when an earthquake rips through the building, trapping the nine characters in the basement. The sense of weariness and mild irritation that had hitherto enveloped them erupts into shock and alarm when walls tumble around them, part of the ceiling caves in, and the earthquake locks these strangers together in dread for their lives.

Their initial basic instinct is understandably to survive, initiating a collective struggle as they share and ration their food supply. Then the office begins to flood. As they sit waiting, with the hope of survival gradually dwindling, Uma, the student, suggests that each tell a personal tale—"one amazing thing" from their lives, which they have never had the occasion to share with anyone before. As their compelling stories unfold, the redemptive nature of cultural narratives in the face of the planetary crisis is brough to the forefront.

The redeeming quality of narrative is also centered in "Lake" that is narrated by Zara. Zara links the disappearance of her sister, Fayza, an activist during President Suharto's regime (1967–98) in Jakarta with the sudden disappearance of Lake Beloye in Central Russia. Zara is a limnologist whose study of lakes takes her to far-flung regions of the planet. When the story opens, she and her colleagues are in a restaurant on the outskirts of Amsterdam. Her creative urge and ecological interests rub shoulders as she confides to her fellow researchers her plan to write a story in memory of Fayza. "All their attention is focused on Zara's plan, which seems so out of place amid the snippets of conversation about changes in the ecosystem, particularly ones resulting from reclamation, sedimentation, and evaporation of lakes" (84). Zara's story is not going to be about ecology, she claims, but about love. "Do any of you have an interesting story about love or life? I want to write a novel in memory of my sister" (84). Her creative energies are presented as firmly separated from her research pursuits. But the story demonstrates precisely the artificiality of such divisions. The narrative opens with a journal entry (signaled through the use of italics) describing a lake created by a landslide. Here geography, geology, despair, wonder, and hope combine:

> *The immense basin entices bees, grasshoppers, and birds, and causes the wind to hasten the union of pollen with the pistils of wild plants that circle its edge [. . .] After a few months have passed and the land that had slid off surrounding slopes begins to harden, an ever-growing number of visitors come to the lake's shore to recollect the massive landslide and to try to calculate how many people had died or were lost; how large an area of land had been displaced; and how many kilograms of asphalt road had been torn up to completely isolate the area. The basin, like an immense earthenware bowl bestowed by nature in just one night, was now filled with water on which lotus flowers would grow, in which fish would come to live, and whose bottom would be covered with algae.* (83; italics in original)

Zara's interest in lakes that disappear and/or appear overnight is emphasized in this passage. But equally significant is the hope that permeates it where the lake, despite being the product of a geographical devastation that caused untold grief, would once again become a beautiful landmark. This points to the core of the angst that drives the plot forward: that Zara's sister Fayza, a social activist, has gone missing with no explanation forwarded by the government or the police. No one knows what has happened to either her or her fellow activists. Ecological hazards and social risks get integrated and are inseparable.

Both texts are apocalyptic in that they depict an environment that is on the brink of collapse or demands concerted effort in order to avert ruination. In *One Amazing Thing*, as the protagonists are under duress to come to terms with their extreme predicament, they slowly but surely accede to the inevitable, turning inward, and at the same time learn to take stock of their lives from a new angle. They also become aware of each other in a deeper way. At first, they appear to be the prototypical protagonists of a stock apocalyptic/adventure narrative. As such, they are positioned as the inheritors of a humanistic, anthropocentric legacy—one that places man at the center of the created world. They appear to rehearse the role of valiant individuals wrestling against the elemental forces of nature to save themselves through their enterprise and agency. Going by Don D'Ammassa's definition of "an adventure [as] an event or series of events that happens outside the course of the protagonist's ordinary life, usually accompanied by danger, often by physical action" (vii–viii), the characters in the novel seem to be focussed on getting over impediments and intent on conquering nature, therefore being presented primarily as the heirs to a solipsistic tradition. But these notions are quickly revised as they are enfolded in their private histories and disclose their inner worlds, shattering their hitherto isolated existence and revealing their vulnerability.

Uma, the primary focalizer in *One Amazing Thing*, understands the trauma this sharing can cause. Later in the novel, after hearing Mrs Pritchett's story which narrates her disappointment in her marriage, she identifies Mr Pritchett's pain as her own. Uma thinks that "[h]ell is other people" (178). She reflects on the essential reserve that characterizes the African-American ex-marine or the "saviour figure" Cameron, who appears to be almost secretive. She wonders, "[w]ho lived within his shuttered inner rooms?" (83) We are made aware of the cultural tensions that can arise when the private worlds that these characters have constructed over years and kept closely guarded are gradually unlocked.

The private and the political, geological catastrophe and personal tragedy also collide in "Lake" but with a difference. While there is pervasive cynicism and apathy about civic activism, geological events are still a matter of mystery and curiosity. The narrative discusses the disappearance of the lake in the Russian village of Bolotnikovo.

> *At the base of the lake are a church and the houses that had mysteriously vanished seventy years before. And now the lake had disappeared, in just a single night, like a huge bathtub whose stopper had been pulled and its waters sucked out by a mysterious force . . . But what happened to the fish, the moss, the algae and tadpoles? . . . An elderly woman says apathetically, "This is all America's doing."* (86)

The apocalyptic imagery of the lake disappearing overnight blends well with the mystery and anxiety that ends on a note of abrupt irony: "This is all America's doing." The mood that pervades the entire narrative is a strange mixture of missionary zeal when it comes to uncovering ecological facts versus a cynicism bordering on apathy when it comes to discussing sociopolitics. This mood is explained by Melanie Budianta in the introduction to the collection: "'Lake' reminds us of the New Order political climate [in Indonesia], in which the Soeharto [*sic*] regime (1966–1998) ruled by suppressing critical voices. This was a time of centralized government and corrupt petty officials" (xiii). As Zara ponders the strange superstitions that she recorded in Bolotnikovo in the course of her research, and wonders if Fayza would like her stories of "the mysterious beings that lived in the lake and who were said to appear only to abduct human beings" (87), the tone shifts abruptly and now the italicized sentence that follows swerves sharply away from natural mysteries to ponder cultural ones: "*And just what kind of being was it that abducted you, Fayza?*" (87) Thus, the political abduction of Fayza and the lake's disappearance converge to set up connections between risk to individual lives and risk to the well-being of the planet. The complex problems, both social and ecological, refuse to be reduced to bucolic simplicity. The pastoral seems far removed from these complexities. As Zara waits for her flight at Schiphol Airport, she ponders Earth's mysteries. "She thought of the two lakes in two different places: one created almost instantly, following an earthquake and massive landslide; the other ingested in an instant by a secret cavern in the Earth's belly, which had taken into its maw everything that had once been above it" (87). At the airport lounge, she sees a man reading a book titled *The World is Flat*. Implied is the irresponsibility of humanity to face truths and take action though when they do, dangerous things happen to them. The troubling questions surrounding Fayza's fate do not go away: "*What kind of stories and people must she create to accompany Fayza's own horrific tale?*" (87) Personal worries mingle with Zara's ecological passions. The text's apocalyptic rhetoric is balanced by a social consciousness in what Huggan labels an eco-cosmopolitan understanding of planeterity, which "forces collective acknowledgement of the social and environmental threats that face us" (*Nature's Saviours* 88). Zara's figure combines her parallel identity as a nature investigator and culture warrior.

Similarly, Cameron, the African-American in *One Amazing Thing*, in one sense fits the prototype of the archetypal hero of any narrative of progress, the doer and the fixer who would be, by way of his nature (and barring his race), the natural protagonist of apocalyptic adventures—the hero who would pit his wits against the elements and "conquer" them. Yet despite his initiative and resilience, his vulnerability as an asthma patient and dependence on his inhaler signal a different narrative emphasis: "He checked his pants pockets. The right one held his inhaler. He pulled it out and shook it carefully. There were maybe five doses left . . . If Cameron was careful, five doses could last him for days" (11). This description of his defenselessness is an early indication that the narrative is pitched to undermine transcendental narratives of achievement and predicated on the intrepidity of humankind. A story that pivots around an ecological disaster could easily proceed to resurrect the heroic nature of those who struggle to survive. But there are no heroes in this novel, only victims of a greater or lesser order. Therefore, in piecing together this splintered portrait, the narrative seems to display a level of skepticism for anything other than fragmented visions of reality. The patchy, incomplete stories that are shared by the characters undercut the idea of the conventional "grand narrative" that is used to reaffirm the stature of the human protagonist, striding tall against the backdrop of a chaotic natural world. On the contrary, the plural, diverse narrators of these tales only convey discontinuity and disenchantment with life. Far from affirming human stature and culture, these narratives problematize them, reaffirming the inadequacy of humans to deal with the environmental crisis they are faced with.

In "Lake," too, Zara's vulnerability does not register her as heroic. Her colleague is concerned about her, wondering if her depression "from all the days she had spent noting in her journal fluctuations in temperature and soil acidity, along with changes in vegetation [. . .] had instilled in Zara the inspiration to convey a noble message, like a holy man after finishing a long term of meditation" (85). Zara, however, is no messiah. While she toys with the idea of writing about ideal love, her motivations are more pragmatic and rooted in the real. Her scientific curiosity is centered on conveying facts: "*In the past, Fayza, the site of Schiphol Airport was a lake. People called it 'Haarlemmermeer.' It was not a calm and refreshing lake [. . .] but a fierce and raging battlefield for Dutch and Spanish forces*" (89).

Her attempts at creative writing notwithstanding, Zara rarely strays from established facts. She recalls that it was because of her sister that she learnt to love lakes and study "lakes, ponds, reservoirs: any kind of land-based recess in which fresh water pooled" (88–89). But paradoxically Fayza "chose to live a life behind resistance banners" (89). The narrative, traversing between apocalyptic images and Beck's risk society seesaws between two kinds of consciousness-raising: about the state of the politically corrupt nation and the state of the unstable planet. The two intersect in Fayza, the point of origin of both. Fayza's vision catalyze her little sister Zara's awareness of both the environmental apocalypse-to-come and the political crises in the nation. Zara's words to Fayza before her disappearance are therefore timely and critical. Not only do they explain her love of lakes but also the probable cause of her sister's activism and disappearance:

> *Almost since time immemorial, Fayza, people have been eliminating the lakes of this planet in order to expedite their ever more evil and greedy plans. In this country, lakes are filled in to become farmland. Swamps are transformed into industrial zones and toll roads. But when a lake disappears, the landscape's brilliance also vanishes, bringing tears to the eyes of the hunters of light in this lowland area.* (90)

Civic irresponsibility is linked squarely to environmental and ecological ruin.

Back in Jakarta, Zara accompanies her parents to the eighth annual memorial for the nine missing activists, including her sister. Their families and friends commiserate with each other and angry voices demand acknowledgment, reparation, and an apology from the government. Zara recalls the final exchange with her sister with bitter irony: "'*Be careful, Fayza . . .*' . . . '*You're the one who should be careful, Zara, living in a foreign country*'" (92). Zara wants so much to return to that moment. She regrets never having really expressed her fear. "*Fayza, you are the one who should be more careful in our own homeland [. . .]*" (92). Zara's thoughts at the end of the memorial service merge the two concerns (environmental and sociopolitical) that propel the narrative forward: "Zara [. . .] recalled the lake in Bolotnikovo, which had vanished in the night. The same thing that had happened to Fayza" (91). Thus, apocalyptic narratives in risk society uncover an intricate network of connections surrounding power at macro and micro levels that contribute to ecological destruction and sociopolitical perils. All these subjects become central concerns of the powerless.

We realize that the dialogic community of *One Amazing Thing* is also constructed entirely by the voices of the marginalized: the Indian girl whose parents are on the brink of a divorce; the African-American male whose academic merit fails him crucially when he needs it the most; the Chinese girl whose distraught parents discover that their lives built around their children's successes is unraveling; the Muslim-American youth who apprehends at last that he will always be an alien in the land of his birth; the Chinese grandmother whose teenage love affair with India and an Indian boy came to naught. These are the voices of the disillusioned. All the characters in the novel are marked by their marginal status in society, distanced from the center of power by capitalism and patriarchy. This underscores the interconnectedness of systems of oppression. Risk is equally pervasive and connects with power in insidious ways, and the narrative takes pains to emphasize these interconnections. Risks that emerge from both nature (the earthquakes/that swallow lakes) and culture (the various threats and setbacks in life that the characters face or repress) reveal the extent to which these are interlocked. But these marginal characters, when brought together, attest to a certain cultural dysfunctionality inherent in today's globalized world.

When apprehending a common danger, the surface solidarity amongst these voices is oftentimes broken up by conflict and anxiety. This is the flipside of the communal harmony emphasized in *Rani in Search of a Rainbow*. As a Muslim and an African-American, respectively, Tariq and Cameron, for example, inhabit highly polemical social spaces. Not unremarkably, Tariq reenacts the social anxieties of the marginalized which prods him to see Cameron as an antagonist—autocratic and dictatorial. As the traditional homemaker, Mrs Pritchett also occupies an undervalued domestic space which, viewed through a feminist lens, is a space deprived of legitimate empowerment under patriarchy. Her narrative that exposes her feelings of betrayal, that her husband has cheated her of a meaningful life, would again have a strong resonance among feminists. Zara as the disenfranchised citizen; Tariq as Muslim-American; and Mrs Pritchett as the disillusioned homemaker are examples of people who are consistently marked as "other" in hegemonic patriarchal discourses. Hence each of these narratives conveys an ironic disenchantment with contemporary society.

The narrative focuses on corporeality—the body's mortality, fragility, and link to all other organic life forms. Thus, Fayza is dead. Lack of fresh air, Uma realizes, is slowing her reflexes (Banerjee Divakaruni 146) while for Mrs Pritchett, "[t]he last few times, it had been hard to climb on and off the desk—her arthritis was acting up—but she hadn't wanted to ask for help, hadn't wanted anyone to know her body was betraying her" (148). This focus on human fragility brings to the surface a pervasive nature/culture dualism in order to raise some pertinent questions in line with ecofeminist Ynestra King's view that "[t]he consideration of the place of human beings in nature, formerly the terrain of religion, becomes a crucial concern for all human beings" (116).

Human embedment in and dependence on nature emerges progressively from the novel's opening, where nature is absent from human imagining:

> When the first rumble came, no one in the visa office, down in the basement of the Indian consulate, thought anything of it. Immersed in regret or hope or trepidation (as is usual for persons planning a major journey), they took it to be a passing cable car. Or perhaps the repair crew that had draped the pavement outside with neon-orange netting, making entry into the building a feat that required significant gymnastic skill, had resumed drilling. (1)

The mundane preoccupations that crowd our thoughts when a catastrophe is minutes away present in microcosm the deeper irony that plays out in the macrocosm of our modern civilization—that, preoccupied with mundane pursuits, we turn our minds away from the imminent environmental catastrophe waiting to happen. "Lake" has Zara pondering whether her novel would be a single volume or a trilogy (84). In *One Amazing Thing*, too, all the indelible markers of culture from its more enduring creative art forms like literature (such as a reference to *The Canterbury Tales* [1]) to its passing irritations ("I missed a big test today" [3]), are brought to the foreground in the first few pages. The narratives seem completely taken up with examining the human predicament from the vantage point of culture, so much so that when the natural catastrophe occurs it comes as a bolt from the blue, taking the characters completely by surprise.

Their struggle to survive illustrates Harold Fromm's idea that dwelling in crisis embeds one in nature. The nagging, embarrassing persistence of bodily needs that Fromm points to—if one "carted one's own excrements out to the fields or emptied chamberpots out of the window" (543), oscillating between hunger and fear of death, to the disposal of bodily wastes—that occurs in the wake of the natural disaster can drive away romance and adventure fairly quickly. In the text, the conditions after the earthquake drive the characters who are trapped in the basement into a state of pre-cultural incompetency very rapidly. With the rising water level in the basement, locating a toilet becomes a priority. So, when Malathi reveals the fact that there is an en-suite bathroom tucked away for the high-commissioner's use, "people immediately suspect Mangalam (the high commissioner) of having suppressed this crucial bit of information on purpose" (Banerjee Divakaruni 36).

The imperative to transcend this entrapment, which persistently reminds them of their imminent death and basic bodily needs, is what leads to their storytelling. But storytelling is intrinsically a communal act, an exchange of histories. Their narratives reconstruct their histories from the vantage point of death. But their narration is constantly punctuated by the rumble of the earthquake, shifting attention from the cultural to the natural and setting up a dialectic where both emerge as equal partners and protagonists in the unfolding drama, nature henceforth refusing to be marginalized by culture. As each character narrates their story, nature reinstates its active status in the midst of these acts of cultural affirmations and consonance: "Uma thought she heard a sound above, as when someone turns over in an old, creaky bed. She stiffened and looked around, but the others were engrossed in the story [. . .] She forced her attention away from the ceiling's mutterings and to the painful inevitability of Tariq's tale" (Banerjee Divakaruni 131–32).

Nature's relentless violation of this precious [cultural] space reaffirms human embedment in nature, which is as much a part of the biosphere as the rest of the natural world. Moreover, the cultural world that is depicted is not *affirming* but filled with personal failures. Nature, as an elemental force, also seems to be a space of dis/ease for these humans. As such, the narrative shows these humans trapped by both nature and culture. Nevertheless, at the climax of their lives, these captives of culture and history realize that their lives are ruled by nature, that they can never find a place outside it.

The narrative also prioritizes a sense of place in both texts. In "Lake" Zara feels a deep sense of entrapment in Jakarta, which becomes the reason for her travels to remote places in search of disappearing lakes. In his essay "Bakhtinian Road to Ecological Insight," Michael J. McDowell argues that Mikhail Bakhtin's concept of the chronotope—a twentieth-century neologism combining *chronos* (time) and *topos* (place) and which Bakhtin defines as "the intrinsic connectedness of temporal and spatial relationships that are artistically expressed in literature" (*The Dialogic Imagination* 84)—is particularly useful to a dialogic analysis of landscape writing as it helps explore how place is tied to narrative. In both texts, the overwhelming sense of place, where the characters are rooted, indeed trapped, is tied to the narrating selves, linking their stories and planetary geographies together. Critics like Neil Evernden (are persuaded that this is the way forward for ecological writers (19). Right from the beginning of the novel the sense of place is paramount, rooting the events in a specific location: "Jakarta" or "the visa office, down in the basement of the Indian consulate" (Banerjee Divakaruni 1).

The phenomenon of entrapment has been studied extensively. In *Landscapes of Fear* human geographer Yi-Fu Tuan describes as a "sense of place" the peculiar connection that occurs between human consciousness and a location, where at times these locales can become abodes of terror: landscapes filled with the dark images of the mind. Tuan states that it is not unusual for such latent fears of drought, earthquake, flood, famine, and disease to be shared by members of a community. In "Lake," ecological anxieties are overtaken by the dread caused by political terrorism while in *One Amazing Thing* the basement room becomes concretely and literally an abode of terror for the entire dialogic community of the novel. In fact, the place exudes fear for Uma even before the earthquake occurs that could possibly end her life. She confesses to having felt an overwhelming urge to exit the room prior to the earthquake:

> Minutes before the second rumble, Uma felt a craving to see the sun. Had the gossamer fog that draped the tops of the downtown buildings when she arrived that morning lifted by now? [. . .] Suddenly she needed to know [. . .] Later she would wonder at the urgency that her pulled her out of her chair and to her feet. Was it instinct like the one that made zoo animals moan and whine for hours before natural disasters struck? (Banerjee Divakaruni 7–8)

It is only minutes later that her "topophobia" is justified when "[i]t was as though a giant had placed his mouth against the building's foundation and roared. The floor buckled, throwing Uma to the ground. The giant took the building in both his hands and shook it" (9). Similarly, it is the topophobia induced by Jakarta that has Zara escape to Russia and Amsterdam. Paradoxically, the terror that the places of entrapment invoke brings out the characters' unacknowledged but fundamental affinity with nature. In *One Amazing Thing*, when the cracked ceiling reveals the sky after days in the dark room, even Lily, the completely urbanized teenager, is struck with awe: "Is that sunlight?" Lily whispered; her face full of wonder" (134).

These pastoral yearnings of the characters are interestingly fostered by idyllic alter images: in "Lake" it is mysterious nature with its disappearing and reappearing lakes and in *One Amazing Thing*, it is images of India. India is the place of desire, the goal of the journey. In a very tangible way, it is their wish to visit India that has placed all of them in the basement to procure an Indian visa, when the earthquake strikes. Thus, both "topophobia" and "topophilia" are tropes that run through the entire narrative. The two spaces in the novel, urban America and India, are juxtaposed and balanced against each other. The concrete basement room becomes the residual if basic cultural emblem while India becomes the imagined other. But interestingly, despite their pastoral yearning, India is not pastoral. On the contrary, all their recollections of India are of a constricted urban dwelling heaving with the weight of humanity, hardly a rural retreat that celebrates the ethos of rusticity over an ethos of metropolitanism. So, in one sense, the yearning for India becomes anti-pastoral, a desire to "dwell in crisis" so that the apocalyptic trope is prophetically extended.

In exploring the tradition of anti-pastoralism in African-American literature, Michael Bennett discusses the way in which marginalized peoples in culture have a distinctly different relationship to the pastoral based on its formal generic features (195). Like the American slaves that Bennett argues were not the shepherds but the sheep of the pastoral—those who lacked souls and could therefore be "owned"—these marginal characters too are not the pensive shepherds of the pastoral but the sheep. *Thus risk, apocalypse, and the anti-pastoral get integrated and become predominant tropes that drive the plot forward.*

The ethos of the anti-pastoral is further reinforced by the sense of displacement or *unheimlich* that the characters experience, which fills them with restlessness and a longing to escape. They inhabit the "uncanny," defined by Sigmund Freud as "in reality nothing new or alien, but something which is familiar and old-established in the mind and which has become alienated from it only through the process of repression" (241). Friedrich Wilhelm Joseph von Schelling's definition of the uncanny as that "which ought to have remained hidden but has come to light" (Freud 224) becomes symbolic of India, a space which articulates the "return of the repressed" in different ways for each of the characters. For instance, after a lifetime in America, Jiang astounds her granddaughter by unveiling her knowledge of English, which she has repressed as it is linked to a traumatic phase in India when she was hounded out of the only homeland she had known and rushed into marriage to a stranger after being abandoned by her Indian boyfriend. Also, Mrs Pritchett's death wish and attempted suicide is linked to her trip to India in a primal way. Recovering in hospital, she decides to go to India to escape her unhappy disappointing marriage: "once I got there, I planned to leave Mr Pritchett. I planned to dive into that roiling ocean of one billion people, all our karmas fitting together like jigsaw puzzle pieces, and begin anew" (176).

Mrs Pritchett allows the repressed emotions and regrets of a lifetime to emerge at what she considers her hour of death. She harks back to a what-might-have-been scenario. India then becomes the land where the familiar and the unfamiliar mingle: the place of Freud's *unheimlich*. However, this is not the only sense in which the "uncanny" is evoked. All the characters experience a sense of cognitive dissonance to a greater or lesser degree. Considering that they believe themselves to be at the juncture between life and death, this is not surprising. Cameron, struggling without his inhaler toward the end, repeatedly imagines an inner voice apostrophizing him to "Give up Seva," Seva being his "sponsored daughter" (178). This is his "*unheimlich*" moment when an incident from his past, when he forced his pregnant girlfriend to abort their unborn son, comes back to haunt him. On the advice of his spiritual friend Jeff, he sponsors Seva, a little girl in India, to make amends for his "sinful" act. Thus, the repetitive voice becomes an instance of the "uncanny." These instances of cognitive dissonance emphasize the deep-rooted cultural discord or dis/ease that these characters expose. In *The Posthuman Condition*, Robert Pepperell posits that:

> consciousness (Mind) and the environment (Reality) cannot be separated. They are integrally linked. There is nothing external to a human because the extent of a human cannot be fixed. If we accept that the mind and body cannot be absolutely separated, and that the body and the environment cannot be absolutely separated, then we are left with the apparently absurd, yet logically consistent, conclusion that consciousness and the environment cannot be absolutely separated. (4)

Pepperell's postulations are not alien to the ideas that inhabit both narratives. For by constantly showing human interconnections with both culture and nature, both *One Amazing Thing* and "Lake" appear to emphasize the fundamental tenet that humans, nature, and culture are all inseparable and that in risk society, this awareness needs to be heeded.

Bakhtin believes that all meaning is determined by the context of an utterance. For Bakhtin, "context" includes all earlier texts as well as the great multiplicity of contemporary voices and even those of the future ("Response to a Question" 4). The contexts of *One Amazing Thing* and "Lake" are provided by the earthquake. But they are contained within the larger thematic of environmental disasters. The characters in peril become representative of endangered humanity. There is a polyphony of voices, especially in the novel, each contributing his or her history and eliciting responses, their resonance reaching out to the past and to the future. Nature, an actant, is presented as constantly overflowing, literally and metaphorically, into the boundaries erected by culture.

> It was as though the giant in the earth had heard Cameron speak his name. Before he could complete his sentence, before his listeners could compare his story to theirs [. . .] the building shuddered and groaned. Something crashed upstairs, and above their heads a ripple went through the ceiling as though it were made of paper. (Banerjee Divakaruni 190)

These constantly reiterated dialogic moments of interaction between culture and nature—that interrupt human narratives—serve to dissolve previous binaries. In "Lake," too, the mysteries of nature—vanishing lakes—get entangled with the mystery of Fayza's disappearance. Thus, both texts dare to push beyond the conventions of a cultural narrative to incorporate a primal nature as a dialogic member. The narrative does not ignore the primeval undercurrent: the "wild earth" that demands a greater acknowledgement and role in the cultural domain, a demand that is acknowledged and granted. By doing so, the pervasive rhetoric of risk that emanates from an active nature is allowed to overflow into the puny ramparts erected by human civilization, revealing its fragility.

In "A Short History of Environmental Apocalypse," Buell discusses how levels and consciousness of risk have escalated such that "risk today is not finally manageable or limitable. Increased consciousness of it haunts us far more than any sense of ends to come" (30). He observes how the conversion of "the rhetoric of apocalyptic irrevocability" into "temporal irresolution of world risk society" has deep implications. The uncertainties of risk "opens up new sites for action and coalitions for change." This, he claims, reveals "the creeping spread of crisis" into the "physical, social and psychological spaces" of our everyday life (31). Zara's description of the plight of the bereaved families near the conclusion of "Lake" approximates to this "creeping spread of crisis." Her comment can be extrapolated to all environmentally conscious humans. "[. . .] the people here had remained trapped in a mysterious tunnel so long that there was no sign of light at its end" (Farid 90). To return then to Jameson for an exploration of the representational quality of these texts that emerge from the margins and are rooted in specific events in their communal and/or personal histories, is to arrive at the idea that these specific moments predict or set up warnings about our present and possible future(s).

These scenarios give glimpses of the unpredictable futures to come . . . that can also be our *present*. "Roar of a Distant War" signposts the fact that people in developing countries are placed far closer to war and other apocalyptic scenarios due to the implacable binaries erected between the privileged nations of the West and other underprivileged nations. *Rani in Search of a Rainbow* reveals the impact of extreme weather on the subdominant, the focus being on the stoicism of their communities. *Wave* demonstrates precisely the opposite: the false sense of control over nature and her surroundings that the representative "elite academic" from a Western institution of privilege entertains all her life, and how it is blown apart in a single instance of climate catastrophe. Both "Lake" and *One Amazing Thing* teach us the truth: that in the face of an increasingly unpredictable nature and a planet at risk, the one important tool to initiate change, and a power that is within reach of the subdominant is that of narrating human responsibilities, the unevenness of risk, and nature's intractability. All the texts discussed bring to the surface the pervasive risk that suffuses both nature and culture.

Finally, all five texts also negotiate the Third Space as a mode of articulation. Their narrative space is productive, going *beyond the reflective to activate the fictional and the real for future action*. The accounts of Ketavong, Deriniyagala, Abdullah, and Farid are based on their own lives or documented history, extrapolating from this "authentic" space to an ethical one that agitates for more consolidated global awareness and action about marginal and compromised locations. This ethical space is what Banerjee Divakaruni's novel, albeit purely fictional, also functions within. This becomes a Third Space that calls for and engenders new possibilities. It is an "interruptive, interrogative, and enunciative" space (that calls for new forms of cultural meaning and production (Bhabha, *The Location of Culture* 179). These texts challenge and blur the limitations of existing boundaries, calling into question established categories of culture and identity.

Concluding Thoughts

In this chapter, I explored Asian apocalyptic narratives with a difference, those where the narrative temporality is poised in a "future-past." As they revolve around both individual and communal histories, I triangulated the apocalyptic mode with the pastoral in "risk society." I came to realize that there are distinct differences in the ways in which the apocalyptic moment is rehearsed in these Asian texts as opposed to most Western apocalyptic fictions. But there are similarities too. In all five narratives, humans and their environment are shown to be at odds. Nature appears to be "other" to humans in decided ways. In "The Roar of a Distant War," Ketavong describes ways in which the beauty of the natural world appears at best alien and at worst an irrelevance, and oftentimes a threat to the survival of Nanda and her family. In *Rani in Search of a Rainbow*, torrential rain and floods drive Rani, her family, and their community of friends from their homes into refugee camps where they are bereft of all their belongings. In *Wave*, the protagonist loses her entire family in one fell blow to the tsunami. *One Amazing Thing* leaves us with people dying in the basement in the aftermath of an earthquake, and the apocalyptic rhetoric of disappearing lakes in Farid's text converges with the crisis in the sociopolitical terrain of the nation-state. In all the narratives, nature represents something irreducibly non-human with the potential to harm and decimate human lives. The cultural spaces in "Lake," "The Roar of a Distant War," and *Wave* are equally terrifying. To echo the words of eco-materialist Jeffrey Jerome Cohen, "[a]gency is distributed among multifarious relations and not necessarily knowable in advance: actions that unfold along the grid surprise and then confound" (xxiv).

These texts, however, also emphasize the redemptive nature of human narratives and their capacity to bridge the gap between nature and culture, though these efforts are not always successful. All the narratives also simultaneously underline the interrelatedness of the human with the environment and the impossibility of insulating the individual from her ecosystem. As Evernden observes: "There is no such thing as an individual, only [. . .] individual as a component of place, defined by place" (101, 103). Does one then have to concede with Jeffers that, in the final analysis, the vastness and power; the very "isness" of nature provides a perspective on the insubstantiality of even the most apocalyptic events in human life?

The next chapter takes up this question through a focus on foundational texts and how their legacies have contributed, even legitimized, the oppression and silencing of subdominant groups such as women, tribal groups, and, indeed, even nature.

CHAPTER FIVE

The Sacred, the Subalterns, Women, and Literary Legacies

❧

> Religion, Society, and Nature - these are the three struggles of man.
> —Victor Hugo
>
> We have been talking about the environment as if it is something different from us, but we are the environment. The non-human elements are our environment, but we are the environment of non-human elements, so we are one with the environment. We are the environment.
> —Thich Nhat Hanh, Buddhist Monk

In the last chapter, I discussed the redemptive nature of human narratives. In this chapter, I explore the role and legacy of scriptural and other impactful cultural narratives. In her essay, "A Feminist Philosophical Perspective on Ecofeminist Spiritualities," Karen J. Warren envisages ecofeminist spirituality—despite the wide-ranging controversies raging within and about it amongst theorists—as offering an important corrective to a dysfunctional system like patriarchy. She describes a belief system as "a network of interconnected values, attitudes, assumptions, myths, judgments, beliefs, and 'facts' that characterize a group, culture, or society" (125). In this chapter, I look at several texts from both South and Southeast Asia that engage with the idea of the sacred, and link them with environmental concerns. Emerging from Hindu, Islamic, and Catholic religious backgrounds, these texts confront ideologies within these belief systems and the long-standing impact they have had on women and the subdominant. I also examine narrative perspectives and their significance in engaging with social and natural ecologies.

Texts and Their Legacies

If there is an argument to be made that the current environmental crisis predates industrialization and in fact originates with the invention of agriculture, deforestation, and the eradication over centuries of large mammals (Clark, *Criticism on the Edge* 3) then one could say that the ancient Hindu epics, the Ramayana and the Mahabharata, register and elucidate this cultural process, where we see the burning of forests and other forms of ecological ruination. "It is said that yaksha's (demon) strength is trivial, and this is a yakshii, a female. How then can this yakshii, frail by her femininity, exert the strength of a thousand elephants?" (Ramayana 1-25-2) These lines, uttered by Rama as he and his brother Lakshmana are being led by sage Vishwamitra to annihilate the demoness Tataka in the Sanskrit epic the Ramayana, is an important entry point to a highly value-laden world that not only links women and the marginalized with land and nature in specific ways but also offers justifications for their oppression or destruction. Additionally, that Dravidian leaders of the twentieth century like E. V. R. Periyar and Anna Durai, castigated these (Indo-Aryan) epics of demonizing Dravidian races,[1] further complicates the issue. Mahasweta Devi opens up this world for scrutiny while presenting the plight of the Indian "tribals,"[2] and often specifically women tribals, in her powerful short stories and novels about contemporary India. Thus, *this chapter opens up questions regarding the power of ideology; language and its slippages in communicating crisis; and textual legacies and their influence in today's world.*

The leftist ideologies of Mahasweta Devi[3] (henceforth referred to as Mahasweta) and her commitment to activism are rendered visible not only through her factual reports about tribal life but also, and in fact, mainly, through her fictional works. Her short stories, in particular, lend themselves to ecofeminist readings because they center the plight of the marginalized (women and tribals) and also emphasize a fundamental tenet of the green movement: that humanity is embedded within local ecosystems. Mahasweta's fictional works, though made popular in the Anglophone world, largely through Gayatri Chakravorty Spivak's translations of her Bengali works into English, have long been acclaimed in India and throughout Asia. Her stark, often brutal, short stories are strengthened by the insights she gained as a social activist. She learnt the languages of the various groups of *adivasi*s (aboriginal tribal people) whom she lived with for long stretches of time, sometimes coming to the city only to fight for their cause with obscurantist government agencies and recalcitrant officials. Mahasweta's short stories can be understood better if one learns how she ironically references and deconstructs the world of Hindu myths to show that the sad plight of the *adivasi*s—who are placed lowest in the social hierarchy and habitually located outside of culture—is one that has come to be accepted, even justified, and inscribed into the social imaginary from the time of the ancient Hindu epics. Her narratives underscore the importance of reflecting on traditions to cognize how ideology, subalternity, and nature are interconnected.

Filipino writer Rosario Cruz-Lucero, an academic at the University of the Philippines, has lived in Manila all her adult life, and her home island of Negros provides her with a trove of material for most of her writing. Her short story "The Death of Fray Salvador Montano, Conquistador of Negros" was awarded the first prize at the Don Carlos Palanca Memorial Awards 2001 and was shortlisted for the N. V. M. Gonzalez Award. Set in the nineteenth century, when Spanish priests were engaged in mass conversion of the natives in the Philippines, this whimsical narrative delves into the despair and confusion of one sincere priest and the gradual devolution of his zeal and faith while isolated in the island province of the Visayas with the "natives." It is paradoxically both humorous and moving. While it is centrally concerned with tribal people, marginal cultures, language, signifiers, and the signified, the text addresses and extrapolates on problems caused when slippages occur in language use, and outlines the hardships involved in the very act of attempting to convey abstract concepts to a skeptical and/or ignorant audience. The text delves into textual politics by way of the use of metonymy, metaphor, and analogy. It reveals how slippages in meaning are an inherent aspect of language use, and that a relentless pursuit of logocentrism is opposed to the spontaneous plenitude of nature and runs counter to its innate unpredictability.

Another useful text, "The Money Makers" by Danish-Filipino writer Nita Umali-Berthelsen, centers on "classism" and the politics of othering and is especially pertinent as it is narrated from the point of view of a child. The innocent recital by the young child demonstrates Martha Nussbaum's idea of the capacity of literature to substitute our understanding of judgement as an abstract and universalized exercise, perceiving it as a reflective activity that is receptive to specific situational complexities (*Poetic Justice* 2). The young girl's relative lack of ideological affiliation is also noteworthy.

The final text that I examine in this chapter is *The Baromashi Tapes*, a novel-length narrative by writer, editor, and translator Niaz Zaman, who is an academic at the University of Dhaka, Bangladesh. The text takes its title from the well-known folk genre of the Baromashi, the twelve-month song,[4] excerpts from which are provided as an epigraph to each chapter. The folk genre organizes the form of the text, each chapter being named after a month both from the Gregorian calendar and the Bangla calendar: July is juxtaposed with Sravan, May with Jyaistha, and so on, with twelve chapters to represent the full year. The text delves into the familiar theme that richer nations and the rich within each nation are able to defend themselves better from environmental hazards. The longing for a return to a premodern way of life, stress-free existence, and a holistic, small-scale community that is invoked in one part of the text is juxtaposed with the reality of risk that pervades the global labor market in the other.

I bring together these texts since they are important for the ways in which each of them mine their respective literary traditions and/or foreground narrative perspectives to make important connections between ideologies, contemporary societies, and their cultural legacies, and the "environmentalism of the poor." These texts comment forcefully on how language, ideology, and the cultural imaginary are all linked.

Julia Corbett emphasizes the use of narratives that can work to convert human relationship to nature from "unrestrained instrumentalism" to "transformative ideologies" (28), that can replace anthropocentrism with ecocritical relationships. What she highlights is the import of communicating catastrophes effectively such that people are galvanized into action or, at least, empathy. The texts that I examine in this chapter describe different kinds of social catastrophes that impact land, the subdominant, and the environment. The implicit message that emerges is that ideology dictates whose lives can be put at risk, even who "deserve" it. People learn to accept ideology or attempt to resist it. In many instances, their response to problems reveals the extent of their internalization of ideology. Ideologies that link hazards and punishment *can* and often *do* emerge from religious systems. Religion can indoctrinate followers to certain preconditioned perceptions and practices.

I begin with Mahasweta's works to illustrate how the cultural imaginary is firmly circumscribed by ideology, which dictates who is expendable and who should be sheltered.

Mahasweta Devi: Tribals, Land, and Ideologies

Hindu philosophical systems are often said to conceive of the physical world as illusory, a projection of Cosmic Intelligence or *Brahman*. The fundamental precept of *maya* from the Upanishads has been misunderstood to mean an "illusory" nature.[5] But as Troy Wilson Organ clarifies in *The Hindu Quest for the Perfection of Man*:

> The world is *māyā*, but to describe it as illusory or false is not to tell the whole story. The world is an appearance, but it is a *false* appearance only when man forgets that it is an appearance and takes it for reality. Then its "reality" is false.[6] [. . .] From the point of view of man the pluralization of Brahman in a space-time world cannot be said to be non-purposive, for only under such conditions can man exist, i.e., man, the being whose essence is to become, can become only in such a world. (156)

Hence, in most Hindu *darshana*s (visions) or philosophies, particularly in the non-dualistic *Advaita*, the physical world is considered essentially sacred, inviolate, and vital for human spiritual evolution. So, the mind/matter binary is differently cognized by the insistence on its interdependence. However, this view that is endorsed by Vedic literature is severely compromised in the epics, where the sociopolitical dimension is predominant. The world as depicted in the epics, which center the Indo-Aryan dynasties and their political strife, is material and solid. This world is peopled by races that constantly pose a threat to the Aryans.

In the eclectic Hindu world, esoteric philosophies are accessed only by the intellectual elite. It is the exuberant world of the epics that fills popular imagination. Therefore, one could credibly argue that in large part the two epics, the Ramayana and the Mahabharata, were foundational in forming the Hindu imaginary and were therefore instrumental in disseminating discursively an idea of nature that rationalized, even justified, its destruction. For example, in one episode of the Mahabharata, Agni, the fire god, entreats Krishna and the warrior Arjuna to feed him a forest. Despite the protests of all the animals, birds, and trees in the forest, Arjuna and Krishna enable Agni to feed off the forest. The epics also sanction social hierarchies that permit exploitation of the socially disenfranchised. Mahasweta's writings reflect her understanding of the importance of the cultural imaginary and how ideology can impact and shape it. She is tuned to the hierarchical thinking that is entrenched in the epics and makes this connection in her conversation with Chakravorty Spivak:

> The tribal population of India is about one-sixth of the total population of the country. The tribes are divided into many groups. India belonged to these tribals before the incursion of the Aryan-speaking peoples. The *Ramayana*, one of India's two ancient epics, seems to contain evidence of how they were oppressed, evicted from their homeland, and then forced to occupy the lower reaches of the mainstream culture. (ix)

Mahasweta hence instantiates critical links between the epics and her short stories, which are designed to question and expose the roles these epics play in formulating a certain type of Hindu cultural imaginary that works to justify the appalling social discriminations and ecological rampage that are currently occurring in India. Therefore, before I analyze her texts, it is essential that I examine the section in *Bala Kanda* (the seventh book) of the original Ramayana by Valmiki (5th–4th century BCE) to reveal how Mahasweta identifies some entrenched ideologies of power in the Ramayana and challenges them through her writing.

In Book 7, sage Vishwamitra takes Rama and his brother Lakshmana to vanquish the demoness Tataka. Despite their reservations as warriors (*kshatriyas*) about to fight against a woman, the sage persuades them that it is a "just war" to wage.[7] Parsing the relevant passage from the Ramayana (n. 44) reveals its endorsement of the hegemonic view that punishing rebels who prove harmful to the status quo is justifiable, even necessary.[8] Several disturbing features emerge, such as the justification of social hierarchies: the idea that nomadic women who threaten Brahmins are dispensable; that the comfort of sages is more important than that of demons and demonesses. Equally significant are the gaps in the text (for example, between stanzas 1-25.9 and 1-25.10); it baldly states that Tataka's husband Sunda was destroyed by sage Agastya's curse but not *why*. Innate narrative contradictions emerge that are never acknowledged nor explained: the "gem-like daughter" Tataka, born after penance by her father, is wed to Sunda who is killed by sage Agastya's curse. But it is never disclosed why Mareecha, Tataka's son, was cursed to become a demon. However, when Sunda's wife and son turn against sage Agastya to avenge Sunda's death, they are deemed monstrous. The gaps in the narrative are vital and render them significantly political. The perspective is that of the powerful sage Vishwamitra describing the plight of his fellow sage, Agastya, to royal princes. Therefore, not only ethics but the very coherence of the text is compromised by the agenda of the dominant class that dismisses and neglects to cogently connect those aspects of the tale that are considered irrelevant to the interests of the powerful. Finally, a direct link is made, repeatedly in this passage (and throughout the Ramayana), between "sinners" and fallow land. The abode of "demons" is also a land of turbulent weather, drought, and fallow land, devolving into desertification. Parallels to contemporary ideologies of power are patent.

Through the deep irony that laces her narratives and by mirroring the conceptual gaps in these texts in her own, Mahasweta exposes the power and structural anomalies evident in these origin tales. She undermines their claims to logic by revealing the political underbelly of these "scriptural" tales[9] generated *by and for* the status quo. By echoing in her stories the incoherence found in the epics and their inconsistent logic, Mahasweta exposes their ideological spine.

Her short story "Salt" focuses on the exploitation of tribals as "wageless" labor by the "caste Hindus." It poignantly presents this irrevocable breakdown in communication between *adivasi*s and *diku*s ("outsiders" or the so-called "caste" Hindus) (Chakravorty Spivak ix). In the story, the Oraon and Kol tribes live on land that belongs to Uttamchand Bania, a trader and moneylender (124). In order to repay the debt of their forefathers, the gullible tribals have been tricked into unpaid labor for the past several generations. Year after year at harvesting time, the tribals trudge 12 miles to Uttamchand's village to offer "wageless" (unpaid) labor for a meal and a handful of crops. But when Balkishan, an ardent young teacher, arrives at the local primary school, he, along with the "youth-team" of the Tribal Welfare Board, fights with Uttamchand against the illegal "wageless labor" and demands that the *adivasi*s work for money and half the crop. While Uttamchand pretends to agree, he vows vengeance on the *adivasi*s. He declares to Purti Munda, the most vocal amongst the tribals, that he would kill them with salt or its lack thereof. After the welfare officers have left for town, Uttamchand stops selling salt to the tribals. Since he is the only shopkeeper anywhere near the village the tribals have no means of obtaining salt, despite it being the cheapest of condiments and the only flavoring that they have used for generations in their *ghato* or food. Without the essential sodium chloride in their diet, the *adivasi*s gradually develop all the symptoms of salt deficiency including nausea, dizziness, and muscle cramps. The alarmed villagers at first attribute their illness to angry gods as punishment for challenging their "master." However, when one of the welfare officers informs them about the scientific facts, Purti, the most enterprising of the villagers, discovers that elephants and deer in the reserve forest receive salt licks from the forestry department and so they begin stealing these. When an *ekoa* or lone tusker attacks the village, the tribal elders are convinced that he had seen the tribal youth stealing from his salt lick and has come to take revenge. When Purti asserts staunchly, "[h]e hasn't seen us. If he had, wouldn't we have known, wouldn't we have seen him? Is an elephant a rabbit?" (141), the elders rebuke him roundly: "An elephant is an ant—an elephant is a butterfly—an elephant is the breeze! Such a huge body, but when it wants, it can creep up unnoticed and squash your head with its foot, and you won't even know. You fool! You shit-eating insect! You didn't see him, he saw you. Why else would he come?" (141) So, the *adivasi*s stop stealing salt licks and, strangely, the rogue elephant never comes to the village again. But forced by circumstance and needing salt in their diet, after an interval, the tribal youth, led by Purti, return to the salt lick again, only to be killed by the rogue elephant.

The forestry officials' complete incomprehension when they are informed that the tribal boys were trampled on by the rogue elephant when they were out stealing salt licks, reveals the vast gulf that separates mainstream Indians and the *adivasi*s. "They died trying to steal salt-earth? Salt-earth? [. . .] Finally, the *daroga* [police officer in charge] says—They must have been drunk" (144). In a scene reminiscent of George Orwell's short story "Shooting an Elephant," the *ekoa* is shot dead by a commissioned hunter. However, Mahasweta ends the story with some difficult questions, questions that are shown to flit hazily through the mind of the village elder: "All this because of mere salt! They couldn't get salt. If they could buy salt, three men and one elephant would still be alive" (144). But because "his thought process is hazy and because his stock of words is limited, he cannot explain anything to anyone" (145). Through their absolute separation from mainstream society and in their inability to communicate, the *adivasi*s, sadly, appear to more closely resemble animals than humans. Their action zoomorphizes the tribals and, on the contrary, the elephant in its canniness is humanized. The tribals accept their fate as divinely ordained and are passive about the injustices they are exposed to. Their internalization of ideologies that leaves them feeling unworthy of procuring "salt" even legitimately, is closely linked to their state of abjection and the absolute power of the status quo.

Their passivity can be traced back to the Hindu epics and the derivative caste system. Indeed, one feature that makes the narratives in the Hindu epics complicated is the subtle, unstated idea of social hierarchy that permeates their narratives which, however, is never explicitly addressed. M. S. S. Pandian discusses a feature he labels "transcoding" that he argues is intrinsic to Hindu discourses relating to caste:

> The subtle act of transcoding caste and caste relations into something else—as though to talk about caste as caste would incarcerate one into a pre-modern realm—is a regular feature one finds in most upper caste autobiographies. Caste always belongs to someone else; it is somewhere else; it is of another time. *The act of transcoding is an act of acknowledging and disavowing caste at once.* (6; emphasis in original)

Pandian points out that "in marked contrast to the upper caste autobiographies, the self-definition of one's identity, as found in the autobiographies of the lower castes, is located explicitly in caste as a relational identity"[10] (6–7). This "acknowledging and disavowing caste at once" (6), Mahasweta's narratives reveal, is constantly at work in Hindu interactions with the tribals, who are marked as Dalits or "outcastes." I would claim that this is a feature that is intrinsic to the Hindu epics as well. Indeed, it has been widely discussed by Dr B. R. Ambedkar,[11] the Dalit leader and a father of the Indian constitution, as well as the Dravidian leader E. V. Ramasamy Naicker,[12] who argue that the Ramayana presents a world deeply inscribed by binaries, where notions of virtue and evil are closely tied to caste, race, and social identity. This view exposes an ideological positioning that Abdul R. JanMohamed terms as "the economy of Manichean allegory."

These social reformers argued in the early half of the twentieth century that in the epics, particularly the Ramayana, the world "beyond civilization" was perceived as "uncontrollable, chaotic, unattainable and ultimately evil," a trope associated commonly with the "colonized other" (Ashcroft et al. 149–50), demonstrating that colonialism began very early in the Indian subcontinent. These community leaders, often seen as dissidents by the Hindu mainstream, argue that this world of non Indo-Aryans (specifically, Dravidians) was the world that the Aryan princes Rama and Lakshmana set out to demonize and to then "conquer." According to their view, the Ramayana was an archetypal "colonial text" rather than a scriptural one.

In her short stories, Mahasweta shows how this mentality has seeped down from the classical epics and is behind the treatment of *adivasi*s by mainstream

Hindus. In her opinion, the ideological persuasions of the epics also largely dictate Hindu attitude toward the natural world. The tribals, too, Mahasweta believes, have been "educated" to internalize these ideologies to varying degrees, which has had them passively accept abuse.

The lack of cogency that hides the misdeeds of the powerful is clearly glimpsed in Mahasweta's "Seeds" that recounts the story of a poor tribal man who keeps a nightly watch over an arid piece of land donated by his landlord, to the bewilderment of his fellow tribals and the ire of his wife. The narrative gradually reveals the diabolical cunning of the rich landlord and his complete power over the tribal(s). Mahasweta does this by working the stereotype of the "stupid tribal." "Old, his skin gnarled and knotted, a loincloth wrapped around his waist from which a quilt bag hangs [. . .] He strikes a flint stone, lights a *beedi*, and sits on the machan. Every day. When night falls, he spreads a mat and goes to sleep. Every day" (22). The description underlines his subaltern status and the repetition of the words "every day" presupposes his stupidity—that he is mad enough to waste time guarding a worthless piece of land. Therefore later, when certain facts come to light, the readers' complicity with the stereotyping gets exposed, showing the pervasive ideology that prejudices everyone. "Seeds" begins with an observation:

> The land north of Kuruda and Hesadi villages is uneven, arid, sunbaked. Grass doesn't grow here even after the rains. The occasional raised serpent hoods of cactus plants, a few *neem* trees. In the middle of this scorched wasteland where no cattle graze is a low-lying boat-shaped piece of land. Around half a *bigha*. You can spot the land only if you climb a high embankment, and the splash of green appears eerie. (21)

What is not revealed until the end is that Lachman Singh, the landlord, has forced this fallow, barren land on the tribal, Dulan, for his own dark reasons; it is the land where Lachman Singh and his men kill and bury all those who refuse to work as bonded laborers. As Singh's rule of terror continues, the body count increases. Dulan has been forced to guard the land for fear of his own and his sons' lives. But when Dulan's own son finally needs to be buried there, Dulan turns the tables on his master. He kills and buries Lachman Singh. That night the tigers smell the freshly buried corpse, unearth it, ravage the face, and mutilate the body. The following day, the investigating officers see the ravaged body but cannot make a positive identification. Also, no one suspects Dulan despite the fact that Lachman Singh's body was found on his land. This is because, given the rigid social hierarchies in place, "[i]t is natural not to suspect him. It is impossible to imagine Dulan killing Lachman, whatever the circumstances" (55). For once, in a bizarre reversal of fortune, social hierarchies and their rigidly prescriptive roles actually work in favor of the tribal. Refusing to harvest the paddy that has been fertilized by his son's and other village youths' rotting bodies, much to the amazement of his oblivious fellow villagers, Dulan generously offers his paddy as seeds to them. The climax comes when Dulan returns to his land:

> His heart is strangely, wonderfully light today! He stands on the embankment and looks at the paddy.
> Karan, Asrafi, Mohar, Bulaki, Mahuban, Paras and Dhatua—what an amazing joy there is in the ripe green paddy nourished on your flesh and bones! Because you will be seed. To be a seed is to stay alive [. . .] Dhatua, I've turned you all into seed. (56)

Fertilized by Lachman's victims, the once arid land sprouts ripe paddy seeds. The classic association between sinful inhabitants and arid land that is central to the Hindu epics is skilfully subverted here. *The land is rendered fertile because it is linked to murder and exploitation by the rich and the higher castes.* The arid earth "fertilized" by tribal corpses turns fecund and yields rich paddy. A new association is created between "habits and habitats" and the naturalized association, so strongly ingrained in the Hindu imaginary between fertile land and virtue, is challenged. Also, Dulan's paddy hints at an alliance between subaltern bodies and the earth. Dulan's dark knowledge changes his life, turning it around from dumb obedience to planned rebellion.

The style that "Seeds" is written in appears to mimic and mock the classical epic that prioritizes agenda over coherence. Gaps in the narrative highlight how ideology and storytelling are connected. Michel Foucault instructs us in *Discipline and Punish*:

> [. . .] we should abandon a whole tradition that allows us to imagine that knowledge can exist only where the power relations are suspended and that knowledge can only develop outside its injunctions [. . .] Perhaps we should abandon the belief that [. . .] the renunciation of power is one of the conditions of knowledge. We should admit rather that power produces knowledge [. . .] that power and knowledge directly imply one another; that there is no power relation without the constitutive correlation of a field of knowledge nor any knowledge that does not presuppose and constitute at the same time power relations. (27)

Foucault goes on to assert that power and techniques of punishment depend on knowledge that constructs and classifies individuals within society. The insidious relationship between the construction of (social and other) knowledge(s) (by authoritative texts) and their impact on subordinate humans and the natural world is a subtle but persistent theme in Mahasweta's short stories and enables an ecofeminist analysis. As Warren emphasizes: "'Ecological feminism' is an umbrella term which captures a variety of multicultural perspectives on the nature of the connections *within* social systems of domination between those humans in subdominant or subordinate positions, particularly women, and the domination of nonhuman nature" ("Introduction," *Environmental Feminism* 1; emphasis in original).

In "Little Ones" and "The Witch," these "social systems of domination" destroy a whole clan of tribals and cause the near death of a mute, pregnant tribal girl. In "Little Ones," when the Relief Officer (RO), who is handpicked for his honesty, is sent to provide aid to the *adivasi*s in Lohri, he is inducted into the local myths by the Block Development Officer (BDO). The latter reveals that in local lore, the tribals—here, the *Aagariyas*—are believed to descend from the *asura* (demon) clan. The description of the land invokes stereotypes. It is "a burnt-out desert. As if the earth here bears a fire of unbearable heat in her womb. So the trees are stunted, the breast of the river a dried-out cremation ground." "It is no wonder," he asserts, "that their land is barren" (2002: 1). The idea expressed here echoes the sentiments of sage Vishwamitra in the Ramayana, when he informs Rama and Lakshmana that "this wretched forest [. . .] was once a vast province [. . .]designed by gods, known as Malada and Karuusha [. . .] equalling heaven, but deteriorated [. . .] owing to demoness Tataka" (1-24-16b, 17a, 17b, 18a). *Associating arid land with sinful inhabitants is pervasive in Hindu classical tradition.* Tataka's land is described as arid and dry before her death, following which it becomes effulgent ("On that very day the forest of Tataka was released from the curse and it shone forth like the luxurious heavenly garden of Kubera, namely Chiatra Ratha" [1-26-35b, c]). Again, the passage from the Ramayana that describes the demon Viradha's habitat from the *Aranyakandam* makes a similar association: "Carrying Rama and Lakshmana, the demon entered into a baffling forest that was like a dark cloud in its aspect, which contained a variety of massive trees. Flocks of vulturine birds spanned the skies overhead. Wild jackals and other predacious animals were roaming around" (3-3-26). Evil persons are usually believed to inhabit wild or arid land. But Mahasweta's stories ironically invert this association, *revealing the sly hand of power that is instrumental in naturalizing such associations at both the literal and discursive levels.* It is the "higher" castes that, with governmental help, drive out the tribals from lands that originally belonged to the tribals to faraway, arid, uncultivable ones. They then ensure that these associations are naturalized at the discursive level through myths and "holy" texts that yoke "habitats with habits," driving home the idea that *adivasi*s karmically "deserve" to live only in arid lands.

In her conversation with Chakravorty Spivak in *Imaginary Maps*, Mahasweta remarks that "the government of India has pauperized [tribals]":

> They have to beg for everything they need. They do not understand mainstream machination, so although there are safeguarding laws against land-grabbing, tribal land is being sold illegally every day, and usurped by mainstream society all over India. In North Bengal, extensive lands are being converted into tea gardens, fruit orchards. They can't keep their land; there is no education for them, no health facilities, no roads, no way of generating income [. . .] The tribals of India are denied everything . . . (x–xi)

Mahasweta shows that this association between arid land and tribals is persistent. In "Little Ones," the tribals, who are traditionally iron miners, come to be associated with "demons" of the underworld. According to local lore, their king fought with the "sun god" who burnt their land. Thus the "benighted" land is rumoured to be haunted. The RO is warned about strange "otherworldly" children who come at night, steal the food, and disappear into the forests. Ghostly tales of officials and drivers going mad with the sighting of these "children" abound until the RO, who is at first skeptical, is astonished one night to find these beings scuttling around and stealing the aid. He gives chase only to discover that they are none other than *Agariya* tribals, who several decades ago had rebelled against the government and run off to the jungles to hide. The lack of food and sunlight (in the dense jungles) stunted their growth until their shrunken and shrivelled bodies resembled those of children. It is not divine ordination but social usage that has "othered" the *Agariya*s.

Similarly, in "The Witch," rumours of a *daini* (witch) set off a whole chain of events, with families and neighbors checking on each other to ensure that one of them has not turned into a *daini*. Suspicions abound that result in son turning against mother and brothers turning against sister. "What does a *daini* do? She casts an evil eye from afar, or uses her evil magic to curdle milk, kill cows-goats, destroy crops, bring drought, cause famine, take the lives of little children, lure menstruating women into her coils, enter the wombs of pregnant women" (102). We learn that all "husbands-fathers-brothers-sons were compelled to keep watch upon the women" (60). The extreme predicament of the triply colonized tribal women is forcefully brought home to us. Finally, when a stark naked young woman with a strangely distended stomach is spotted eating raw flesh, there is no doubt in the villagers' minds that the *daini* has at last been spotted and must be destroyed. All the men from the surrounding villages set forth with torches to destroy or drive the *daini* out. It is only when they are close that the *pahaan* (tribal priest) of

Tura village recognizes his mute, "simple" daughter, who had been sent to work in the upper-caste Hanuman Misra's house, where she had been raped by his son and had gone missing. Hunger had driven the pregnant girl to eat raw flesh. It is significant that it is Misra who has started the *daini* rumor in the first place.

Both narratives relentlessly expose the iniquities of the powerful landlords in whose hands *adivasi* men and women are exploited. They also illustrate how nature cannot be extricated from the coils of ideology. In "The Witch," through (upper-caste) patriarchal machinations, the violated and pregnant girl has come to be embedded in the natural world as the "other." The girl is caught in a matrix of oppression in which tribal men are almost equally participants, and has been rendered as voiceless as the natural world.

Another curious feature that bears scrutiny in "The Witch," which parallels the Ramayana, is the preoccupation with the weather prior to the introduction of *asuri*s and/or *daini*s. Almost always in the epics, the very elements portend the arrival of the "evil other." In the Ramayana, before the introduction of the demoness Shurpanakha, Lakshmana describes the inclement winter weather as they proceed along with Sita to bathe in the Godavari river. "These days the dew is harsh on human bodies; earth is overlaid with crops, [the cold] water is unenjoyable; only fire is delightful" (4-16-5). Similarly, "The Witch" begins thus: "No rain in the month of *Chaitra*. A fiery *Baisakh* and *Jaisthya* come and go, and the monsoon month of *Ashad* is as fierce as Dhumavati. Clouds play hide and seek. Kuruda's philosophical pessimist Budhni Oraon says—Oh, this time we'll have drought for sure, and famine as well, I just know it" (57). These pronouncements about the weather by a royal prince in the Ramayana are echoed in "The Witch" by the omniscient narrator; both are equated to authority. It is also noteworthy that the inauspicious and portentous signs displayed by the atmospheric conditions appear to adversely affect only the culturally "othered." As the war between the demons that is led by Khara, Shurpanakha's brother, and the royal princes Rama and Lakshmana, is about to commence, nature appears malignant: "A mass of tumultuous grey cloud rained ill-omened bloody water" (3-23-1); "despite the even roads scattered with flowers, Khara's fast-paced horses totter to the earth" (3-23-2); "the sun appears eclipsed by a blackish corona with a blood-red outer circle resembling a fireball" (3-23-3); "an eagle has perched on top of Khara's chariot's mast" (3-23-4); "the cacophony of carnivorous predators and vultures filled the land" (3-23-5). The natural calamities listed are endless: meteors fall and the day darkens to reveal stars. All nature appears to be afflicted. The demon Khara is finally defeated. It appears as though nature itself has resolved to turn against him. It is only when Rama has valorously defeated the demon that nature once again returns to its natural state. *The link between morality and climate change, mentioned earlier, is vividly captured here.*

Similarly, at the end of "The Witch," when (at least some of) the *adivasi*s have painstakingly worked out how they had been fooled and distracted by their "master" into chasing after nonexistent *daini*s, suddenly nature, which had seemed blighted thus far by the presence of a *daini*, appears to be effulgent again. The text foregrounds the idea that deep-seated ideologies have the ability to distort one's (individual and social) perceptions about even something as basic as the weather. The following passage in "The Witch" pauses to mark that epiphanic moment when the *pahaan* realizes this.

> The *pahaan* of Hesadi would look around at intervals, amazed, as if he was seeing things for the first time [. . .] he had realized the wind was as fragrant, the forest as green, as before. Because the oppressive cloud of terror had dissolved, the *pahaan* knew in his heart that everything was as before. The colour of the sky had never changed. The wind had never stopped blowing. Nature was exactly as she had always been in a dry year. It was only because the *pahaan* had changed that everything seemed to have changed, too. (122)

This passage most effectively emphasizes humans' ambivalent (often malevolent) relationship with nature. Here, it is not nature reacting to human actions but only humans "reading" into *their* text called "nature." However, in its refusal of human meaning, nature seems to effectively stand outside of human constructions of it, bound to an immutable law that is opaque to human emotion or the mind. The narrative of "The Witch" demonstrates the immutability of natural laws, exposing the ways in which the epics invoke a version of the pathetic fallacy, another trope that reveals the link between power and narrativization. As Mary Mellor reiterates, "for ecofeminisms, the natural world of which humanity is a part has its own dynamic beyond human construction or control" (7). Mahasweta, in preserving nature's autonomy, shows a commitment to this view. Such epiphanic moments serve to drive home the point that so-called "knowledges" are calibrated by the status quo to befuddle the subalterns and retain them in their powerless position.

A lesson well-learned from the epics is that *perspective is key*, and it is the only means through which some irreconcilable contradictions that could undermine the status quo can be resolved. In Valmiki's Ramayana, the inherent contradictions that shadow the epic, which struggles to reconcile the roles of the ever-compassionate, divine Vishnu who is always at hand to help his devotees, and his human avatar, Rama, the valorous king who has to willy-nilly kill people in combat to establish the supremacy of his dynasty, is often palpable. Both the destruction of the demon, Viradha, at the beginning of the *Aranya Kanda* in the Ramayana, and even more controversially, the wrongful slaying of the valiant Vaali in the *Kishkantha Kanda*, illustrate this tussle. Note these crucial moments when Rama approaches the dying Vaali in the following two stanzas from the Ramayana:

> On seeing the brave Vali fallen, drowsy, like extinguished tongues of flames, the two valiant brothers, Rama and Lakshmana, approached him with due honour. (4-17-12b, 13)
> On seeing Rama and the mighty Lakshmana, the vanquished and dying Vali spoke these sardonic but meaningful words to the victorious Rama, . . . (4-17-14, 15)

Vali asks Rama what right he has to interfere in an internal feud between his brother and himself and kill him "unrighteously" in war.[13] Rama can advance no convincing reply to this query. This climactic moment that threatens to undermine the very righteousness and nobility of the protagonist, which indeed is the driving force of the epic narrative, can only be resolved in the aftermath of Vali's logical accusations by the latter eventually conceding that Rama, the "greatest of humans," knows best, and he, a mere *vānarā* (of the monkey tribe), cannot presume to judge Rama's actions.

This notion of social status as insulating one's actions from critical inquiry is one that is deeply embedded in the epics. It is also one that Mahasweta establishes as very prevalent in contemporary India where, in popular opinion, higher-caste status and accumulation of good karmic deeds (*punya*) are often equated. Hence social interactions with nature (fauna and flora) and marginalized tribes become complex and multilayered, both being viewed by "caste Hindus" as exploitable commodities since these are deemed not just inferior in the evolutionary chain but are also in the karmic hierarchy.

In "Arjun," a less-known short story of Mahasweta's, she brings together the scattered themes of sustainability, deforestation, corruption, and the fate of the powerless subalterns. The story records the significance of a perspectival shift. "Arjun" is a story with an interesting denouement, wherein the subaltern tribes are able to subvert the machinations of the powerful who seek to destroy the Arjun tree that is sacred to the tribes. The tribals use myths and dreams as tools to defeat their materialistic, corrupt, and greedy masters.

Ketu Shabar is routinely asked by his two "masters," Bishal Mahato, the Panchayat (local self-government) chief and his hand-in-glove political "opponent" Ram Halder, to clear the protected jungles for their profiteering. When the two neocolonial "masters" need money, they instruct the hapless tribals to fell trees from the protected forests, which they then secretly cart away to sell for their private gain. Since felling trees contravenes the forestry department's rules, Ketu and his tribesmen are regularly sent to prison. The palpable dispensability of the tribals is clearly spelt out in the omniscient narrator's ironic words: "If you were born in the Shabar tribe of Purulia, you *had* to cut down the trees. And you *had* to go to jail. It could be no other way. If one Ketu was in jail, and something needed to be done, Haldar could always find another Ketu" (Mahasweta Devi 123; emphasis in original). If this is the fate of the men, the doomed destiny of their womenfolk are beyond words and can only be evoked in silence, in the ellipses between words: "The last time Ketu had been jailed for cutting down the trees of the Forest Department, Mohoni [his wife] had gone out looking for work. And who knows what happened . . . In spite of the inevitability of the situation, Ketu couldn't face the prospect of returning to an empty hut" (123). The tragedy lies in the complete acceptance of the vulnerability, indeed dispensability of the womenfolk and the tribals. Like the trees, the women and tribals cannot articulate their fate. The climactic moment is when Bishal asks Ketu to cut down their sacred tree.

> "You have to cut down the Arjun tree," Bishal said.
> "Why, babu?" Ketu was startled.
> "Just do what I say."
> "Please babu, I've just come out of jail, babu."
> "If I wanted to send you back, would you be able to prevent it?"
> asked Bishal Mahato. (124)

But Ketu and his friends are loath to aid in the hacking down of "the only surviving relic of the Bandihi jungles." "When the jungles were not jungles in name only, the Shabars had been forest-dwellers. Gone were those days when they scampered off like rabbits into its dark depths the moment they heard or saw a stranger approaching" (125). But now, cheated of their lands, they wander around homeless. Ketu is deeply troubled by Mahato's order since the "elders of the tribe still revered the arjun tree. They believed that it was a manifestation of the divine. Now Ketu was to be responsible for its death" (125–26). "Hadn't Diga's father said that the tree had medicinal properties?" (126) Ketu is racked by doubt and guilt about cutting down this precious tree.

> Against the backdrop of the deep blue sky, the majestic arjun tree stood with its head held high—like a guardian of the village, keeping vigil from its lofty vigil post. Once upon a time, this land used to be guarded by hundreds of leafy sentinels. One by one they have all gone, leaving no trace. Only the arjun is left now. Alone, to guard this devastated, neglected, humiliated land . . . (129)

But the characteristic duplicity of their neocolonial masters constantly defeats the simple tribals. Ram Halder's business does not stop with one or two trees. First, he puts up posters of "Save the Forests" then vandalizes the jungles. Hands that wield the axe are rewarded with "torches, wristwatches, gleaming radios, cassette players, cycles and of course, unlimited quantities of liquor" (126). But the fallout is that whether innocent or guilty, the Shabars are repeatedly prosecuted by the forest department or the police. Now the tribals are hard put to save the tree. "That one tree is the entire jungle for us. And our few families, the children of the forest. Now Mahato wants that very tree?" (128) There is a deep poignancy in the tribals' predicament as revealed in Mahasweta's words: "[T]he Sobors (the hunting tribes) will beg forgiveness if they are forced to fell a tree: You are our friend. I do this because my wife doesn't have any food, my son doesn't have any food, my daughter starves. Before they killed an animal, they used to pray to the animal: the bird, the fish, the deer" (Chakravorty Spivak x). Unlike the confused elder in "Salt" who is even more remote from the mainstream systems, here the Shabars put their heads together to plot against their masters' diabolical scheme. Diga, the canniest Shabar, who has attended four whole days at the non-formal education center, devises a plan. "Bishal Babu is going to town. We must collect the cash [for illegal felling] from him before he leaves" (128). Bishal babu is assured that by the time he returns from town, the job would be done. But when Bishal Mahato returns, the sight that met his eyes made "his head reel" (129). "All around boomed the sounds of the *dhol-dhamsa-damak* and the strains of the *nagra*. An agitated Bishal Mahato rushed into the village. A huge crowd had gathered around the arjun. Its trunk was covered with *aakondo* garlands" (129).

The bemused Mahato questions Ram Haldar, his partner-in-crime:

"What happened?" asked Mahato.
"The gram-devata [village deity] had made them do it" answered
   Haldar.
"What? Which ill-begotten fellow says so?"
"Diga had a dream, it seems. You paid him money in the dream and
   instructed him to build a concrete base around the tree. People
   from all the tribes—Santhal, Khedia, Shohish, Bhumji—have
   now gathered to make their offerings." (130)

The story ends on an interesting not when the corrupt neocolonial master realizes, for the first time, the latent power that is in the hands of the subalterns when they work as a collective. "Bishal was suddenly afraid. This tree, these people—he knew them all. He knew them very well. And yet, today, they seemed like strangers.

Fear. An uncomprehending fear gripped him" (130). Though the author reinstates the dignity and agency of the tribals in "Arjun," she also reveals their extreme limitations and the behemoth system they are up against. In the introduction to *Bitter Soil* she remarks that "the sole purpose of my writing is to expose the many faces of the exploiting agencies: The feudal-minded landowner, his henchmen, the so-called religious head of the administrative system, all of whom, as a combined force, are out for lower-caste blood" (ix).

Mahasweta not only discloses the risks that the tribals are routinely exposed to, her stories collectively unmask the power of ideology in determining who is deemed expendable and who is sheltered. Risks are always represented and experienced unevenly, as we see in the epics. William Cowper's "World at a Distance," discussed in Chapter 4, exposes the racist dimensions of danger: "Thus sitting and surveying thus at ease/The globe and its concerns, I seem advanced/To some secure and more than mortal height,/That liberates and exempts me from them all."

"The Hunt" exposes the endless harassment that the tribal women are exposed to from "upper-caste" Hindu men. In it is recounted the story of how one tribal girl, Mary Oraon, born of Dixon, a white Australian, and a tribal woman, is hunted by the "upper-caste" *tehsildar*. When he tries to woo her with a sari, Mary boldly confronts him. "Tehsildar was sitting in the tent paying the men and women. Lots of people. Mary enters and throws the sari at him. She says, 'You think I'm a city whore? You want to grab me with a sari? If you bother me again, I'll cut off your nose.' She goes off proudly, swinging her arms" (11). Mary's threat refers to Lakshmana's mutilation of the demoness and Ravana's sister Shurpanakha, whose nose Lakshmana cuts off for desiring his brother Rama. Mary's words at once associate the *tehsildar* with the demon clan. His relentless pursuit of Mary finally turns her into a righteous "hunter" at par with Rama and Lakshmana, though she is hunting an "upper-caste" man. Thus, *the traditional association between virtue and upper caste status is deftly inverted*. On the tribal women's hunting day, Mary ignores the hares and the small prey and goes for the "big beast," the *tehsildar*, here akin to Ravana.

> Mary laughed and held him, laid him on the ground. Tehsildar is laughing. Mary lifts the machete, lowers it, lifts, lowers . . . Mary stands up. Blood? On her clothes? She'll wash in the cut. With great deftness she takes the wallet from Tehsildar's pocket. A lot of money [. . .] She undoes the fold in the cloth at her waist and puts the money with her own savings. Then, first she throws Tehsildar in the ravine, his wallet, cigarettes, his handkerchief. Stone after stone. Hyenas and leopards will come at night, smelling blood. Or they won't. (17)

The *tehsildar*'s body that is cast in the ravine, followed by Mary casting "stone after stone"[14] on the corpse, is an act of justice and a reprisal for the endless ills that the tribals have to face from "caste" Hindus on a daily basis. This "rough justice" is the only one they have access to. If we take all of Mahasweta's stories to be "speaking as a unit" then the stones that Mary casts at the *tehsildar* seem to be in retaliation for the stones cast at the poor *daini* girl; the exploitation of tribals as "wageless labor"; the deaths of the tribal boys at the hands of their "*diku* masters"; and tribal deaths caused due to lack of mere "salt." Mary's act "The Hunt" becomes a gesture that, above all, exorcises the innumerable humiliations that the *adivasi*s are habitually subjected to.

Thus far, I have examined several short stories by Mahasweta Devi to discuss how ideology, and social and natural ecologies, are closely allied, and hegemony and caste/race work to secure the status quo. Mahesweta's stories reveal mainstream (Hindu) India's complicity in the cruelty inflicted on the marginalized tribals and on nature.

Next, I examine two texts from the Philippines, which are important because they emphasize Catholic legacy, hegemony, and slippages in language, and foreground the significance of narrative perspective.

Language and Its Pitfalls in "The Death of Fray Salvador Montano, Conquistador of Negros"

Rosario Cruz-Lucero's story begins with the arrival of Fray Salvador Montano in the island province of the Visayas in the Philippines to replace Fray Duertas, who, "desperate with loneliness and suffocating with envy" at the unrepentant concupiscence of the natives, "had finally asked to be reassigned elsewhere" (Cruz-Lucero 2). Fray Duertas keeps himself and the natives busy on the island, shielded from the Devil through strenuous good works. It is his stern belief that "[l]aziness, drunkenness, and lust" (3) are the enemies of civilization. He warns his successor earnestly:

> Never let Them take over these *indios* souls, although I must warn you, they are so easily afflicted. So keep them busy, keep them working. Next thing you know they'll be doing it like snails. Then where will your mission be? Clear the forests, build roads and bridges, plant fruit trees. That church [that he built] still needs a nave and a taller belfry. (3; uppercase in original)

The priest's passionate tone is a forewarning of the ironic reversals to come for it is the soul of Fray Montano that appears to run amok at the end of the narrative.

What is important to note is that both friars operate on what Homi K. Bhabha identifies as "cultural difference," which is "the process of the enunciation of culture as *knowledgeable*, authoritative, adequate to the construction of systems of cultural identification" ("Cultural Diversity"; italics in original). For the friars who operate on the European/native binary, a culture is a closed system that one can master. The friars are undone precisely because they do not allow for the Third Space, which Bhabha explains as follows: "The act of interpretation is never simply an act of communication between the I and the You designated in the statement. The production of meaning requires that these two places be mobilized in the passage through a Third Space" (206). Bhabha describes this space as implicated in "unconscious performance" which introduces "an ambivalence in the act of interpretation" (206). Hence their *lack* of "ambivalence in interpretation" and an absolute insistence on "authoritative [. . .] constructions of cultural identification" trips up the friars despite their best intentions.

Montano is a pious friar who, "ever since he was six . . . knew God was calling him. He saw himself kneeling on stones in the tropical sun to atone for the world's sins; he would fell but one tree to build his little prayer hut of thatch and wood" (Cruz-Lucero 2–3). Fray Duertas, who is keen to move from this province of licentious natives, welcomes his successor most warmly. But there is another reason for his eagerness. During the months prior to Fray Montano's arrival, the other friars on the island are interested in learning about Fray Duertas' achievements in building a church and wonder how he has erected "such a heavy structure on such shifty soil in this typhoon-and-earthquake-ravaged land." Fray Duertas gives several private lectures and finally decides "he might as well publish the sketches and the secret of his engineering principle" (3). He sends his manuscript to the bishop for the *imprimatur*—the official license issued by the Roman Catholic Church to print an ecclesiastical book—and Fray Duertas is keen to read the bishop's reply that Fray Montano is hand-carrying. But shockingly, the license is denied by the bishop "on the grounds that it contains several obscene words and tends to conjure indecent imagery." Instead, the bishop orders Fray Duertas to publish a dictionary of Hiligaina, the Visayas' language. The deeply bewildered and humiliated friar decides to humbly leave this "devil's work" behind and enjoins his colleague, Fray Montano, to burn it. "It is the work of the devil and I have allowed myself to be his plaything," he cries out in despair (4).

After Fray Duertas departs, his successor, renewing his faith in Church and God, carries on his missionary work zealously. But he cannot bring himself to burn Fray Duertas' architectural manuscript that "lay deep in the drawer of his *escritorio*" (5). After several months, an occasion arises when he needs to consult the manuscript for, all of a sudden, bird droppings have begun falling on the congregation on Sundays. Montano needs to know the church's design in order to seal the roof. On opening the book along with a native construction worker, his curious eyes seek the passages that had caused offence and comes across the following description by Fray Duertas that is heavily underscored in censorious red.

> The top layer of riverbank soil is all sand. But if we want our churches to be tall and massive fortresses, these cannot be built on sand. In the case of the Buyonan Church, the bedrock on which its foundation rests is 29 feet beneath. This means that hardwood piles 29 feet long were driven all the way down to the bedrock. Hence, the grip of the sand on the whole length of each pile is as important as having the pile rest on the bedrock. *Just as a tightly clenched fist can grip a quill,* so the sand has a vise-like grip on each pile, thus assuring a solid foundation for the church to be built on. (6; emphasis added)

The offending (sexual) imagery that this description evidently evokes, together with the "sketch of the hardwood pile thrusting through the sand and another detailed sketch of the sand's vice-like grip on a pile" (6–7) has obviously been (mis)read by the bishop as a double entendre implying lust and licentiousness. The slippage that occurs between authorial intention and the emergent meaning, although hilarious, more seriously mirrors the problems that Bhabha identifies: "The intervention of the Third Space, which makes the structure of meaning and reference an ambivalent process, destroys this mirror of representation in which cultural knowledge is continuously revealed as an integrated, open, expanding code" ("Cultural Diversity" 207). But for Fray Montano, who is trained in the colonial Catholic mores of exactitude and the singularity of the *logos*, semantic ambivalence is not an option.

The avidly interested native, Pedro, the construction worker threatened by the punishment of everlasting fire and brimstone, refrains from gossiping about the contents of the passage but instead composes and sings a *loa* that hints at Fray Duertas' excesses. More and more stanzas are added to Pedro's *loa* by the audacious natives that paints a torrid picture of Fray Duertas, until the helpless Fray Montano approaches Estrella, the recently baptized shaman of the village, for advice on how to stop them. Estrella persuades him to permit the people to sing their old epics again and thus wean them off the salacious *loa*. However, when the triumphant Estrella begins her song, she discovers that reviving the epic is not that simple. "She could not go on" (Cruz-Lucero 10) because the nether spirits, lacking an audience, did not stir to the call of the epic song.

This unhappy image is juxtaposed beside the hilarious efforts of Fray Montano, who decides that the only way he can counter the snide comments of the Negros is by learning their language. He then discovers that Fray Duertas had, in fact, compiled a fairly comprehensive dictionary of the language which, owing to his *imprimatur* being denied, he was too ashamed to own up to having put together. Therefore, Fray Montano decides that he just needs to add the missing, lascivious words to the dictionary to understand what the natives are chanting about Fray Duertas and put a stop to it. But the task is nowhere as straightforward as he believes it to be.

> As Montano compiled his vocabulary, he found more and more categories to divide the *indio* language into. Words missing from Duertas' dictionary were those which conjured images of orifices, phalluses, attitudes of naughtiness, certain kinds of laughter, ways of eating and drinking, positions of verticality, horizontality and perpendicularity, spirals and arrows, numbers and games, weapons and tools, dryness and wetness. (Cruz-Lucero 12)

In fact, increasingly, no word in the language appears to be innocent. As his list of words lengthens, Fray Montano, trapped in the polysemy of words, believes that he now begins to understand the *indios*' world, and "what had been its daunting unpredictability became simply a matter of singular inevitability" (12). As the priest sinks deeper into the never-ending list of sinful words, he drowns in a mire of lust of his own making. The bewildered priest finally dies in the lap of the shaman, confused between Yawa the Consummator, the pagan spirit or the devil, and Yahweh, the jealous, self-righteous Judeo-Christian God.

Driven by his single-minded goal, namely, to net and contain all the lustful words in the language, Montano wants to nail a definitive meaning to every word that links it to lust and sin. Caught in the jouissance of words, the friar seeks a closure that does not exist. As Roland Barthes reminds us:

> The Text is plural. Which is not simply to say that it has several meanings, but that it accomplishes the very plural of meaning: an irreducible (and not merely an acceptable) plural. The Text is not a co-existence of meanings but a passage, an overcrossing; thus it answers not to an interpretation, even a liberal one, but to an explosion, a dissemination. (159)

The plurality of the text is signaled in its refusal to be reduced to any one interpretation but, in fact, counters this effort by generating an explosion of "signified[s]." What is interesting about the story is that it rehearses this notion of plurality both within and through its narrative. The text, in fact, is layered and modulated by deliberately signaling the impossibility of containing meaning.

Thus, Fray Duertas' architectural manuscript, filled with what appears to some as rather innocuous engineering explanations, strikes the bishop and the censors at the Catholic Church as sinister metaphors and images of lust that have wormed their insidious way into the pages of this friar's writing. The friar is disconcerted when he realizes that this is an/other perfectly legitimate way of reading the text, leading him to "suddenly fall on his knees after reading the bishop's letter, beating his breast and muttering ejaculations that Fray Montano could only hope was the litany to Our Lady of the Immaculate Conception" (Cruz-Lucero 4). The mischievous use of the word "ejaculations" in the passage quoted here as well as Montano's suspicions about Fray Duertas' prayers already signal the irreducibility of meaning. Both Fray Duertas and Fray Montano, schooled to logocentrism through church doctrines, never think to question the plurality of the signifiers in question and thus to challenge the censors. Again, Montano's excursions into completing the Hiligaina dictionary by entering all the left-out lustful words leads him into precisely this morass of the plenitude of the "signified" that refuse to be contained. We are told that "he forced his mind to dwell on harmless things—but everything had lost its innocence" (13).

Fray Montano, in fact, constantly exercises logocentric practices. When his sacristan, a young *indio*, confesses that "I have been playing with myself, Padre. I am so ashamed and so afraid. I have begun to forget the answers to the catechism" (13), Montano rushes to reassure and correct him. "One has got nothing to do with the other, *hijo*; playing with yourself and forgetting your prayers are simply two separate sins" (13). This rigid compartmentalization echoes the innate problems of communicating abstract facts. It is also Fray Montano's undoing when it comes to completing the dictionary with sinful Hiligaino words: "Fray Montano, in fact, was now caught in a conundrum. Every night, his list of words for the day haunted him and refused to let him sleep. They invaded his mind in words coupling like dogs, jellyfish, lady and lordbugs, even papaya trees, and the shrinking mimosa" (13). Every word appears to have a lustful dimension to it. Fray Montano's literality, that makes him add "nine-more strokes to his nightly ritual of self-flagellation" and to recite "all the litanies to all the saints, legendary and real" (13) only draws him further and further away from resolving the practical problem of sealing the church roof.

Thus, Cruz-Lucero's text exuberantly and with consummate skill illustrates Barthes' idea that "[t]he plural of the Text depends . . . not on the ambiguity of its contents but on what might be called the stereographic plurality of its weave of signifiers (etymologically, the text is a tissue, a woven fabric)" (159; parenthesis in original). Here the narrative weaves together problems of textuality, playing the phallogocentric world of the Catholic priests against the plenitude of the *indios*' mythic world. The world of plenitude and imagination, though initially curtailed, ultimately appears to overtake the disciplined but arid world of the priest's imagination. Despite their faith and ardor, both the friars, trained as they are to privilege the singularity of the *logos*, are tripped up precisely because of the polysemy of words and their inability to comprehend the intrinsic plurality of meanings that texts generate.

Central to this problem then is Bhabha's notion of the Third Space. Fray Montano's experience with Hiligaino words is strikingly reminiscent of Robert J. C. Young's linguistic interpretation of Bhabha's Third Space. "It winks at us and draws us in; but as soon as we try to grasp it or to map it, like the real itself, it begins to elude us" ("The Void of Misgiving" 81). Young's description echoes Montano's bewilderment. In his earliest discussions of the Third Space, Bhabha cites renowned Guyanan writer Wilson Harris, who invokes colonial history. He observes that there is "a certain 'void' or misgiving attending every assimilation of contraries" in colonial encounters. Bhabha observes: "This meditation by the great Guyanan writer Wilson Harris on the void of misgiving in the textuality of colonial history reveals the cultural and historical dimension of that Third Space of enunciations which I have made the precondition for the articulation of cultural difference" ("Cultural Diversity" 209). Bhabha is emphasizing the importance of hybridity. The friars are unable to reach an understanding about "the inscription and articulation of culture's hybridity." So, they descend into what Bhabha describes as "the spiral of différance." For Bhabha this is:

> the third space, the space which is a non-space, hooked into the fractured moments of the event of splitting which happens instantaneously upon speaking, and which . . . becomes in some sense the non-place of the subject itself, a place which is no place, a space through which you spiral downwards, down into the depths of the void . . . a vast, bubble-shaped empty space, Sunyata, into an emptiness more extreme and exploratory than mere vacant or "negative" space can ever accommodate ("Anish Kapoor" 39)

This is the space that Fray Montano descends into: a space where "the plenitude of meaning" signifies to him "the loss of all meaning." The hilarious yet poignant story describes a crisis of the soul that occurs because of the mis/reading of a passage on "soil quality and church building" as lascivious. But its lightheartedness notwithstanding, the fray's "soul in crisis" becomes an example of how religious traditions, in insisting on a clear Manichean binary, ideologically manipulate the lives of unsuspecting individuals. The pious Fray Duertas and Fray Montano are both broken by the discourse of the religion that they have blindly served all their lives. Both friars live and die in mortal fear of losing their souls to the devil. They operate within the Catholic metanarrative of sin and eternal damnation. The more they strive to "contain and fix" the "sinful" words, the more slippery the meaning gets. Thus Cruz-Lucero's story, an ostensibly humorous account about the peccadillos of two friars, can be parsed as a metonymic text that illuminates the dangers involved in refusing to acknowledge the Third Space of enunciation and its refusal to essentialize meaning. An ironic vision presents the risks that open up in cultural gaps, which suck in unsuspecting human crusaders who do not dare to cross ideological boundaries unsanctioned by their religious systems.

Narrative Perspective in "The Money Makers"

The ensuing story that is told from the first-person perspective of a child underscores the significance of voice and narrative perspective. Though set in the Catholic Philippines, it is important to augment my thesis because the guileless narrator has not yet been successfully interpellated by ideology[15] and so is able to inhabit what Young labels the "invisible third space outside the structures of power" (93–94).

In recent decades, critics and thinkers have examined the ethical and political value of the narrative voice from diverse theoretical angles, extending the scope of literary works to participate in questions of practical ethics. For instance, Nussbaum's praise of literary imagination for its reflective activity that is receptive to specific situational complexities, as mentioned above, despite having been challenged and qualified, is nevertheless persuasive. It underscores how the plurality and unpredictability of literary narratives enable them to be grounded in lived reality (*Poetic Justice* 1). I examine "The Money Maker," which opens up one such opportunity.

Nita Umali-Berthelsen has published several articles and serialized novels which reveal her social consciousness. Her "The Money Makers" poignantly underscores "classism" and the politics of othering and is especially useful as it is narrated from the point of view of a child who has not yet developed a moral compass from within which to make ethical judgments, innocently recounting incidents and leaving the burden of judgment and ethical evaluation of the characters' actions to the readers. There is mention of a grandmother, a landowner, and a weekend father who works in the city, but no mention of a mother. The primary caregiver seems to be the maid, Karia. The guilelessness of the child substitutes for a "prelapsarian innocence" that witnesses the fall. The child begins by recounting a gory tale: "Karia, our maid [. . .] said the men with jute sacks slung on their backs who walked outside our yard at sunset were moneymakers. Children were inside the sacks. The men took them to a bridge built of bones and there cut off their heads, then squeezed blood from their bodies" (39). Unlike the child, a background to whom we are provided with, we understand that the "moneymakers" are the laborers employed by her grandmother during the paddy harvesting season. Karia's story is meant to scare the young child and prevent her from wandering out of the compound.

Terrified by the possibility of abduction, the little girl crouches in her room every afternoon, waiting out the departure of the "moneymakers." One day, to her horror, the child sees Karia chatting cheerfully to one of the "moneymakers." When she questions Karia, the maid is initially puzzled at her anxiety and then, recollecting the cause, responds with, "'Oh, that' [. . .] 'No, he is not a moneymaker, he is Tino'" (41). Karia reassures the apprehensive child that Tino does not abduct children. One afternoon, Tino comes by earlier than usual and catches the child with Karia. He notices the terrified child looking at the sack and offers to open the sack to reveal its contents. The child is scared and diffident:

> When I shook my head he smiles, "You don't really think I am a moneymaker, do you? Karia has told me, but look into this sack and you'll see." Karia nodded. She had promised that no harm would happen, so I looked inside. It really was rice. "Is it yours?" I asked. A strange look shadowed Karia's face and then neither of them was smiling. "Yes" He sounded angry. (41)

This is the first hint to the readers that Tino, a laborer who is working for the child's grandmother, is perhaps stealing rice from her.

The following day, the grandmother hurries to the granary "to portion out the shares of the rice harvest to the laborers" (41–42). Though old and tiny, she cuts a majestic figure, striding with her late husband's cane in her hand. This cane had one end made of the scales of a *pagi*, a stingray. The old, brown cane's smooth length is covered with knobs and knots. Yet again, the little girl shares Karia's views: "Karia said anyone whipped by the cane, no matter how lightly, would get thinner and wither away. Because Grandma was frail, she needed protection, so it was right she should have it with her when she was alone" (42). Karia and the child reach the granary later in the day and watch the men measuring the golden paddy using large measures. They see a grim Tino standing knee-deep in the midst of the heaped paddy. After all the paddy has been measured, it is past midday, and Grandma, Karia, and the child begin walking back home. Tino walks swiftly behind them, arguing with Grandma to part with more rice. But she firmly refuses. The child-narrator hears her grandmother shouting at Tino: "You're not getting any more rice or money from me so you can marry her. And if you think I will forget her father's debts and let her go without serving her time you are wrong! She sounded very angry" (43). The child-narrator notices in confusion that Karia has "stopped walking" (43) and though Tino turned away, he suddenly turns towards them, "a terrible fierce expression on his face." He shouts at Grandma, "You are killing us. But you will not get your way, you greedy old usurer. You'll see!" (43)

The child's impartial account alerts us to the serious issues centered on the non-status of poor women and the subaltern, and their construction as "ethical non-subjects." As Vandana Shiva points out, for poor rural women of the South, "[. . .] all struggle is ecological struggle" (3). This is palpably true for the subdominant laborers, othered innocently by the child as "moneymakers." They work on the paddy fields and their lives revolve around the planting and harvesting of paddy. Their lives are embedded in nature and "all struggle is ecological struggle" (Shiva 3).

Nussbaum argues that literary imagination improves our ability to judge because it denies us our "refusals to see." The text, unlike life, does not permit those lapses of attention through which we render others "invisible" in real life. She claims that literary imagination forces our attention on aspects of life that we otherwise avoid or prefer not to notice (*Poetic Justice* 1). The unfolding story is an excellent illustration of this point. By filtering the incidents through the innocent, non-judgmental gaze of a child, the reader is forced to construct his/her own meaning of the text. Thus, the text forces the reader to take a moral position as regards the unfolding events.

This crisis of judgment escalates for the reader when we later learn that Tino and the old woman, having exchanged blows, are both seriously injured. It is interesting to see how the impartial narrator's unvarnished recital of events as they occur, continuously modifies and qualifies our own judgment of both Tino and Grandma. When the child, excited at the unprecedented arrival of her father on a weekday, races to meet him, she witnesses her grandmother lying injured in bed. The image painted is startling: "On the floor by Grandma's bed was the white tub in which I used to float toy ducks and boats. Now it was half-filled with cotton and gauze, red and messy with blood" (Umali-Berthelsen 45). As we construct a shocking narrative of the frail old woman being bludgeoned by the young "bully," we hear the reassuring words of the doctor: "She'll be alright." This is followed starkly by: "[t]he blows she gave him were surprisingly strong, breaking his skin." The image we form is then reversed and qualified. But even as we struggle to arrive at a proper judgment, the utterly tangential nature of the young child's evaluation is presented to us.

> "Karia, I think Tino is a moneymaker," I said. She looked at me, then at the window with its square of morning-blue sky. "You said moneymakers made money only out of innocent children, but I think Tino was going to try and make money out of Grandma, wasn't he? Her face twitched as if she was going to cry. I felt sorry for her." (46)

The little girl's tangential reading reveals her inadequate interpellation into ideology. It demonstrates how the girl follows her own unerring logic, which is so at odds with the reality of the situation where hegemonic powers are at work, oppressing laborers. But the text also demonstrates how multiple readings of the situation are rendered possible so that the so-called "irrefutability of logic" is shown as disputable, for contexts are multiple, layered, and localized. As Mellor citing Bill McKibben insists: "Humanity must always be seen as embedded within local and global ecosystems. The ecosystem surrounding any living organism imposes boundary conditions upon it. Humanity's failure to respect the ecological limits of these bounding conditions has caused the present ecological crisis" (1). The narrative underscores how the "cultural imaginary" determines belief. Grandma has hit Tino with the cane, using the *pagi*-end on his body. The resultant injuries, Karia believes, can slowly kill a man, make his body wither and die. Her abject misery, fueled by her belief system, turns the event into an endless tragedy. Karia's and Tino's lives and beliefs are those "hidden from history." Again, this text also attests to how the cultural imaginary is firmly circumscribed by ideology, which dictates who is expendable and who should be sheltered, why some people accept their fate and others resist; it thus highlights the gendered and economic spaces of agency and passivity.

Discussing the ethics of reading in her article, Maša Mrovlje observes that Nussbaum seeks to unearth "not the morality that is caused by reading" but "the morality of the act of reading." The purpose is to delve into the lived experience of reading as a "communal endeavor" by which we are "constituted" as a community of responsible spectators of political events and incited to reflect upon feasible forms of "living together" (164).

In the story the child becomes a transparent, guileless narrator, one who absorbs everything around her and relates it back to the reader without any deliberate filters that an adult consciousness can impose on its observations. The reader is challenged to make sense of the events and is conflicted by the confused ethics involved. The story not only raises the huge class divide in the Philippines, that is not atypical of other nations in Asia, but also underlines the importance of narrative perspective.

Mrovlje explains how Nussbaum, drawing on Aristotle, argues to establish literature as offering important and necessary data to enable judgment because it introduces us to a plethora of events "that might happen," reveals "their impact on human lives," and allows us to evaluate in general terms the "possibilities for being human" (165). In this view, as Veronica Vasterling notes, literature assumes the role of an "ethics lab," where we can train our capacities for a proper response without the impediment of contingency that confronts us in the outer world (84).

To return to Bhabha, the child-narrator, by occupying the "Third Space" that eludes "the politics of polarity" emerges as "the other of itself" ("Cultural Diversity" 209), able to impartially though erroneously arrive at conclusions in a non-partisan way. But the adults are yet to understand this. Both Tino and Grandma are yet to realize that they have entered "the third space [that has] become . . . a space of intersubjective negotiation, a difficult dialogue conducted in different tongues" (Young, "The Void of Misgiving" 89). By this lack of realization, they let an important opportunity for negotiation pass them by. In the final analysis, then, the events in the text are symptomatic of the Third Space, which Young describes as "above all a site of production, the production of anxiety, an untimely place of loss, of fading, of appearance and disappearance" (82).

What is of equal interest to us is that narrative perspective is deftly used to open our eyes to a pervasive problem regarding the commodification of labor, hegemony, and its power over the subalterns, and the vast disparity in economic status.

I now turn to an interesting text from Bangladesh, *The Baromashi Tapes* by Niaz Zaman, to examine literature as reflecting cultural legacy while exposing a troubled ecology.

The Baromashi Tapes: Crisis and Critique

While discussing risk society in the Introduction, I touched upon how, for Ulrich Beck, genetic engineering, ozone depletion, global warming, and toxic contamination all mark a shift from the "first modernity" of industrial society to the "second modernity" of global risk. Beck notes the "democratic" aspects of the new risks, that these are ubiquitous, and that distinctions between rich and poor are redundant. His famous declaration "*smog is democratic*" (*Risk Society* 36) rams home this perspective. However, in his later works, he becomes more aware of the social inequalities that the new risks could amplify. In fact, Beck uses Bangladesh as an example to illustrate the idea that *risk is simultaneously both democratic and hierarchical*. *The Baromashi Tapes* effectively illustrates how globalization can impact the lives of the subalterns and women. Khokon cannot find employment in Bangladesh and works under terrible conditions in a palm-oil estate in Malaysia. He and his bride, Sakina, exchange conversations through audio tapes. Their life becomes illustrative of the privations faced by the downtrodden of this globalized world.

The Baromashi Tapes comprises twelve chapters, each standing for a month which reflects the season. Each chapter is subdivided into three segments. The first segment always begins with a recipe. This is followed by two narratives, which tell the story of a young Bangla couple, Sakina and Khokon, respectively. The chapters' themes revolve around the idea of pining or separation, which is the predominant mood of the Baromashi folk songs, revealing their textual affiliations. The chapters narrate the story of Khokon leaving Sakina and the rest of his family to travel to Malaysia to work as a laborer. Though the primary narrative terrain is Bangladesh, the text oscillates between Bangladesh and Malaysia.

The epigraphs, namely the excerpts from the Baromashi folk songs, are central to the text and reflect certain underlying dualities. Though the harmony and strong sense of community in the rustic setting forms the backdrop, intertwined with this is an underlying sense of vulnerability and a lurking sense of fear of the encroaching global world, which is important to note. The epigraph invokes nature:

> In the month of Sravan [July], the farmer cuts the paddy.
> The kora-bird calls, sitting on the rice stalk.
> Dak calls, damphala calls, bora calls, sitting there.
> The call of the cruel kokil makes my heart ache
> ("Komolar Baromashi," *The Baromashi Tapes* 43)

This allusion to the natural world becomes an intentional act of excavating a regional eco-consciousness through a deliberate recourse to folk tradition. These epigraphs are pivotal to the establishment of a subtext that interestingly contradicts, even contests, the ostensible sentiments expressed in the surface text, thus initiating a textual movement that is precariously balanced between conformity and subversion. A license and female sexual agency is identifiable in the folk songs that elides the patriarchal strictures that attend to the young wife, Sakina. For instance, the singer remarks:

> In this month of Magh [January], coldness is like poison.
> Komola lies in bed, the lep kantha spread over her.
> Why does the room feel so cold?
> The lep kantha spread over her, the pillow on her breast
> Cannot keep the cold away.
> When you were here, I did not need a lep kantha
> Spread over me, nor a cotton pillow clutched to my breast.
> ("Komolar Baromashi," *The Baromashi Tapes* 103)

The folk singer boldly declares her sexual desire that differs considerably from Sakina's chaste registrations of her husband's absence. "Ma [her mother-in-law] was peeling a mango for Baba and said that you loved mangoes. She said that during the mango season, even as a small boy, all you wanted to eat were mangoes

[. . .] I was just going to strip the skin off with my teeth, but, when I heard that, I just could not eat. I put the mango away" (28).

The contrast between the sweet acquiescence and sacrificial passivity of the bride in contemporary Bangladesh, and the bold declarations of the folk singer are striking and help shift the discursive circle and its vision beyond the parochial world of the young, rural wife. The carefully defined restrictions of the Muslim home open up to a multicultural space through the Baromashi. For example, the orthodox Muslim home recognizes Hindu religious festivals: "In the month of Aswin is the Durga festival;/the Brahmin wives offer flowers to the goddess/Let them offer flowers, let them take the offerings home" ("Komolar Baromashi" 65). This extraordinary inclusivity is a sign of the emergence of the Third Space. As Edward Soja explains, this "[t]hirdspace is a meeting point, a hybrid place, where one can move beyond the existing borders." But more appositely, Soja claims that it is also "a place of the marginal women and men, where old connections can be disturbed and new ones emerge. A Thirdspace consciousness is the precondition to building a community of resistance to all forms of hegemonic power" ("Third Space" 56). As such, the story as it unfolds in modern-day Bangladesh and the epigraph together create this Third Space, which becomes a space of resistance.

Therefore, the resentment about her abandonment by her husband, that cannot be expressed by the bride within the traditional confines of the patriarchal home, is vocalized by the folk singer. While the bride's conduct is regulated by the (patriarchal institution of the) family, the folk singer's emotions and words exceed patriarchy's parameters.

> In the month of Phalgun (February), householders sow seeds,
> The girl has a cup full of poison.
> *I shall eat poison. I shall eat venom. I shall die.*
> *But shall never again marry a boatman.*
> *The boatman is a great scoundrel, a slave of his business.*
> *He married me, but went away. He cares nothing about me.*
> ("Komolar Baromashi" 113; emphasis added)

The epigraphs therefore challenge and complicate the subservience expressed by Sakina and hint at subtexts that are opened up by the silence of the conservative young couple.

Each chapter is also balanced between Khokon's and Sakina's narratives. The former recounts the problems he faces in a palm-oil estate in Malaysia and cumulatively paints a picture of an industrialized world where laborers fight desperately for their meager rights while indifferent, corrupt politicians make gestures of appeasement concerning their welfare. *The Baromashi Tapes* becomes a metonymic narrative that while highlighting the particularities of living in a specific ("Third World") location and reflects the pitfalls of globalized capitalism. Even as it narrates the particular problems of the young Bangla couple, it calls for a cosmopolitan coalitional oversight and response to ways in which patriarchal capitalism comes masked as globalization, that puts the "two-thirds world" into the service of the privileged elite.

Paul Crosthwaite observes that:

> "[c]risis" and "criticism" (as well as the latter's immediate cognates—"critic," "criticize," "critical," critique") have their roots in the Greek *krinein*: "to separate, judge, decide." Compacted together at this point of etymological origin is the notion of a decisive conjuncture that is associated with states of crisis and the performance of evaluation, discernment, or discrimination that traditionally lies at the core of the practice of criticism. (1)

The Baromashi Tapes accomplishes both the critique of global risk as well as conveying the crisis.

Sakina's and Khokon's narratives equate to "oral narratives" since both *record* their messages on a tape recorder and send it through a messenger, ironically aligning their efforts with romantic visions of epic lovers exchanging messages through messenger pigeons that abound in classic Indian texts.[16] Their lives—Sakina's in a rural village and Khokon's at a palm-oil plantation—serve to bring forward a comparison of two ways of living and arrive at conclusions that are pertinent to the modern world. The exchange, being firmly embedded in modern technology, also critiques varying aspects of modernity and its crises. Khokon's first exposure to modernity marks the start of a moment of enunciation quite literally:

> I went with Sharif Bhai to a big mall where there were so many shops that my head went round and round. There I bought two tape recorders and some tapes. I recorded all this [i.e. his first narrative] on one tape and I am going to send it to you with Mama [uncle] when he comes. I will also send one tape recorder and a few tapes with him. Bappy [Khokon's younger brother] will show you how to listen to my tape and how to record a tape for me. I want you to record one tape every month and send it to me when you can. I will also try to send one tape to you every month. (Zaman 11)

His narrative begins from the moment of his insertion into the global, late capital workforce as a coolie and marks his shift from being a quasi-member of an agricultural economy to a subaltern member of a global economic imperialist structure. His narratives describe his first plane trip from Dhaka to Kuala Lumpur and thence to a palm-tree plantation in Johor Bahru. The narratives present his violent confrontation with late modernity, tracing his gradual transformation from a wide-eyed naïve villager nursing an uncomplicated hope for a better future into, at first, a hopeful, then gradually a belligerent, and eventually a disillusioned but stoic member of the global workforce. Khokon's life bears out Beck's predictions about the vagaries of the future as not being those of blind fate or meteorites but rather the side effects of modernity come back ironically as a menacing environment with which we are now confronted. His narratives reveal the dark underside of globalization where the subtext of class and race inheres in labor interactions. "I work as a sprayer on the plantation [. . .] the bosses are not good. They promised us 600 ringgits but are deducting 200 for food and board. We are packed in our camps. The bosses took away our passports. They say it is for safekeeping, but it is so that we cannot run away" (Zaman 42). Khokon's silence is that of a subaltern's and resonates with Chakravorty Spivak's now famous query, "Can the Subaltern Speak?"[17] What Khokon omits to tell his wife is that he is spraying "paraquat" without any protective gear. This weed killer is restricted in the USA because it is highly toxic. The NIOSH[18] pocket guide to chemical hazards describes it as an organic compound which is classified as a viologen, a family of redox-active heterocycles of similar structure. Paraquat is manufactured by Chevron. This salt is one of the most widely used herbicides. It is quick-acting and non-selective, killing green plant tissue on contact. Due to its redox activity, which produces superoxide anions, it is also toxic to human beings and animals. It has been linked to the development of Parkinson's disease. It is interesting that the risks surrounding his existence have to be excavated from Khokon's recordings, a feat that is beyond Sakina. Here, risk and silence go hand-in-hand. Khokon's messages inscribe the uneven nature of risk: it reifies truths that surround the international division of labor, the effects of global capitalism on the subdominant, and the subject-production of worker within nation-state ideology.

Contrasted to these are Sakina's narratives that are placed after Khokon's and register a life more deeply attuned to the elements, where one's humanity is valued despite one's poverty. Compared to the almost formulaic phrases that Khokon uses in every one of his "recordings": "I am well. I hope you are well too [. . .] Please give my salams to Ma and Baba" (Zaman 35, 42, 52, 64 etc.), Sakina's are filled with events and emotions that are in touch with the native landscape and its food, art forms, festivities, and seasons, all of which are described with love and care. Her narratives record the everyday occurrences of her life and occasionally the gossip in the neighborhood, imparting the essence of a communal life lived holistically.

Sakina's narratives complément Khokon's in that they bear witness to vicissitudes that affect not only the landscape but also the minds of the people and their gradually shifting customs and traditions; the erosion of the centrality of agricultural economy; the gradual alienation of the younger generation from farming; and cogitations about whether capitalist infusion is necessary for a subsistence economy to thrive. Her impoverishment, but arguably also her viable vision for financial autonomy, is countered by Khokon's embedment as a subaltern laborer in a mass-production cash-crop plantation. Even so innocuous a statement as Khokon's description of the palm tree as one that "looks like coconut tree but their fruits are different" (42) hints at the history of violent displacement that he and his friends have been subjected to. His apprehension of what Heidegger would call a certain kind of "Being-in-the-world" (*Being and Time*) is shown to have been severely threatened by his embedment in a modernity that devalues him. Therefore, we could say that the two narratives are rhetorically codependent. Ironically, the modernity that confronts Khokon is shown as "postnatural." Despite working in plantations, he and his fellow coolies are distanced from nature. This is reflected not only in the content of Khokon's recordings but even in the mechanical tone he increasingly adopts.

> It must be getting cold in Padmapukur. Here the weather is still the same. Perhaps it rains a little more. I am well. I hope you are well too. Please give my salams to Ma and Baba [. . .] Did Baba get the proper amount of paddy from the fields he has given on borga? You and Ma must have been very busy boiling and drying paddy. I miss the smell of harvested paddy and the taste of newly husked rice. The rice we get here has no taste. It is like bhushi. (92)

The impression of a joyless, automated existence seeps through his recordings, which are testament to Theodor Adorno's observation that "alienation is the price human beings have paid for their increasing control and management of nature" (cited in Huggan and Tiffin 202). Sakina's narratives are livelier and trace the gradual transformation of the countryside as it gets mechanized. She tells her husband: "The last few days the whole place has been smelling of newly harvested paddy and throbbing to the noise of the new threshing machines. Yes, people who have bullocks, or a large amount of harvested paddy, still use bullocks for *marai*, but these new machines are slowly becoming popular" (Zaman 14). But her upbeat narratives are later revealed as born out of ignorance of the risks that lurk with the new agri-technologies that do not take changing weather patterns into consideration and make guinea pigs of the poor farmers. We learn that, after a violent storm which uprooted all the paddy plants, Baba's land, along with the other farmers', has not even able to yield rice pods since the husks were empty. The paddy seeds from a new high-yielding variety, they are informed, cannot be kept to grow another crop (125). The traditional farmers lose out on both their present and future yields. The hazards of introducing non-native breeds into local ecosystems and the impact of the global economy and its demands on local, natural resources or farming practices is highlighted. Thus, the narrative oscillates between different kinds of risks, vacillating between hope and despair and depicting the plight of those at the bottom of the economic-chain in Beck's "second-modernity" (Beck, *Risk Society*).

Sakina's narratives also embed "at-risk-ecologies" in cultural contexts. She narrates a feud between neighbors over the chopping of a rare breed of mango tree, the *munsifbabbar*, and the sadness of the whole community in losing the tree. She recounts how an agricultural scientist used its bark and was able to resuscitate the tree and nurture a sapling, much to the wonder and joy of the community. This highlights the raised awareness of native communities to the urgencies of preserving the ecosystem.

Tensions between and within human communities, their respective relations to the natural world, and the extra-discursive reality of nature that is constantly evolving all find a place in Sakina's audiotape narratives. Equally, the family's anxiety that the younger son, Bappy, should study well and matriculate; Bappy's own indifference to farming; and the younger sister Shiuli's migration to the city as a factory worker with the attendant fears of being lured into the sex trade are also part of Sakina's narrative, revealing the many perils faced by those at the bottom end of the global economic hierarchy.

Gradually Khokon's narratives, that at first initiated the entire plot, begin to shrink and to seem more like *intrusions* while Sakina's narratives, like the epigraphs, incrementally but steadfastly gather feminine themes and interests around themselves to unfurl a predominantly woman's world. (Un)Like Thomas Henry Huxley's idea of "man's place in nature," here it is the woman's place that is explored. Despite the fact that their social context is shown as indubitably embedded in patriarchy, what is admirable is the clear space for women that is carved out within its pages. Every chapter, as earlier mentioned, begins with a recipe, underscoring the primacy of *home* cooking (as opposed to gourmet or commercial cooking). With the failing health of Khokon's father, Sakina's mother-in-law progressively takes over as the main breadwinner. She becomes the center of organization, constantly drawing on and contributing to the surroundings. Unlike her son's entry into a dependent economy, she generates an income through independent labor. She is inducted by a local women's group leader to teach other women *kantha* embroidery. What emerges is an economy of interdependence with other women within and outside the community. She also takes Sakina to a play designed to raise consciousness about women's rights and produced by a women's welfare organization.

As the narrative meanders through the twelve months like the Baromashi folksong on which it is based, the "textuality"—linguistically, that which constitutes the text in a particular way—pulls its semantics in the direction of Sakina's world that, eschewing Khokon's, is attuned to the economies of nature. This has deep implications for the importance accorded to an organic, communal world as opposed to a mechanical, capital-driven one.

The Baromashi Tapes is thus a critical text that raises eco-consciousness while bringing about an awareness of the hazards faced by the subdominant classes. The text illustrates Crosthwaite's belief that "[t]he plurality of perspectives within contemporary critical discourse is [. . .] mirrored by a proliferation of crisis scenarios. Indeed, it often seems that the horizons of everyday life are defined, today, by an overlapping series of crises" (3). By juxtaposing different scenarios, some that pervade the global labor market and place the laborer at risk, and others that insinuate themselves into rural agricultural economies, the ubiquitous nature of risk and impossibility of escape in second modernity is brought home to us. Yet, through its textuality, it also opens up a space of possibility which accords with Soja's description of the Third Space and is "contradictory and ambiguous," displaying both "restricting as well as liberating aspects" and existing "as a space of resistance and permanent struggle" (Soja 56).

Concluding Thoughts

Nikolas Kompridis believes that "the experience of crisis may well be the primary inducement to thought in our time, the time of modernity. This is not an accident or some contingent fact about modernity; rather, modernity induces 'crisis thinking' because it is inherently crisis generating." He observes that once we appreciate the deep connection between crisis and critique, we will also come to see "how complexly enmeshed in the self-understanding of modernity are critique, crisis, and the need to begin anew—how deeply they affect modernity's experience of itself" (Kompridis 3–4).

In the texts examined in this chapter, I have made significant connections between crises, language, and textualities. Rosario Cruz-Lucero's metonymic narrative turns the lens on slippages in language use, and how a relentless pursuit of logocentrism stands opposed to the spontaneous plenitude of nature. It also points to the importance of acknowledging and opening up to the Third Space of possibility. The afflictions of the priests—the result of the clash of patriarchal parochialism and the exuberance of an animistic culture—could also be seen as holding a mirror to the afflictions of the human race in responding to the current ecological crisis. The final surrender of the friar to the native shaman priestess can be read as a muted celebration of the female and the spontaneous natural world as well as the polysemy of the text (of nature). In her short stories, Mahasweta Devi brings together issues that deal with environmental destruction and the delegitimating of tribals, revealing the role of ideology in risk distribution. She exposes the hypocrisy and double standards of a Hindu India and demonstrates the ideological complicity of classical Sanskrit texts in the desecration of nature and abuse of the marginal in contemporary India. In "The Money-Maker," Nita Umali-Berthelson foregrounds the challenges that are implicit in reading and responding ethically to narratives. The story foregrounds the huge chasm between the rich and the poor and subtly underscores the ideological challenges that the readers are faced with due to their interpellations into (hegemonic) culture. Niaz Zaman, in *The Baromashi Tapes*, juxtaposes contrasting risk scenarios and reveals the unexpected side effects of modernity that can put communities at risk. The harsh realities of modern life that alienate subsistence communities from nature and women from their husbands once again reveals Beck's observation that "everyone is at risk in second modernity."

Interestingly, in all these texts, the women are placed in what Eric Prieto calls the interstitial place. Prieto observes, "[. . .] as recent reappraisals of interstitial geographical entities like American suburbia and third-world squatter cities have emphasized, such places, despite their very real problems and inadequacies, may also prove to be unexpectedly resourceful loci of innovation and development" (1). In the texts discussed in this chapter, the women are strong. Though faced with various kinds of tribulations, they are resourceful and find ways of negotiating their circumstances. All these authors' works, though emerging from very diverse Hindu, Catholic, and Islamic traditions, respectively, as well as different nations—India, the Philippines, and Bangladesh—use *textual legacies* to trace human estrangement from nature and the risks people face in revealing the pan-cultural scope of their heritage.

In doing so, the texts also emulate Bhabha's ideas about culture as something constantly created and renewed, an imaginative process rather than a reservoir of given values. This view aids us in seeing the hybrid nature of all cultures, the Third Space, where tradition and rebellion, reverence and hilarity, old and new mingle. In all three texts, culture and ethnicity intermix to be dynamically produced and reproduced, creating transformative spaces. The characters "generate" culture through their lived experience rather than mechanically transmitting an unchanging set of "given" values. Their lived experiences create a new cultural space—the Third Space—where there is a confluence of values, challenges, and generative power.

POSTSCRIPT

> Mother Earth, where people belong to different races, follow separate faiths and religions, and speak numerous languages, cares for them in many ways. May that Mother Earth, like a Cosmic Cow, give us the thousandfold prosperity without any hesitation, without being outraged by our destructive actions.
> —"Prithvi Sukta," Kanda 12, Hymn 1, Verse 45; *Atharva Veda*

> We have thought [. . .] of humanity as being a component of nature even as we have conceptualized nature as absolute otherness to humanity. 'Nature' is in this sense both hat which we are not *and* that which we are within.
> —Kate Soper, "The Discourse of Nature" 15

The ancient Hindu epic, the Mahabharata, relates a story about the five good Pandavas, who are banished to the forest by their evil cousins, the Kauravas. One of the Pandavas laments the injustice of the world where the good are punished and the evil rule in triumph. But shorn of their royal duties and luxuries, the Pandavas have time to practice penance and meditation which, it is believed, was made possible by their being embedded in nature and which ultimately led to their victory. This episode from the epic is often narrated to Hindu children to invoke the idea of nature being a healer and a teacher that far surpasses others. It also neatly illustrates the paradoxical views about nature that Kate Soper voices in her essay "The Discourse of Nature," an extract from which forms the epigraph to this chapter. Discourses on nature are indeed conflicting and contradictory since nature is viewed as both external and internal to humans. Furthermore, while it is viewed as a teacher in this episode, it is sometimes treated in less edifying ways in these ancient epics. This text, like several others from Asia, shows how Asians' relationship with nature has always been complicated.

The "Prithvi Sukta," which is mentioned in earlier chapters, emphasizes the idea of unity in diversity. The idea of *Vasudaiva Kudumbakam* or the family of Mother Earth is an ancient concept that is brought to life with our awareness of our planetary ecological connections and unity. As early as in the Vedic Age, the verse in the epigraph above acknowledges human atrocities against nature even as it adulates Mother Earth. It appears that very little has changed in human attitude toward nature.

The over thirty eco-narratives by Asian women writers that I have examined in this book reflect these complex, contrary attitudes that contemporary Asians have inherited. I have discussed these texts under five overarching topics. Though these groupings are convenient they are not definitive. Different kinds of connections could have been made which would have been equally productive. For instance, Viliya Ketavong's "The Roar of a Distant War" and Jean Arasanayagam's *All Is Burning* and even portions of *Wave: A Memoir of Life after the Tsunami* by Sonali Deraniyagala could have been examined together as contemporary responses to the Buddha's "Fire Sermon." This could have led to a discussion of the futility and/or relevance of religious systems to contemporary South and Southeast Asia's relationship with nature. Alternately, *The River's Song* by Suchen Christine Lim and "Lake" by Lily Yulianti Farid could have been grouped with other "littoral" literatures like *A River Sutra* by Gita Mehta or *Fish-Hair Woman* by Merlina Bobis to highlight the concept of an "ecotope." Or again, "The Heartless Forest" by Mya Zin Khin and *The River Sutra* could have been viewed as working out the ancient Sāṃkhya system of *puruṣa* and *prakṛti*, contravening the conventional binaries of the agentic male and the passive female through harking back to indigenous genres or literary devices like *tawlar ratu* and the *sutra* traditions. The combinations and permutations could have been manifold and we might perhaps have taken away slightly differing views about these texts. However, the point is not to fix the meanings emerging from these ecofictions.

Instead, I have demonstrated how this new, exciting corpus, comprised entirely of writing by Asian women, enables us to construct the emerging discourse on cultural and natural ecologies as it concerns women and the subdominant in two major regions of Asia. Many of these can be argued to exist in the Third Space of possibilities and to make connections between the "f/actual and the fictive" in ways that enable an understanding of not only contemporary problems that beset women, subalterns, and the non-human in Asia, but also the crises that many Asian spaces are facing regarding their management of natural resources. In the process, the attitude and treatment of the underclass and nature in many Asian nations come under scrutiny. These narratives by women that are committed to the elimination of the male gender bias, illustrated overtly in texts such as "The Blood of Leaves" by Vietnamese writer Thi Hao Vo and "The Heartless Forest" from Myanmar, further underscore the entanglement of nature and culture.

These narratives show how risks appear to be pervasive across different patriarchies and reappear with minor differences in different societies. They also illustrate how eco-justice issues and the treatment of women are deeply entangled. Equally, however, these texts and contexts interact within a specific culture to generate ecofeminist plots that appear to be a peculiar product of certain histories. Hence, while there are narratives about the civil war in Sri Lanka and the Philippines, the deflections and ramifications of these wars are specific to their cultures and result in narratives that mirror these unique cultural dissonances. Even within a country, some "histories from the underside" can engender completely dissimilar messages as, for instance, Meira Chand's *A Different Sky* about World War II Singapore that is engaged with the idea of nation-building and *The River's Song* that is about postcolonial Singapore eagerly invested in recreating itself as a modern metropolis. Very productively, the ways in which contemporary women writers reclaim ancient concepts such as *prakṛti* and/or Bonbibi folk stories in order to contest patriarchal subjugation, initiate a liberatory rhetoric that is distinctive to these regions and most useful from the ecofeminist perspective in offering alternative perspectives.

Taken together, these narratives provide us with a mosaic that exposes the ecological problems that South and Southeast Asians are grappling with. Some of these problems are perennial, some uniquely contemporary. But all of them center the issues surrounding women–nature connections. An awareness of these problems and these new perspectives emerging from the other side of West-centric power can help us to critically qualify, review, and rewrite ecofeminist perspectives that have emerged in mainstream Anglo-American scholarship.

NOTES

Introduction

1. Scholars like Georg Feuerstein argue that the dates attributed to most of these texts are, in fact, erroneous and that they are from a much earlier period. See his *The Yoga Tradition: Its History, Literature, Philosophy and Practice*.

2. See, for example, Graham Huggan's "Greening Postcolonialism," Rob Nixon's "Environmentalism and Postcolonialism," the later, and influential, *Postcolonial Ecocriticism: Literature, Animals, Environment* by Graham Huggan and Helen Tiffin, and also Laura Wright's *Wilderness into Civilized Shapes: Reading the Posctcolonial Environment*.

3. One of the earliest written literatures in the world are the Vedas. Vedic literature in Sanskrit is generally dated between the mid-to-late second millennium BCE.

4. This is despite the fact that some pioneering ecofeminists like Vandana Shiva hail from South Asia. However, Shiva, a physicist, philosopher, and feminist, has focused primarily on science and developmental issues.

5. Scholars believe that the Uttar Ramayana, which constitutes the final (Kānda) section of the Valmiki Ramayana, is a later addition to the original. For more, see *Uttara Kanda* by Arshia Sattar.

6. Guanyin, Guan Yin, or Kuan Yin is the popular name of the Bodhisattva known as Avalokiteśvara. Widely worshiped in Southeast Asia as the "Goddess of Mercy," Guanyin, short for Guanshiyin, associates her with the material world since in Chinese it means "(The One Who) Perceives the Sounds of the World." For more, see John Blofeld, *Bodhisattva of Compassion*.

7. Dharmic religions such as Hinduism, Buddhism, Sikhism, Jainism, and so forth.

8. See Mark Harvey, "The Secular as Sacred?" and Austin Creel, "The Reexamination of Dharma in Hindu Ethics."

9. My article in this volume is the only one on a woman writer from an ecofeminist perspective.

10. Kakawin Ramayana is an "Old Javanese" rendering of Valmiki Ramayana in "kakawin meter." It is believed to have been written in Central Java (modern Indonesia) around 870 CE during the era of the Medang Kingdom under the reign of Mpu Sindok. The Kakawin Rāmayana is so called since it is written in kakawin, the Javanese form of kāvya, a poetic style in classical Sanskrit.

11. Nirguna Brahman is the substratum of all creation. This universal consciousness is so without quality that the only response to attempts to describe it would be neti, neti (not this, not this).

12. The current pandemic is a singular reminder of this fact.

Chapter One. Colonial, Postcolonial, and Neocolonial Ecologies

1. This well-known phrase is part of their essay title on Enrique Dussel, who is an Argentinian/Mexican writer. He is one of the founders of "the Philosophy of Liberation" movement. His works focus on ethics and political philosophy. Dussel engages in critiquing Eurocentric discourses and postmodernity in his works.

2. For more on the Japanese occupation of Singapore see Peter Thompson's *The Battle for Singapore: The True Story of the Greatest Catastrophe of World War Two*.

3. The Commonwealth War Graves Commission (CWGC) is an intergovernmental organization of six independent member states. Its principal function is to mark, record, and maintain the graves and places of commemoration of Commonwealth of Nations military service members who died in the two world wars. It currently counts 1.7 million as the death toll from British dependencies.

4. For more on this, see Richard Gombrich, *How Buddhism Began: The Conditioned Genesis of the Early Teachings*.

5. The pipa is a four-stringed Chinese musical instrument with a pear-shaped wooden body. It is also known as the Chinese lute.

6. Sarkar in Hindi or Bengali literally means "government." It also used to mean a person in authority and/or possessing power (sarkari).

Chapter Two. Women, Animals, and Animality

1. Anatomo-politics refers to the disciplinary dimension of biopower. According to Foucault, it makes up the second pole of biopower and refers to the regulations and control to which a collective body of individuals ("objectified" and "subjectified" through varying techniques) is subordinate.

2. The novel won the Victorian premier's literary awards: the Sheaffer Pen Prize for First Fiction in 1993 and the New South Wales State Literary Award. It has been translated into several languages. The Australian Book Review describes it as: "'A novel of wonders . . . rich with magic, secrets, dragons, curses, ghosts and most importantly, stories" (The National Library of Australia, Catalogue section: https://catalogue.nla.gov.au/Record/7461866).

3. Adam J. Goldwyn's conception of the anthomorphic appears to be different from my understanding of the anthropomorphic, wherein animals are given human characteristics.

4. For more on Saussure, see Daniel Chandler's book *Semiotics: The Basics*.

5. Her other publications include both short stories and novels such as *Salvation Sea, Black Widow, The Last of the Comedians, The Stories That Should Not Be Read at Midnight*, and *The Pyre*. For more on Va Thi Hao, see https://www.loaphuong.org/2015/05/vo-thi-hao-nhung-chuyen-chua-bao-gio-ke.html and https://iwpuiowa.edu/writers/vo-thi-hao.

6. Velasquez's web details are available online: http://www.dailymail.co.uk/femail/article-3218362/26-year-old-rare-genetic-disorder-labeled-world-s-ugliest-woman-insists-s-better-thanks-cruel-bullies.html.

7. https://www.climaterealityproject.org/blog/how-does-climate-change-cause-forest-fires.

8. I acknowledge my thanks to John Ryan for making this information accessible to me.

9. In Hinduism, Aranyani is a goddess of the forest and protects the animals that dwell there (Aranyaka means "forest" in Sanskrit). The Rigveda has a hymn dedicated to the goddess (hymn 146 of the 10th Mandala). The hymn describes the goddess as elusive, one who dwells in quiet glades in the jungle. The hymn describes her worshiper entreating her to explain the mystery of how she eludes human gaze and lives away from civilization so unafraid. This hymn is repeated in Taittiriya Brahmana. Aranyani is said to be the precursor of later-day forest deities like Bonbibi. See *The Hymns of the Rigveda* by Ralph T. H. Griffith, 1973, hymn CXLVI, p. 640.

Chapter Three. Feminized Rivers, History, and Enchantment

1. *The Times of India*, June 5, 2013, http://timesofindia.indiatimes.com/articleshow/20434043.cms?utm_source=contentofinterest&utm_medium=text&utm_campaign=cppst. Accessed Nov. 11, 2018.

2. https://borgenproject.org/water-pollution-in-the-philippines/. Accessed Nov. 1, 2019.

3. https://www.reuters.com/article/us-bangladesh-rivers-idUSTRE54I04G20090519. Accessed Mar. 8, 2020.

4. https://www.bulatlat.com/2016/04/20/marcos-era-saw-most-rapid-environmental-degradation-biodiversity-loss/. Accessed Nov. 21, 2018.

5. Within Hindu literature, "sutra" denotes a distinct genre and is used as suffix in the title of many texts of this genre as in the Kama Sutra, which then indicates that this sutra is about Kama or sensual or sexual pleasure.

6. http://dilarahashem.net/. Accessed Nov. 1, 2018.

7. See https://www.voabangla.com/a/a-16-2005-08-17-voa3-94375164/1388588.html for a talk show conducted by Hashem. Accessed May 31, 2018. There are other such websites as well that reveal her engagement with such problems.

Chapter Four. Women, Pasts, and the Apocalypse

1. As, for instance, Sujatha's novels in Tamil and Muhammed Zafar Iqbal's in Bengali.

2. See https://www.asianfanfics.com/browse/tag/apocalyptic/O for more on Asian apocalyptic fiction. Accessed Nov. 21, 2018.

3. There are a number of ecologically charged apocalyptic narratives too, such as *Silent Spring* by Rachel Carson; Bill McKibben's *The End of Nature*; *The Revenge of Gaia* by James Lovelock; and *The Enemy of Nature* by Joel Kovel.

4. Shaila Abdullah, based in Austin, Texas, has written many other children's books such as *Saffron Dreams, Beyond the Cayenne Wall, A Manual for Marco: Living, Learning, and Laughing with an Autistic Sibling*, and with Aanyah Abdullah, *My Friend Suhana: A Story of Friendship and Cerebral Palsy*. She is the recipient of the Golden Quill Award and the Patras Bukhari Award.

5. See Cowper's poem "The World at a Distance" below:

'T is pleasant, through the loopholes of retreat,
To peep at such a world; to see the stir
Of the great Babel, and not feel the crowd;
To hear the roar she sends through all her gates,
At a safe distance, where the dying sound   5
Falls a soft murmur on the uninjured ear.
Thus sitting and surveying thus at ease
The globe and its concerns, I seem advanced
To some secure and more than mortal height,
That liberates and exempts me from them all.   10
It turns submitted to my view, turns round
With all its generations; I behold
The tumult, and am still. The sound of war
Has lost its terrors ere it reaches me;
Grieves, but alarms me not. I mourn the pride   15
And avarice that make man a wolf to man,
Hear the faint echo of those brazen throats,
By which he speaks the language of his heart,
And sigh, but never tremble at the sound.

6. The idea that people need to believe that "one will get what one deserves" so strongly that they will rationalize an inexplicable injustice by naming things

the victim might have done to deserve it. Also known as blaming the victim, the just-world fallacy, and the just-world effect (Psych Central. https://psychcentral.com/encyclopedia/just-world-hypothesis/[accessed June 3, 2017]).

7. Lily Yulianti Farid is a journalist and writer born and raised in Makassar, Indonesia. She is deeply committed to the Indonesian arts and literary scene and is the founder/director of Makassar International Writers Festival and Rumata Artspace. She spreads her year between Melbourne, Australia and Makassar, Indonesia.

8. Chitra Banerjee Divakaruni is an author of Bengali origin who currently resides in the USA. She is a poet, and the Betty and Gene McDavid Professor of Writing at the University of Houston's Creative Writing Program. She is an award-winning author of several fictional works.

9. Gerard Genette coined the term "focalization" to replace "perspective" and "point of view." It may be defined as a selection or restriction of narrative information in relation to the experience and knowledge of the narrator, the characters, or other, more hypothetical entities in the story world. https://www.lhn.uni-hamburg.de/node/18.html. Accessed Dec. 11, 2018.

Chapter Five. The Sacred, the Subalterns, Women, and Literary Legacies

1. For more on the Dravidian Movement, see Robert Hardgrave and Karthick Ram Manoharan 1.

2. Tribals in the plural form is used throughout South Asia to refer to members of tribal groups who are subaltern and marginalized economically, socially, and educationally.

3. Mahasweta Devi (1926–2016) was born in Dhaka to an artistic family; her parents and uncles were luminaries in the Bengali art and literary scene. Many in her family were also committed social workers and activists. She was married for a while to renowned playwright Bijon Bhattacharya, one of the founding fathers of the Indian People's Theatre Association (IPTA), a left theatre movement. She is a renowned writer who was honored with several awards including the Sahitya Academy Award (in Bengali), Jnanpith Award, and Ramon Magsaysay Award along with India's civilian awards, the Padma Shri and the Padma Vibhushan.

4. Baromashi or *baromasya* refers to a specific folk narrative device or motif originally from medieval Bengali literature. Basically a feminine narrative with sad connotations, it revolves around a woman expressing pangs of suffering, poverty, and separation from a beloved/husband that pervades every month in the traditional Bengali calendar. This device has been extensively used in religious

lyrics, especially the Vaishnava lyrics (praying to Vishnu/Krishna). Examples are the *Radhar Baromasya/Baromashi* and *Chandimangal*.

5. The word *maya* in Sanskrit means "magic" or "illusion." This is a fundamental concept in Hindu philosophy, notably in the *Advaita* (Nondualist) school of Vedanta. For the Nondualists, *maya* is the cosmic force that presents the infinite *Brahman* (variously referred to as the supreme being or universal consciousness) as the finite phenomenal world. Nondualists believe that maya is reflected in the individual level by human ignorance (*ajnana*) of the reality of *Brahman*.

6. Organ explains that when the world is seen as an appearance of *Brahman*, when it is understood as rooted and grounded in *Brahman*, when it is known as one of the infinite manifestations of *Brahman*, then it is an appearance of Reality. As long as the world is seen as an appearance, and that of which it is an appearance is known, it is not false appearance; it is the Real under the categories of finite human sensation and knowledge. When so viewed, it is valued as a help and not a hindrance to man in his pilgrimage to the Self. The world is the *lila* (play) of Brahman, the joyous proliferation of the plenitude of Being, the necessary manifestation of the all, the non-telic activity of the Absolute (156).

7. Cognize how a female became exceptionally strong because of the bestowal of a boon (1-25-3, 4).

> Once there was a formidable yaksha named Suketu who was childless; therefore he performed a great ascesis (1-25-5).
>
> Blessing his ascesis, the forefather Brahma gave him a gemlike daughter who was renowned by the name of Tataka (1-25-6).
>
> Forefather Brahma also gave the strength of a thousand elephants to her but did not give a son to that yaksha, anticipating that a male would be more hazardous (1-25-7).
>
> When that bright girl grew into a youthful beauty her father Suketu wed her to Jambha's son, Sunda (1-25-8).
>
> Sometime later, the yakshii Tataka delivered an indomitable son named Mareecha, who was cursed to become a demon (1-25-9).
>
> But when Sunda was eliminated by sage Agastya's curse, Tataka along with her son, Mareecha, wished to retaliate against that eminent sage (1-25-10).
>
> With desperation brewing in her, she and Mareecha rushed with a roar towards sage Agastya who firstly cursed Mareecha saying, 'you will attain demon-hood' (1-25-11, 12a).
>
> Sage Agastya also cursed Tataka, saying, "forthwith divested of this form of a beautiful female, oh, great yakshii, you shall become a man-eater with your form distorted, face contorted, and shape monstrous" (1-25-12b, 13).
>
> Frenzied by the curse and convulsed in fury, Tataka is hence vandalising this auspicious province which sage Agastya once inhabited (1-25-14).
>
> Hence, Rama, you shall eliminate the atrocious Tataka filled with malevolence, whose conduct is horrific, for the welfare of Brahmins and cows (1-25-15) (Valmiki's *Ramayana*).

8. This passage, a complex and highly debated *sarga* (canto) in the Ramayana, is often seen as the first test administered to Rama to see if his compassion would overcome a righteous call to duty; whether he would quail in killing a (destructive) female and thereby disclose his unfitness to be a just ruler.

9. Hinduism is not a founded religion. There is no overarching authoritative body that determines what texts are scriptural and what are not. This means that the epics are usually believed to be part of a body of scriptural texts.

10. For example, the autobiographical renditions of Bhama or Viramma, two Dalit women from the Tamil-speaking region, the poignant autobiographical fragments of Dalits from Maharashtra, put together by Arjun Dangle in his edited volume *Corpse in the Well*, and Vasant Moon's *Growing up Untouchable in India* are all suffused with the language of caste Contrast these with the autobiography of R. K. Narayan, the famous Brahmin writer, *My Days* (1973), in which Narayan's caste is never overtly mentioned but almost everything relating to his life is largely influenced by his awareness of it.

11. Bhimrao Ramji Ambedkar (1891–1956) was a jurist, economist, politician, and social reformer. He inspired the modern Buddhist movement and was a crusader of Dalits, women, and the marginalized. He was India's first law minister and the principal architect of the Constitution of India. Ambedkar was educated at Columbia University and the London School of Economics. In 1956 he converted to Buddhism, initiating mass conversions of Dalits.

12. E. V. Ramasamy Naicker (1879–1973) was the founder of the Dravidian Movement or *Dravida Kazhagam*. Popularly known as "Periyar," he propagated the principles of rationalism, self-respect, women's rights, and eradication of caste. He opposed the exploitation and marginalization of the non-Brahmin Dravidian peoples of South India and the imposition of what he considered the Indo-Aryan social order. He advocated against the caste system and indicted Brahmins of Aryan descent as propounding the caste system. He was also against Sanskrit texts such as the Ramayana and the Mahabharata, which he said nurtured social discrimination and hierarchy through their narratives.

13. Vali has been blessed that he can never be killed in combat by an opponent who faces him. So, Rama hides behind a tree and shoots from behind—a non-valorous act in the *kshatriya* code.

14. No doubt there are also resonances to the Biblical Mary of Christianity. This is further emphasized by the phrase "casting stone after stone" that echoes Jesus' words: "[L]et him who is without sin cast the first stone," thus attributing an untainted innocence to the tribal, Mary.

15. According to Marxist French philosopher Louis Althusser, "interpellation" describes the process by which ideology, that is embodied in major social and political institutions such as the family and church in the private domain (which

he terms "ideological state apparatus") and police and military in the public domain (which he terms "repressive state apparatus"), constitutes the very nature of individual subjects' identities. According to Althusser, "ideology 'acts' or 'functions' in such a way that it 'transforms' the individual into subjects" ("Ideology and Ideological State Apparatuses" 11].

16. See Patyal.
17. See Chakravorty Spivak 1988.
18. National Institute for Occupational Safety and Health.

BIBLIOGRAPHY

Abdullah, Aanyah, and Shaila Abdullah. *My Friend Suhana: A Story of Friendship and Cerebral Palsy*. 2014.
Abdullah, Shaila. *Beyond the Cayenne Wall*. Bloomington, IN: iUniverse, 2005.
———. *A Manual for Marco: Living, Learning, and Laughing with an Autistic Sibling*. Ann Arbor, MI: Loving Healing Press, 2015.
———. *Rani in Search of a Rainbow: A Natural Disaster Survival Tale*. Kindle ed., Ann Arbor, MI: Living Healing Press, 2014.
———. *Saffron Dreams*. Ann Arbor, MI: Loving Healing Press, 2009.
Achebe, Chinua. *Things Fall Apart*. 1958. New York: Hungry Minds, 2001.
Ackerman, Jennifer. *Notes from the Shore*. New York: Penguin Books, 1995.
Agamben, Giorgio. *Homo Sacer: Sovereign Power and Bare Life*. Translated by Daniel Heller-Roazen. Stanford, CA: Stanford UP, 1998.
Alaimo, Stacy. *Bodily Natures: Science, Environment, and the Material Self*. Bloomington, IN: Indiana UP, 2010.
Alaimo, Stacy, and Susan Hekman. *Material Feminisms*. Bloomington, IN: Indiana UP, 2008.
Alcoff, Linda Martin, and Eduardo Mendieta, editors. *Thinking from the Underside of History: Enrique Dussel's Philosophy of Liberation*. New York: Rowman and Littlefield, 2000.
Alexander, Richard, and Arran Stibb. "From the Analysis of Ecological Discourse to the Ecological Analysis of Discourse." *Language Sciences*, vol. 41, Part A, 2014, pp. 104–10.
Alfar, Dean Francis. *Outpouring: The Typhoon Yolanda Relief Anthology*. Kindle ed., New York: Kestrel & Flipside, 2014.
Althusser, Louis. "Cremonini, Painter of the Abstract." *Lenin and Philosophy and Other Essays*. Translated by Ben Brewster. New York: Monthly Rev., 2001, p. 1.
———. *For Marx*. 1965. London: Verso, 2005.
———. "Ideology and Ideological State Apparatuses: Notes towards an Investigation." *Lenin and Philosophy and Other Essays*. London: Verso, 1971.
Amiel, Henri-Frédéric. *The Project Gutenberg EBook of Amiel's Journal*. Translated by Mrs Humphrey Ward, 2003, https://www.gutenberg.org/files/8545/8545-h/8545-h.htm. Accessed Nov. 11, 2017.
Anderson, Benedict. *Imagined Communities: Reflections on the Origin and Spread of Nationalism*. 1983. London and New York: Verso, 2006.

Ankersmit, Frank, Eva Domanska, and Hans Kellner. *Re-figuring Hayden White*. Stanford, CA: Stanford UP, 2009.

Arasanayagam, Jean. *All Is Burning*. New Delhi: Penguin Books, 1995.

———. "I am an Innocent Man." *All Is Burning*. New Delhi: Penguin Books, 1995.

———. "Man without a Mask." *All Is Burning*. New Delhi: Penguin Books, pp. 97–115.

Arnoldi, Jacobi. *Risk*. New York: John Wiley and Sons, 2013.

ASEAN Post Team, The. "Southeast Asia's Widening Inequalities." *The ASEAN Post*, July 17, 2018, https://theaseanpost.com/article/southeast-asias-widening-inequalities. Accessed Feb. 27, 2021.

Ashcroft, Bill, Gareth Griffiths, and Helen Tiffin. *The Empire Writes Back*. London and New York: Routledge, 1989.

Attenborough, Sir David. Epigraph to Introduction. *Population Matters*, https://populationmatters.org/our-patrons. Accessed Mar. 11, 2021.

Atwood, Margaret. *The Handmaid's Tale*. Merchantville, NJ: Houghton Mifflin, 1986.

Australian Book Review. *Vagabond Press*, 1993, http://vagabondpress.net/products/copy-of-beth-yahp-the-red-pearl-other-stories. Accessed Nov. 11, 2016.

Avatar. Directed by James Cameron. Lightstorm Entertainment/Dune Entertainment/Ingenious Film Partners/20th Century FOX, 2009.

Ayroso, Dee. *Bulat Lat: Journalism of the People*, Apr. 20, 2016, https://www.bulatlat.com/2016/04/20/marcos-era-saw-most-rapid-environmental-degradation-biodiversity-loss/. Accessed Nov. 11, 2018.

Baines, Gary. "Apocalypticism in American Folk Music." *Media and the Apocalypse*, edited by Kylo-Patrick R. Hart and Annette M. Holba. New York: Peter Lang, 2009.

Bakhtin, Mikhail M. *The Dialogic Imagination: Four Essays*, edited by Michael Holquist. Translated by Caryl Emerson and Michael Holquist. Austin, TX: U of Texas P, 1981.

———. "Response to a Question from Novy Mir." *Speech Genres and Other Late Essays*, edited by Caryl Emerson and Michael Holquist. Translated by Verne McGee. Austin, TX: U of Texas P, 1970.

Bale, Kevin. *Disposable People: New Slavery in the Global Economy*. Berkeley, CA: U of California P, 2004.

Bambara, Toni Cade. *The Salt Eaters*. 1980. New York: Vintage, 1981.

Barthes, Roland. "From Work to Text." *Image, Music, Text*. 1977. Translated by Stephen Heath. London: Fontana Press, 1977, 155–64.

Beard, Mary. "Risk and the Humanities." *Risk*, edited by Layla Skinns, Michael Scott, and Tony Cox. Darwin Lecture Series. Cambridge: Cambridge UP, 2011.

Beck, Ulrich. "Cosmopolitanism as Imagined Communities of Global Risk." *American Behavioral Scientist*, 2011, pp. 1346–61.

———. *The Cosmopolitan Vision*. Cambridge: Polity Press, 2006.

———. *Risk Society: Towards a New Modernity*. Translated by Mark Ritter. London: SAGE Publications, 1992.

———. "World Risk Society and Manufactured Uncertainties." *IRIS*, [S.l.], pp. 291–99, Oct. 2009, http://fupress.net/index.php/iris/article/view/3304/2906. Accessed Mar. 28, 2018.

Beck, Ulrich, Wolfgang Bonss, and Christopher Lau. "The Theory of Reflexive Modernization." *Theory, Culture & Society*, vol. 20, no. 2, 2003, pp. 1–33.

Benjamin, Walter. "Theses on the Philosophy of History." *Illuminations*. Translated by Harcourt Brace Jovanovich. New York: Shocken Books, 1968, pp. 253–64.

Bennett, Jane. "Systems and Things: On Vital Materialism and Object-Oriented Philosophy." *The Nonhuman Turn*, edited by Richard Grusin. Minneapolis, MN: U of Minnesota P, 2015, pp. 223–39.

———. *Vibrant Matter: A Political Ecology of Things*. Durham, NC: Duke UP, 2010.

Bennett, Michael. "Anti-Pastoralism, Frederick Douglass and the Nature of Slavery." *Beyond Nature Writing: Expanding the Boundaries of Ecocriticism*, edited by Karla Armbruster and Kathleen R. Wallace. Charlottesville, VA, and London: UP of Virginia, 2001, pp. 195–210.

Berger, John. *Ways of Seeing*. London: British Broadcasting Corporation and Penguin Books, 1972.

Bhabha, Homi K. "Anish Kapoor: Making Emptiness." *Anish Kapoor: With Essays by Homi K. Bhabha and Pier Luigi Tazzi*. London: Hayward Gallery, 1998, pp. 11–41.

———. "Cultural Diversity and Cultural Difference." *The Postcolonial Studies Reader*, edited by Bill Ashcroft, Gareth Griffiths, and Helen Tiffin. 1995. London and New York: Routledge, 2006, pp. 155–57.

———. *The Location of Culture*. New York: Routledge, 1994.

Biehl, Janet. *Finding Our Way: Rethinking Ecofeminist Politics*. Montreal: Black Rose Books, 1991.

Bigo, Didier. "Security and Immigration: Toward a Critique of the Governmentality of Unease." *Alternatives*, vol. 27, no. 1, 2002, pp. 63–92.

Birkeland, Janis. "Ecofeminism: Linking Theory and Practice." *Ecofeminism*, edited by Greta Gaard. Philadelphia, PA: Temple UP, 1993.

Biswas, Damyanti. *Suchen Christine Lim Talks about Writing in Singapore*. Singapore, Dec. 5, 2013, http://www.damyantiwrites.com/2013/12/05/suchen-christine-lim-talks-about-writing-in-singapore/. Accessed Aug. 11, 2016.

Blofeld, John. *Bodhisattva of Compassion: The Mystical Tradition of Kuan Yin*. Boston, MA: Shambhala, 1988.

Blumberg, Hans. *Paradigms for a Metaphorology*. Translated by Robert Savage. 1960. Ithaca, NY: Cornell UP, 2010.

Bobis, Merlinda. *Fish-Hair Woman*. Manila: Anvil Publishing, 2013.

Boccacio, Giovanni. *The Decameron*. 1353. Translated by G. H. McWilliam. London: Penguin Classics, 1987.

Botkin, Daniel B. *Discordant Harmonies: A New Ecology for the Twenty-first Century*. Oxford: Oxford UP, 1990.

Braidotti, Rosi. *The Posthuman*. Cambridge: Polity Press, 2013.

Brontë, Charlotte. *Jane Eyre*. 1847. Oxford: Oxford UP, 2016.

Buckles, Mary Parker. *Margins: A Naturalist Meets Long Island Sound*. New York: North Point Press, 1998.

Budianta, Melanie. "Introduction." *Family Room* by Lily Yulianti Farid. Jakarta: Lontar, 2010, pp. ix–xii.

Buell, Frederick. *From Apocalypse to Way of Life: Environmental Crisis in the American Century*. London and New York: Routledge, 2003.

———. "A Short History of Environmental Apocalypse." *Future Ethics: Climate Change and Apocalyptic Imagination*, edited by Stefan Skrimshire. London: Continuum International, 2010, pp. 13–36.

Buell, Lawrence. *The Future of Environmental Criticism: Environment Crisis and Literary Imagination*. Malden, MA: Blackwell, 2005.

———. "Toxic Discourse." *Critical Inquiry*, vol. 24, no. 3, 1998, pp. 639–65.

Burley, Mikel. *Classical Sāṃkhya and Yoga: An Indian Metaphysics of Experience*. New York: Routledge, 2007.

Butler, Judith. "Contingent Foundations: Feminism and the Question of 'Post modernism.'" *Feminists Theorize the Political*, edited by Judith Butler and Joan W. Scott. New York: Routledge, 1992.

Cambridge English Dictionary. Cambridge: Cambridge UP, 2021.

Cameron, Sharon. "Writing Nature: Henry Thoreau's Journal." Oxford and New York: Oxford UP, 1985.

Carrier, Martin, and Alfred Nordmann. *Science in the Context of Application*. Dordrecht, London, and New York: Springer, 2011.

Carson, Rachel. Acceptance speech for the John Burroughs Medal. April 1952. *Lost Woods: The Discovered Writing of Rachel Carson*, edited by Linda Lear. Boston, MA: Beacon Press, 1999.

———. *The Edge of the Sea*. New York: Houghton Mifflin Harcourt, 1955.

———. *The Sense of Wonder: A Celebration of Nature for Parents and Children*. 1956. New York and London: Harper Perennial, 1998.

———. *Silent Spring*. Boston, MA: Houghton Mifflin Harcourt, 1962.

Caruth, Cathy. *Unclaimed Experience: Trauma, Narrative, and History*. Baltimore, MD: The Johns Hopkins UP, 1996.

Chakrabarty, Dipesh. "The Climate of History: Four Theses." *Critical Inquiry*, vol. 35, 2009, pp. 197–222.

Chakravorty Spivak, Gayatri. "Can the Subaltern Speak?" *Marxism and the Interpretation of Culture*, edited by Cary Nelson and Lawrence Grossberg. Champaign, IL: Illinois Press, 1988, pp. 271–313.

———, editor. *Imaginary Maps: Three Stories by Mahasweta Devi*. Translated by Gayatri Chakravorty Spivak. New York: Routledge, 1995.

Chand, Meira. *A Different Sky*. London: Vintage, 2011.

Chandler, Daniel. *Semiotics: The Basics*. 2001. London and New York: Routledge, 2003.

Chanter, Tina. "Looking at Hegel's Antigone through Irigaray's Speculum." *Between Ethics & Aesthetics: Crossing the Boundaries*, edited by Dorota Glowacka and Stephen Boos. Albany, NY: SUNY P, 2002, pp. 29–48.

Chase, Steve, editor. *Defending the Earth: A Dialogue Between Murray Bookchin and Dave Foreman*. New York: Southend Press, 1991.

Chatterjee, Partha. *Nationalist Thought and the Postcolonial World: A Derivative Discourse*. Minneapolis, MN: U of Minessota P, 1986.

Chaucer, Geoffrey. *The Canterbury Tales*. 1342. London: Penguin Classics, 1996.

Chin, Grace V. S. "Angry Ghosts: The Furious Power of the Marginalized Other in Beth Yahp's *The Crocodile Fury*." *Outskirts: Feminisms along the Edge*, vol. 4, May 1999.

———. "Reading the Postcolonial Allegory in Beth Yahp's *The Crocodile Fury*: Censored Subjects, Ambivalent Spaces, and Transforming Bodies." *Nebula*, vol. 6, no. 1, 2009, pp. 93–103.

Chua, Beng Huat. *Communitarian Ideology and Democracy in Singapore*. New York and London: Routledge, 1995.

Clark, Nigel. "Volatile Worlds, Vulnerable Bodies: Confronting Abrupt Climate Change." *Theory, Culture & Society*, vol. 27, no. 2–3, 2010, pp. 31–53.

Clark, Timothy. *The Cambridge Introduction to Literature and the Environment*. Cambridge: Cambridge UP, 2010.

———. *Ecocriticism on the Edge*. London: Bloomsbury, 2015.

———. *Literature and the Environment*. Cambridge: Cambridge UP, 2011.

———. *The Value of Ecocriticism*. Cambridge: Cambridge UP, 2019.

Clifford, Hugh. "On Malayan Rivers." *Stories by Sir Hugh Clifford*, edited by William R. Roff. Kuala Lumpur: Oxford UP, 1966, pp.170–85.

Clifford, Hugh. "The East Coast." *Stories by Sir Hugh Clifford*, edited by Will R. Roff. Kuala Lumpur: Oxford UP, 1966, pp. 10–22.

Cohen, Jeffrey Jerome. "Introduction: Ecology's Rainbow." *Prismatic Ecology: Ecotheory Beyond Green*, edited by J. J. Cohen. Cambridge: Cambridge UP, pp. xv–xxxvi.

Collins, Suzanne. *The Hunger Games*. New York: Scholastic, 2008.

Conrad, Joseph. "The Lagoon." *Joseph Conrad: The Eastern Stories*, edited by Ban Kah Choon. New Delhi: Penguin Books, 2000, pp. 43–58.

Cook, Barbara J. "Introduction." *Women Writing Nature: A Feminist View*, edited by Barbara J. Cook. New York: Lexington Books, 2008.

Coole, Diana, and Samantha Frost. "Introduction." *New Materialisms: Ontology, Agency, and Politics*, edited by Diana Coole and Samantha Frost. Durham, NC: Duke UP, 2010, pp. 1–45.

Cooper, Nicola, and Stephen McVeigh. "Introduction: Men at War: Masculinities, Identities and Cultures." *Journal of War and Culture Studies*, vol. 5, no. 3, 2013, pp. 245–48.

Corbett, Julia. *Communicating Nature: How We Create and Understand Environmental Messages*. Washington, DC: Island Press, 2006

Cory, Pamela Libré. "Love, Land, and Language: An Erotics of Place," May 2012, http://rwwsoundings.com/wp-content/uploads/2012/05/Cory-1.pdf. Accessed Aug. 10, 2016.

Cottle, Simon. "Ulrich Beck, 'Risk Society' and the Media: A Catastrophic View?" *European Journal of Communication*, vol. 13, no. 1, 1998, pp. 5–32.

Coward, Jonathan. "How's That for an Ending?' Apocalyptic Narratives and Environmental Degradation: Foreclosing Genuine Solutions, or Rhetorical Necessity?" 2013, http://www.academia.edu/5431894/_How_s_that_for_an_ending_Apocalyptic_narratives_and_environmental_degradation_Foreclosing_genuine_solutions_or_rhetorical_necessity. Accessed Aug. 1, 2016.

Cowper, William. "The World at a Distance." *Poems of Places*, edited by Henry Wadsworth Longfellow. Bartleby.com, 1993, http://www.bartleby.com/270/1/10.html. Accessed Aug. 12, 2016.

Creel, Austin. "The Reexamination of Dharma in Hindu Ethics." *Philosophy East and West*, vol. 25, no. 2, 1975, pp. 161–73.

Crosthwaite, Paul. "Introduction." *Criticism, Crisis, and Contemporary Narrative: Textual Horizons in an Age of Global Risk*, edited by Paul Crosthwaite. London and New York: Routledge, 2011, pp. 1–13.

Cruz-Lucero, Rosario. "The Death of Fray Salvador Montano, Conquistador of Negros." *Collected Stories* by Rosario Cruz-Lucero. Manila: Philippines Free Press, 2001.

Cuddon, J. A. *Dictionary of Literary Terms and Literary Theory*, 5th ed. 1977. Hoboken, NJ: Wiley-Blackwell, 2012.

Currie, Mark. "Introduction." *Metafiction*, edited by Mark Currie. London and New York: Longman, 1995, pp. 1–18.

D'Ammassa, Don. *Encyclopedia of Adventure Fiction*. New York: Facts on File, 2009.

Dangle, Arjun. *A Corpse in the Well: Translations from Modern Marathi Dalit Autobiographies*. New Delhi: Disha Books,1992.

Das, Bhagavan. *A Science of Social Organisation, Vol. 1*. Chennai: Theosophical Publishing House, 1932.

Deckard, Sharae. "Jungle Tide, Devouring Reef: Postcolonial Anxiety and Ecocritique in Sri Lankan Literature." *Postcolonial Green: Environmental Politics and World Narratives*, edited by Bonnie Roos and Alex Hunt. Charlottesville, VA and London: U of Virginia P, 2010, pp. 32–48.

Dening, Greg. 1980. *Islands and Beaches: Discourses on a Silent Land, Marquesas 1774–1880*. Honolulu, HI: U of Hawai'i P.

Deraniyagala, Sonali. *Wave: A Memoir of Life after the Tsunami*. New York: Vintage, 2013.

Derrida, Jacques. "The Animal That Therefore I Am (More to Follow)." *Animal Philosophy: Ethics and Identity*, edited by Peter Atterton and Matthew Calarco. London: Continuum, 2004, pp. 113–28.

De-Shalit, Avner. *The Environment: Between Theory and Practice*. Oxford: Oxford UP, 2000.

Devi, Mahasweta. "Arjun." *The Picador Book of Modern Indian Literature*, edited by Amit Chaudhuri. Translated by Mridula Nath Chakroborty. London: Picador, 2002, pp. 122–30.

———. *Breast Stories*. Translated by Gayatri Chakravorty Spivak. Calcutta, London, and New York: Seagull Books, 1997.

———. "The Hunt." *Imaginary Maps: Three Stories by Mahasweta Devi*. Translated by Gayatri Chakravorty Spivak. New York and London: Routledge, 1995, pp. 1–18.

———. "Little Ones." *Bitter Soil* by Mahasweta Devi. Translated by Ipsita Chanda. Calcutta: Seagull Books, 2002, pp. 1–20.

———. "Salt." *Bitter Soil* by Mahasweta Devi. Translated by Ipsita Chanda. Calcutta: Seagull Books, 2002, pp. 124–45.

———. "Seeds." *Bitter Soil* by Mahasweta Devi. Translated by Ipsita Chanda. Calcutta: Seagull Books, 2002, pp. 21–55.

———. "The Witch." *Bitter Soil* by Mahasweta Devi. Translated by Ipsita Chanda. Calcutta: Seagull Books, 2002, pp. 57–123.

Divakaruni, Chitra Banerjee. *One Amazing Thing*. New Delhi: Hamish Hamilton, 2010.

DN. "Women and Forests." *Economic and Political Weekly*, vol. 25, no. 15, Apr. 1990, pp. 795–97.

Doubiago, Sharon. *Hard Country*. 1982. New Mexico: U of New Mexico P, 1999.

———. "Mama Coyote Talks to the Boys." *Healing the Wounds: The Promise of Ecofeminism*, edited by J. Plant. London: Green Print, 1989.

Dube, Saurabh. "Modernism in South Asia." *Routledge Encyclopedia of Modernism*, https://www.rem.routledge.com/articles/overview/tousled-temporalities. Accessed Sept. 15, 2017.

———. "Modern Subjects: An Epilogue." https://doi.org/10.7765/9781526105134.00012, Jan. 20, 2017. https://www.manchesteropenhive.com/view/9781526105134/9781526105134.00012.xml?print.

Dworkin, Andrea. *Pornography: Men Possessing Women*. New York: Dutton Signet, 1989.

Eagleton, Terry. *Ideology: An Introduction*. 1991. London and New York: Verso, 2007.

"Ecology." *Science Daily*, 2010, http://www.sciencedaily.com/articles/e/ecology.htm. Accessed Nov. 24, 2014.

Eliot, T. S. "Hamlet and His Problems." *The Sacred Wood*. 1921, Bartleby.com.

———. *The Wasteland*. 1922. New York: Renassaince Classics, 2012.

Emel, Jody. "Are You Man Enough, Big and Bad Enough? Ecofeminism and Wolf Eradication in the USA." *EPD: Society and Space*, vol. 13, no. 6, 1995, pp. 707–34.

Escobar, Arturo. *Encountering Development: The Making and Unmaking of the Third World*. Princeton, NJ: Princeton UP, 1995.

Estok, Simon C., and Won-Chung Kim, editors. *East Asian Ecocriticisms: A Critical Reader*. New York: Palgrave Macmillan, 2013.

Evernden, Neil. "Beyond Ecology: Self, Place, and the Pathetic Fallacy." *The Ecocriticism Reader: Landmarks in Literary Ecology*, edited by Cheryl Glotfelty and Harold Fromm. Athens, GA: U of Georgia P, 1996, pp. 92–104.

Farid, Lily Yulianti. "Lake." *Family Room*. Jakarta: Lontar, 2010, pp. 83–92.

Feinberg, Matthew and Robb. Willer. "Apocalypse Soon? Dire Messages Reduce Belief in Global Warming by Contradicting Just-World Beliefs." *Psychological Science*, vol. 9, no. 12, 2010, pp. 34–38. http://www.climateaccess.org/sites/default/files/Feinberg_Apocalypse%20Soon.pdf. Accessed Aug. 1, 2016.

Feuerstein, Georg. *The Yoga Tradition: Its History, Literature, Philosophy and Practice*, Kindle ed. Chino Valley, AZ: Hohm Press, 2013.

Flaubert, Gustave Flaubert. *Salammbo*. 1862. London: Penguin Classics, 1977.

Forster, E. M. *A Passage to India*. New York: Haskell House Publishers Ltd, 1969.

Fortun, Kim. *Advocacy after Bhopal: Environmentalism, Disaster, New Global Orders*: Chicago, IL: U of Chicago P, 2001.

Foucault, Michel. *Discipline and Punish: The Birth of the Prison*. 1975. Translated by Alan Sheridan. New York: Vintage Books, 1995.

———. *"Society Must Be Defended": Lectures at the Collège de France, 1975–1976*. London: Penguin Books, 2003.

———. *The Will to Knowledge: The History of Sexuality*, vol. 1. New York: Vintage Books, 1990.

Frank, Pat. *Alas Babylon*. Philadelphia, PA: JB Lippincott & Co., 1959.

Freud, Sigmund. "The Uncanny." *The Complete Psychological Works, Vol. XVII*. 1919. London: Hogarth Press, 1955, pp. 217–56.

Fromm, Harold. "From Transcendence to Obsolescence: A Route Map." *Georgia Review*, vol. 32, no. 3, Fall 1978, pp. 543–52.

Fudge, Erica. *Perceiving Animals*. New York: Palgrave Macmillan, 2000.

Garrard, Greg. *Ecocriticism*. London and New York: Routledge, 2004.

Gautam, Pradeep Kumar. "Kautilya's Arthashastra and the Panchatantra: A Comparative Evaluation." *World Affairs: The Journal of International Issues*, vol. 18, no. 2, Apr.–June 2014, pp. 64–73.

Genette, Gérard. *Narrative Discourse. An Essay in Method*. 1972. Oxford: Blackwell, 1980.

Ghosh, Amitav. *The Great Derangement*. Chicago, IL: U of Chicago P, 2018.

———. *The Hungry Tide*. Boston, New York: Houghton Mifflin Harcourt, 2005.

———. *Sea of Poppies*. New Delhi: Viking, 2008.

Gifford, Terry. "Pastoral, Anti-Pastoral, and Post-Pastoral." *The Cambridge Companion to Literature and the Environment*, edited by Louise Westling. Cambridge: Cambridge UP, 2013, pp. 17–30.

Gilligan, Carol. *In a Different Voice: Psychological Theory and Women's Development*. Cambridge, MA: Harvard UP, 1982.

Gilman, Charlotte Perkins. *Herland*. Gutenberg e-book, 1915, http://www.gutenberg.org/files/32/32-h/32-h.htm. Accessed Dec. 2014.

Glotfelty, Cheryll. "Introduction: Literary Studies in an Age of Environmental Crisis." *The Ecocriticism Reader*, edited by Cheryll Glotfelty and Harold Fromm. London and Athens, GA: U of Georgia P, 1996, pp. xv–xxxvii.

Goldwyn, Adam J. "A Case Study in Byzantine Ecocriticism: Zoomorphic and Anthomorphic Metaphors in the Medieval Greek Romance."

Interdisciplinary Studies in Literature and Environment, vol. 23, no. 2, Spring 2016, pp. 220–39.

Gombrich, Richard. *How Buddhism Began: The Conditioned Genesis of the Early Teachings*. New York: Continuum International Publishing Group, 1996.

Gore, Al. *Earth in the Balance: Forging a New Common Purpose*. London: Houghton Mifflin and Earthscan Publications, 1992.

Greimas, Algirdas Julien. *Structural Semantics: An Attempt at a Method*. Translated by Daniele McDowell, Ronald Schleifer, and Alan Velie. 1966. Lincoln, NE: U of Nebraska P, 1983.

Grinnell, R. *Just-World Hypothesis*. Psych Central, 2016, https://psychcentral.com/encyclopedia/just-world-hypothesis/. Accessed June 3, 2017.

Gruen, Lori. "Dismantling Oppression: An Analysis of the Connection between Women and Animals." *Ecofeminism: Women, Animals, Nature*, edited by Greta Gaard. Philadelphia, PA: Temple UP, 1993, pp. 60–89.

Gunasekara, Romesh. *Reef*. London: Granta Books, 1994.

Gupta, Bina. "The *Sāṃkhya* Darshana." *An Introduction to Indian Philosophy: Perspectives on Reality, Knowledge, and Freedom*. New York: Routledge, 2012, pp. 130–43.

Haekel, Ernst. *A Visit to Ceylon, 1883*. Translated by Clara Bell. Colombo: Asian Educational Services, 1995.

Hardgrave, Robert. *The Dravidian Movement*. Bombay: Popular Prakashan, 1965.

Harris, Wilson. *Tradition, the Writer and Society: Critical Essays*. 1967. London: New Beacon Books, 1998.

Harvey, Mark. "The Secular as Sacred?" *Modern Asian Studies*, vol. 20, no. 2, 2016, pp. 321–31.

Hashem, Dilara. "Immersion." *Galpa: Short Stories by Women from Bangladesh*, edited by Niaz Zaman and Firdous Asim. Translated by Saeeda Karim Khan. London: Saqi, 2005.

Hazlitt, William. *Characters of Shakespeare's Plays*. Produced by Steve Harris and Charles Franks, n.d., http://www.gutenberg.org/cache/epub/5085/pg5085-images.html. Accessed Nov. 11, 2016.

Hegel, Friedrick. *Aesthetics. Lectures on Fine Art*, 2 vols. Translated by T. M. Knox. Oxford: Clarendon Press, 1975.

Heidegger, Martin. *Being and Time*. 1927. New York: Harper Perenennial, 2008.

———. "Building Dwelling Thinking." 1971. *Martin Heidegger: Basic Writings*, edited by D. F. Krell. New York, NY: Harper & Row, 1993, pp. 343–64.

Heilmann, Anne and Mark Llewellyn. "Introduction." *Metafiction and Metahistory in Contemporary Women's Writing*, edited by Anne Heilman and Mark Llewellyn. Basingstoke and New York: Palgrave, 2007.

Heise, Ursula K. "The Hitchhiker's Guide to Ecocriticism." *PMLA*, vol. 121, no. 2, 2006, pp. 503–16.

———. *Sense of Place and Sense of Planet: The Environmental Imagination of the Global.* Oxford: Oxford UP, 2008.

Hiltebeitel, Alf, and Kathleen M. Erndl. "Introduction: Writing Goddesses, Goddesses Writing, and Other Scholarly Concerns." *Is the Goddess a Feminist? The Politics of South Asian Goddesses*, edited by Alf Hiltebeitel and Kathleen M Erndl. New York: New York UP, 2000, pp. 11–23.

Huggan, Graham. "Australian Literature, Risk, and the Global Climate Challenge." *Literature Interpretation Theory*, vol. 26, 2015, pp. 85–105.

———. "'Greening' Postcolonialism: Ecocritical Perspectives." *Modern Fiction Studies*, vol. 50, no. 3, Fall 2004, pp. 701–33.

———. *Nature's Saviours: Celebrity Conservationists in the Television Age.* London and New York: Routledge, 2013.

Huggan, Graham, and Helen Tiffin. *Postcolonial Ecocriticism: Literature, Animals, Environment.* London and New York: Routledge, 2010.

Huxley, Thomas Henry. *Man's Place in Nature.* London: Williams and Norgate, 1863.

Internet Archives. *Mahabharata.* Translated by Kisari Mohan Ganguly. Lichtenberg Press, n.d., https://holybooks.com/mahabharata-all-volumes-in-12-pdf-files/. Accessed Nov. 11, 2017.

Iovino, Serenella, and Serpil Oppermann. "Theorizing Material Ecocriticism: A Diptych." *Interdisciplinary Studies in Literature and Environment (ISLE)*, vol. 19, no. 3, 2012, pp. 448–75.

Jabri, V. "Michel Foucault's Analytics of War: The Social, the International, and the Racial." *International Political Sociology*, vol. 1, no. 1, 2007, pp. 67–81.

Jameson, Fredric. "Progress Versus Utopia; Or, Can We Imagine the Future?" *Science Fiction Studies, Special Issue: Utopia and Anti-Utopia*, vol. 9, no. 2, 1982, pp. 147–58.

JanMohamed, Abdul R. "The Economy of Manichean Allegory: The Function of Racial Difference in Colonialist Literature." *Critical Inquiry*, vol. 12, no. 1, 1985, pp. 59–87.

Jeffers, Robinson. "Sharing Poetry 'Credo,'" 1927, http://sharingpoetry.tumblr.com/post/33540443260/robinson-jeffers-credo. Accessed Aug. 1, 2016.

Jeyaratnam, Philip. *Abraham's Promise.* 1995. Singapore: Marshall Cavendish, 2010.

Johnson, Alan. "Sacred Forest, Maternal Space and National Narrative in Mahasweta Devi's Fiction." *Interdisciplinary Studies in Literature and Environment (ISLE)*, vol. 23, no. 3, 2016, pp. 506–25.

Johnson, Sarah. *Historical Fiction: A Guide to the Genre.* Westport, CT: Libraries Unlimited, 2005.

Joshi, Ruchir. *The Last Jet Engine Laugh.* New York: Flamingo, 2000.

Kellert, Stephen R. *The Value of Life: Biological Diversity and Human Society.* Washington, DC: Island Press, 1996.

Kellert, Stephen R., and Joyce K. Berry. "Attitudes, Knowledge, and Behaviors toward Wildlife as Affected by Gender." *Wildlife Society Bulletin*, vol. 15, no. 3, Autumn 1987, pp. 363–71.

Kermode, Frank. "Introduction to Tempest." 1954. *Arden Shakespeare.* London and New York: Routledge, 1994, pp. xi–lxxxviii.

Ketavong, Viliya. "The Roar of a Distant War." *A Rainbow Feast: New Asian Short Stories*, edited by Mohammad A. Quayum. Singapore: Marshall Cavendish, 2010, pp. 96–110.

Kheel, Marti. "From Heroic to Holistic Ethics: The Ecofeminist Challenge." *Ecofeminism: Women, Animals, Nature*, edited by Greta Gaard. Philadelphia, PA: Temple UP, 1993, pp. 243–71.

Khin, Mya Zin. "Heartless Forest." *Heartless Forest: An Anthology of Burmese Women Writers*, edited by Mon Mon Myat and Nance Cunningham. Translated by Nance Cunningham. Yangon: Myanmar: Pansodan Books, 2013, pp. 41–50.

———. *Kaungkin Moe Tain Wuttu-to Mya* (Clouds Over the Sky and Others Short Stories). https://www.wikiy.org/en/Myanmar_National_Literature_Award-8084886404.

King, Stephen. *The Stand.* New York: Doubleday, 1978.

King, Ynestra. "Healing the Wounds: Feminism, Ecology and Nature/Culture Dualism." *Gender, Body, Knowledge: Feminist Reconstructions of Being and Knowing*, edited by Allson M. Jaggar and Susan R. Bordo. New Brunswick, NJ: Rutgers UP, 1992, pp. 115–43.

Kompridis, Nikolas. *Critique and Disclosure: Critical Theory between Past and Future.* Cambridge: MIT Press, 2006.

Kovel, Joel. *The Enemy of Nature: The End of Capitalism or the End of the World?* Winnipeg: Fernwood Publishing, 2002.

Kumar, Deepak, Vinita Damodaran, and Rohan D'Souza, editors. *The British Empire and the Natural World Environmental Encounters in South Asia.* Oxford: Oxford UP.

Lahiri, Jhumpa. "Jhumpa Lahiri: By the Book." Interview. *Sunday Book Review*, Sept. 5, 2013.

Lazarus, R. J. "Super Wicked Problems and Climate Change: Restraining the Present to Liberate the Future." *Cornell Law Review*, vol. 94, no. 5, 2009, pp. 1153–234.

Le Clézio, J. M. G. *The Mexican Dream Or The Interrupted Thought of Amerindian Civilizations.* Translated by Teresa Fagan. Chicago, IL: U of Chicago P, 1993.

Le Guin, Ursula K. *The Left Hand of Darkness*. New York: Ace Books, 1969.
Lee Kuan Yew. *From Third World to First: The Singapore Story, 1965–2000*. New York: HarperCollins, 2000.
———. *The Singapore Story: Memoirs of Lee Kuan Yew*, Times New Edition, Singapore Press Holdings, Singapore, 1998.
Lee, Martha F. *Earth First: Environmental Apocalypse*. Syracuse, NY: Syracuse UP, 1995.
Lemm, Vanessa, and Miguel Vatter. "Michel Foucault's Perspective on Biopolitics." *Handbook of Biology and Politics*, Gloucestor and Northampton, MA: Edgar Elgar Publications, 2017, pp. 40–54.
Leopold, Aldo. *A Sand County Almanac and Sketches Here and There*. Oxford: Oxford UP, 1968.
Leskanich, Alexandre. "The Great Derangement: Climate Change and the Unthinkable—Book Review." *LSE Business Review*, July 30, 2017.
Lessing, Doris. "Old Chief Mshlanga." *African Stories*. New York: Simon and Schuster, 1965.
Li, Huey-li. "A Cross-Cultural Critique of Ecofeminism." *Ecofeminism: Women, Animals, Nature*, edited by Greta Gaard. Philadelphia, PA: Temple UP, 1991, pp. 272–94.
Lim, Suchen Christine. *The River's Song*. Singapore: Aurora Metro Books, 2013.
Lincoln, Bruce. *Theorizing Myth: Narrative, Ideology, and Scholarship*. Chicago, IL: U of Chicago P, 1999.
Lindbergh, Anne Morrow. *Gift from the Sea*. New York: Pantheon Books, 1955.
Ling, Ma. *Severance*. New York: Farrar, Straus and Giroux, 2018.
Lo, Miriam Wei Wei. "Shaking a Few Tales: The Dialectics of Hybridity and Beth Yahp's *The Crocodile Fury*." *Hecate*, vol. 25, no. 1, 1999, pp. 56–62.
Lovelock, James. *The Revenge of Gaia : Why the Earth is Fighting Back and How We Can Still Save Humanity*. Harmondsworth: Penguin Books, 2006.
Lukács, Georg. *The Historical Novel*. 1936. Translated by Hannah and Stanley Mitchell. London and Lincoln, NE: U of Nebraska P, 1962.
Macey, David. "Rethinking Biopolitics, Race and Power in the Wake of Foucault." *Theory, Culture & Society*, vol. 26, no. 6, 2009, pp. 186–205.
Macherey, Pierre. "The Text Says What It Does Not Say." *Literature in the Modern World: Critical Essays and Documents*, edited by Dennis Walder. Oxford: Oxford UP, 2004, pp. 252–59.
———. *A Theory of Literary Production*. London: Routledge & Kegan Paul, 1978.
Maøecki, Wojciech, Boguslaw Pawøowski, and Piotr Sorokowski. "Literary Fiction Influences Attitudes toward Animal Welfare." *PLoS ONE* vol. 11, no. 12, 2016, e0168695. Accessed Mar. 30, 2017.

Manes, Christopher. "Nature and Silence." *Environmental Ethics*, vol. 14, Winter 1992, pp. 339–50.

Manoharan, Karthick Ram. "Freedom from God: Periyar and Religion." *Religions*, vol. 11, no. 1, 2020, pp. 10–21.

Manto, Sadat Hasan. *Fifteen Stories* selected by Nandita Das. New Delhi: Rajkamal Prakashan, 2018.

McCarthy, Cormac. *The Road*. New York: Vintage, 2006.

McClintock, Anne. *Imperial Leather: Race, Gender, and Sexuality in the Colonial Context*. London and New York: Routledge, 1995.

McDowell, Michael J. "The Bakhtinian Road to Ecological Insight." *The Ecocriticism Reader*, edited by Cheryll Glotfelty and Harold Fromm. Athens, GA: U of Georgia P, 1996, pp. 371–89.

McKibben, Bill. *The End of Nature*. New York: Random House, 1989.

Meeker, Joseph. *The Comedy of Survival: Studies in Literary Ecology*. New York: Charles Scribner's, 1974.

Mehta, Gita. *A River Sutra*. New Delhi: Penguin Books, 1993.

Mellor, Mary. *Feminism and Ecology*. Cambridge: Polity Press, 1997.

Mentz, Steve. "Brown." *Prismatic Ecology: Ecotheory Beyond Green*, edited by Jeffrey Jerome Cohen. Minneapolis, MN and London: U of Minnesota P, 2013, pp. 193–212.

Merchant, Carolyn. *The Death of Nature: Women, Ecology, and the Scientific Revolution*. New York: HarperCollins, 1980.

———. *Earthcare: Women and the Environment*. New York: Routledge, 1995.

Moon, Vasant. *Growing Up Untouchable in India: A Dalit Autobiography*. Translated by Gail Omvedt. Lanham, MD: Rowman & Littlefield, 2001.

Morton, Timothy. "Material Ecocriticism." *Cambridge Companion to Ecocriticism: Cambridge*, edited by Louise Westling. Cambridge: Cambridge UP, 2014, pp. 111–36.

Moser, Keith. "Is Preserving Indigenous Languages and Cultures the Key to Avoiding the Impending Eco-Apocalypse? An Eco-linguistic Reading of Le Clézio's Le Rêve Mexicaine." *The Journal of Ecocriticism: A New Journal of Nature, Society and Literature*, vol. 7, no. 1, 2015, pp. 1–11.

Mrovlje, Maša. "Beyond Nussbaum's Ethics of Reading: Camus, Arendt, and the Political Significance of Narrative Imagination," *The European Legacy*, vol. 24, no. 2, 2019, pp. 162–80.

Mukherjee, Upamanyu Pablo. "Arundhati Roy: Environment and Uneven Form." *Postcolonial Green: Environmental Politics and World Narratives*, edited by Bonnie Roos and Alex Hunt. Charlottesville, VA and London: U of Virginia P, 2010, pp. 17–31.

———. *Postcolonial Environments: Nature, Culture, and the Contemporary Indian Novel in English*. London: Palgrave Macmillan, 2010.

Murray, John Stuart. "Thanatopolitics." *Bloomsbury Handbook to Literary and Cultural Theory*, edited by J. R. Di Leo. London: Bloomsbury Books, 2018, pp. 718–19.

Nanda, Akshita. "Review of The River's Song." *The Sunday Times*, Nov. 3, 2013, p. 16.

Narayan, R. K. *My Days*. New York: Viking Press, 1974.

Nelson, Barney. *The Wild and the Domestic: Animal Representation, Ecocriticism and Western American Literature*. Reno, NE, and Las Vegas, NE: U of Nevada P, 2000.

Nixon, Rob. "Environmentalism and Postcolonialism." *Postcolonial Studies and Beyond*, edited by Ania Loomba, Suvir Kaul, Matti Bunzl, Antoinette Burton, and Jed Esty. Durham, NC: Duke UP, 2005, pp. 233–51.

———. *Slow Violence: The Environmentalism of the Poor*. Cambridge, MA: Harvard UP, 2011.

Nkrumah, Kwame. *Neo-Colonialism, The Last Stage of Imperialism*. London: Thomas Nelson & Sons, Ltd. New York: International Publishers Co., 1965.

Nussbaum, Martha. *Cultivating Humanity: A Classical Defense of Reform in Liberal Education*. Cambridge, MA: Harvard UP, 1997, pp. 87, 91–92, 96–98, 34.

———. *Poetic Justice: The Literary Imagination and Public Life*. Boston, MA: Beacon Press, 1995, pp. xiv–xvi, 1–12.

Oreskes, Naomi. "The Scientific Consensus on Climate Change: How Do We Know We're Not Wrong?" *Climate Change: What It Means for Us, Our Children, and Our Grandchildren*, edited by Joseph F. C. DiMento and Pamela Doughman. Cambridge, MA: MIT P, 2007, pp. 65–99.

Organ, Troy Wilson. *The Hindu Quest for the Perfection of Man*. 1970. Eugene, OR: Wipf and Stock Publishers, 1998.

Ortner, Sherry. B. "Is Female to Male as Nature is to Culture?" *Woman, Culture, and Society*, edited by M. Z. Rosaldo and L. Lamphere. Stanford, CA: Stanford UP, 1974, pp. 68–87.

Orwell, George. "Shooting an Elephant." *New Writing*, The Literature Network, 1936, http://www.online-literature.com/orwell/887/. Accessed Mar. 21, 2015.

Pandian, M. S. S. "One Step Outside Modernity: Caste, Identity Politics and Public Sphere." SEPHIS-CODESRIA Working Paper. Amsterdam, 2002. Reprint *Economic and Political Weekly*, vol. 37, no. 18, May 4, 2002.

Patyal, Hukam Chand. "Pigeon in Vedic Mythology and Ritual by Hukam Chand Patyal." *Annals of the Bhandarkar Oriental Research Institute*, vol. 71, no. 1/4, 1990, pp. 310–17.

Pearson, Michael N. "Littoral Society: The Concept and the Problems." *Journal of World History*, vol. 17, no. 4, 2006, pp. 353–73.

Pepperell, Robert. *The Posthuman Condition*. Exeter: Intellect, 1997.

Pham, Chi, Chitra Sankaran, and Gurpreet Kaur, editors. *Ecologies in Southeast Asian Literatures: Histories, Myths and Societies*. Wilmington, DE: Vernon Press, 2019.

Pillai, Shanthini. "Occidental Echoes: Beth Yahp's Ambivalent Malaya." *Hecate*, vol. 33, no. 1, 2007, pp. 174–86.

Plumwood, Val. "Androcentrism and Anthrocentrism: Parallels and Politics." *Ethics and Environment*, vol. 1, no. 2, 1996, pp. 119–52.

———. "Decolonizing Relationships with Nature." *Decolonizing Nature: Strategies for Conservation in a Post-Colonial Era*, edited by William H. Adams and Martin Mulligan. London: Earthscan, 2003, pp. 51–78.

———. *Feminism and the Mastery of Nature*. London: Routledge, 1993.

Prieto, Eric. *Literature, Geography, and the Postmodern Poetics of Place*. New York: Palgrave Macmillan, 2012.

Radhakrishnan, Sarvepalli, and C. A. Moore. *A Source Book in Indian Philosophy*. Princeton, NJ: Princeton U, 1957.

Rajan, Chandra. "Introduction." Sharma, Vishnu. *The Panchatantra*, Vishnu Sharma. Translated by Chandra Rajan. New Delhi: Penguin Books, 1993, pp. 1–6.

Rao, Seshagiri. "The Five Great Elements (Pancamahabhuta): An Ecological Perspective." *Hinduism and Ecology*, edited by Christopher Key Chapple and Mary Evelyn Tucker. Cambridge, MA: Harvard UP, 2000, pp. 23–38.

Renn, Ortwin. *Risk Governance: Coping with Uncertainty in a Complex World*. London: Routledge, 2008.

Repo, Jemima. "Thanatopolitics or Biopolitics? Diagnosing the Racial and Sexual Politics of the European Far-right." *Contemporary Political Theory*, vol. 15, no. 1, 2016, pp. 110–18.

Rhys, Jean. *Wide Sargasso Sea*. 1966. London: Penguin Books, 2001.

Roff, William R. "Introduction." *Stories by Sir Hugh Clifford* by Hugh Clifford. Oxford: Oxford UP, 1966, pp. vii–xxviii.

Roosevelt, Theodore. Cited in *Wilderness and the American Mind* by Roderick Frazier Nash. New Haven, CT: Yale UP, 1967.

Rosen, S. A. C. "Littoral Women Writing from the Margins." *Women Writing Nature: A Feminist View*, edited by Barbara J Cook. New York: Lexington Books, 2008.

Roser-Renouf, Connie, Edward Maibach, and Anthony Leiserowitz. *Global Warming's Six Americas 2009: An Audience Segmentation Analysis*. New Haven, CT, and Fairfax, VA: Yale Project on Climate Change, 2009.

Roy, Arundhati. *The God of Small Things*. New York: Random House, 1997.

Rueckert, William. "Literature and Ecology: An Experiment in Ecocriticism." *Iowa Review*, vol. 9, no. 1, 1978, pp. 71–86.

———. *Literature and Ecology: An Experiment in Ecocriticism*. Athens, GA, and London: U of Georgia P, 1996.

Ryan, John C., editor. *South East Asian Ecocriticism: Theories, Practices, Prospects*. New York: Lexington Books, 2017.

Sachs, Wolfgang. "Environment and Development: The Story of a Dangerous Liaison." *The Ecologist*, vol. 21, no. 6, 1991, pp. 252–57.

Said, Edward. *Orientalism*. New York: Vintage Books, 1979.

Salleh, Ariel. *Ecofeminism as Politics: Nature, Marx and the Postmodern*. London: Zed Books and New York: St Martins Press, 1997.

———. "The Ecofeminism/Deep Ecology Debate: A Reply to Patriarchal Reason." *Environmental Ethics*, vol. 14, 1992, pp. 195–216.

Sandilands, Catriona. *The Good-Natured Feminist: Ecofeminism and the Quest for Democracy*. Minneapolis, MN: U of Minnesota P, 1999.

San Juan, E. "Preface to Pierre Macherey and an Aesthetics of 'Imaginary Relations.'" Oct. 28, 2008. *The Philippines Matrix Project*, https://philcsc.wordpress.com/2008/10/28/marxist-aesthetics-on-macherey-althusser/. Accessed Nov. 15, 2016.

Sankaran, Chitra. "Women, Rivers and Serpents: Reifying the Primordial Link in Gita Mehta's A River Sutra." *Journal of Commonwealth Literature*, vol. 47, no. 3, 2012, pp. 429–46.

Sarmiento, Irene Carolina A. "Maharlika." *Hoard of Thunder: Philippine Short Story in English 1990–2008*, edited by Gemino H Abad. Manila: U of the Philippines P, 2004, pp. 218–36.

Sattar, Arshia. *Uttara Kanda*. Maryland: Rowman and Littlefield, 2016.

Schlegel, Friedrich. "Dialogue on Poetry" (Selections). *German Romantic Criticism*, edited by A. Leslie Willson. Translated by Ernst Behler and Roman Struc. New York: Continuum, 1982.

Sebald, W. G. *After Nature*. Harmondsworth: Penguin Books, 2013.

"Sermon on the Not-Self Characteristic, The." *Anattalakkhana Sutta, Samyutta Nikaya*, vol. XXII, no. 59. http://santipada.co.nz/wp-content/uploads/2019/05/Anatta-lakkhana-Sutta.pdf. Accessed Nov. 21, 2018.

Shahraz, Qaizra. "The Zemindar's Wife." *A Rainbow Feast*, edited by Mohammad A. Quayum. Singapore: Marshall Cavendish, 2010, pp. 266–85.

Shelley, Mary. *The Last Man*. 1826. Edited by Pamela Bickley and Keith Carabine. London: Wordsworth Editions Ltd, 2004.

Shiva, Vandana. *Staying Alive: Women, Ecology, and Development*. London: Zed Books, 1989.

Singer, Peter. *Animal Liberation: A New Ethics for Our Treatment of Animals*. New York: Harper Collins, 1975.

———. *The Expanding Circle: Ethics and Sociobiology*. Oxford: Oxford UP, 1983.

Singh, Karan. "The Hindu Declaration on Nature." *The Assisi Declarations*. Gland, Switzerland: World Wide Fund for Nature (WWF), Sept. 29, 1986, https://www.silene.org/en/documentation-centre/declarations/the-hindu-declaration-on-nature#The_Assisi_Declarations.pdf. Accessed Mar. 12, 2021.

Sinha, Indra. *Animal's People*. London and New York: Simon & Schuster Paperbacks, 2007.

Sîn-lēqi-unninni, editor. *The Epic of Gilgamesh*. Mesopotamia: Assyrian International News Agency Books Online, 1300–1000 BCE, http://www.aina.org/books/eog/eog.pdf. Accessed July 7, 2016.

Slovic, Scott. "Introduction." *Critical Insights: Nature & the Environment*, edited by Scott Slovic. Salem, MAA: EBSCO Publishing, 2013, pp. 1–14.

———. "Oh, Lovely Slab: Robinson Jeffers, Stone Work, and the Locus of the Real." *Essays in Ecocriticism*, edited by Nirmal Selvamony and Alex Rayson. New Delhi: Sarup and Sons, 2007, pp. 82–113.

Slovic, Scott, Swarnalatha Rangarajan, and Vidya Sarveswaran. *Ecocriticism of the Global South*. New York: Lexington Press, 2015.

Slovic, Scott, and Paul Slovic, editors. *Numbers and Nerves: Information, Emotion and Meaning in a World of Data*. Corvallis, OR: Oregan State UP, 2015.

Soja, Edward. *Thirdspace: Journeys to Los Angeles and Other Real-and-Imagined Places*. Oxford: Basil Blackwell, 1996.

———. "Third Space: Toward a New Consciousness of Space and Spaciality." *Communicating in the Third Space*, edited by Karin Ikas and Gerhard Wagner. New York: Routledge, 2009, pp. 49–61.

Sollors, Werner. *Neither Black Nor White Yet Both: Thematic Explorations of Interracial Literature*. Cambridge, MA: Harvard UP, 1997.

Solnit, Rebecca. *Hope in the Dark: Untold Histories, Wild Possibilities*. New York: Nation Books, 2006.

Soper, Kate. "The Discourses of Nature." *What is Nature? Culture, Politics and the Non-Human*. Cambridge, MA: Blackwell Publishing, 1995, pp. 15–36.

Sørensen, Mads P., and Allan Christiansen. *Ulrich Beck: An Introduction to the Theory of Second Modernity and the Risk Society*. London and New York: Routledge, 2014.

Sovern, Jeff. "The Risks of Unfettered Capitalism," *New York Times*, Aug. 15, 2016, https://www.nytimes.com/2016/08/16/business/dealbook/the-risks-of-unfettered-capitalism.html. Accessed Feb. 18, 2018.
Still, John. *The Jungle Tide*. Edinburgh and London: William Blackwood and Sons Ltd, 1930.
Stoker, Bram. *Dracula*. 1897. New York: Dover Publications, 2000.
Stone, Alison. "Friedrich Schlegel, Romanticism, and the Re-enchantment of Nature." *Inquiry: An Interdisciplinary Journal of Philosophy*, vol. 1, no. 48, 2005, pp. 3–25.
Subramanian, K. R. *The Origins of Saivism and Its History in the Tamil Land*. New Delhi and Chennai: Asian Educational Services, 2002.
Tal, Kali. *Worlds of Hurt: Reading the Literatures of Trauma*. Cambridge: Cambridge UP, 1996.
Thompson, Damien. *The End of Time: Faith and Fear in the Shadow of the Millennium*. New Hampshire: UP of New England, 1997.
Thompson, Peter. *The Battle for Singapore: The True Story of the Greatest Catastrophe of World War Two*. London: Portrait Books, 2005.
Thornber, Karen Laura. *Ecoambiguity: Environmental Crisis and East Asian Literatures*. Ann Arbor, MI: U of Michigan P, 2012.
Titumir, Rashed Al Mahmud, and Jakir Hossain. *Disability in Bangladesh: Prevalence, Knowledge, Attitudes and Practices*. Dhaka: Unnayan Onneshen, 2005.
Tuan, Yi-Fuan. *Landscapes of Fear*. New York: Pantheon, 1979.
Umali-Berthelsen, Nita. "The Money-Makers." *Songs of Ourselves: Writings by Filipino Women in English*, edited by Edna Zapanta Manlapaz. Santa Monica, CA: Philippine American Literary House, 1994, pp. 39–46.
Valmiki. *Ramayana*, n.d., http://www.valmikiramayan.net/. Accessed Feb. 11, 2015.
Vasterling, Veronica. "Cognitive Theory and Phenomenology in Arendt's and Nussbaum's Work on Narrative." *Human Studies*, vol. 30, no. 2, June 2007, pp. 79–95.
Vo, Thi Hao. "The Blood of Leaves." *Family of Fallen Leaves: Stories of Agent Orange by Vietnamese Writers*, edited by Charles Waugh and Lien Huy. Athens, GA, and London: U of Georgia P, 2010, pp. 134–46.
Waites, Elizabeth A. *Trauma and Survival: Post-Traumatic and Dissociative Disorders in Women*. New York: Norton, 1993.
Wallace, Molly. *Risk Criticism: Precautionary Reading in an Age of Environmental Uncertainty*. Ann Arbor, MI: U of Michigan P, 2016.
Warren, Karen J. "Feminism and Philosophy." *American Philosophical Association Newsletter*, Fall 1991, pp. 108–16.

———. "A Feminist Philosophical Perspective on Ecofeminist Spiritualities." *Ecofeminism and the Sacred*, edited by Carol J. Adams. New York: Continuum, 1995, pp. 119–32.

———. "Introduction." *Ecological Feminism*, edited by Karen J. Warren. London and New York: Routledge, 1994, pp. 1–7.

———. "Introduction." *Environmental Philosophy: From Animal Rights to Radical Ecology*, edited by J. Baird Callicott, George Sessions, Karen J. Warren, John Clark, and Michael E. Zimmerman. NJ: Prentice-Hall, 1993, pp. 1–14.

Waugh, Charles. "Introduction." *Family of Fallen Leaves: Stories of Agent Orange by Vietnamese Writers*, edited by Charles Waugh and Huy Lien. Athens, GA and London: U of Georgia P, 2010, pp. 1–16.

Waugh, Patricia. "What is Metafiction and Why are They Saying Such Awful Things About it?" *Metafiction*, edited by Mark Currie. London and New York: Longman, 1995, pp. 39–54.

Weisman, Alan. *The World Without Us*. New York: Picador, 2007.

Welch, Sharon, D. *A Feminist Ethic of Risk*, rev. ed. Minneapolis, MN: Fortress, 2000.

Wells, H. G. *The War of the Worlds*. 1897. Alabama, AK: Mockingbird Classics Publishing, 2015.

Wenzel, Jennifer. "Epic Struggles over India's Forests in Mahasweta Devi's Short Fiction." *Alif: Journal of Comparative Poetics,* Special Issue: Post-Colonial Discourse in South Asia, vol. 18 , 1998, pp. 127–58.

———. "Reading the Politics of Survival in Mahasweta Devi's 'Dhowli.'" *Postcolonial Ecologies: Literatures of the Environment*, edited by Elizabeth DeLoughrey and George B. Handley. New York: Oxford UP, 2011.

Westling, Louise. "Literature, the Environment, and the Question of the PostHuman." *Nature in Literary and Cultural Studies: Transatlantic Conversations on Ecocriticism*, edited by Catrin Gersdorf and Sylvia Mayer. Amsterdam and New York: Rodopi, 2006, pp. 25–47.

What Happened to Monday? Directed by Tommy Wirkola. Written by Max Botkin and Kerry Williamson. SND/Vendome Pictures/Raffaella Productions, Nexus, Umedia, 2017.

Wikipedia. *Littoral Zone*. Definition. New York: Environment Agency Grey Literature, 2013, http://ea-lit.freshwaterlife.org/fedora/repository/vocabpref:19194. Accessed Jan. 7, 2015.

Williams, Terry Tempest. *Refuge*. New York: Pantheon Books, 1991.

———. *An Unspoken Hunger: Stories from the Field*. New York: Vintage Books, 1995.

Willmot, Glenn. *Reading for Wonder: Ecology, Ethics, Enchantment*. New York and London: Palgrave Macmillan, 2018.

Wilson, Elizabeth A. *Psychosomatic Feminism and the Neurological Body*. Durham, NC, and London: Duke UP, 2004.

Wisner, Ben, Peirs Blaikie, Terry Cannon, and Ian Davis. *At Risk: Natural Hazards, People's Vulnerability and Disaster*, 2nd ed. London and New York: Routledge, 2004.

Wolfe, Cary. "Old Orders for New: Ecology, Animal Rights and the Poverty of Humanism." *Diacritics*, vol. 28, no. 2, 1998, pp. 21–40.

Woolf, Leonard. *The Village in the Jungle*, edited by Yasmine Gooneratne. 1913. Lewiston, Queenston, and Lampeter: The Edwin Mellen Press, 2004.

Wright, Laura. *Wilderness in Civilized Shapes: Reading the Postcolonial Environment*. Athens, GA: U of Georgia P, 2010.

Wynn, Le Le. "The Role of Myanmar Poems in Environmental Conservation." Irrawady Literary Festival, Feb. 3, 2013.

Yahp, Beth. *The Crocodile Fury*. New South Wales: Angus and Robertson, 1992.

Young, Robert J. C. *Postcolonialism: An Historical Introduction*. Oxford: Blackwell, 2001.

———. "The Void of Misgiving." *Communicating in the Third Space*, edited by Karin Ikas and Gerhard Wagne. London and New York: Routledge, 2009, pp. 81–95.

Zaman, Niaz. *The Art of Kantha Embroidery*. Dhaka: The UP Limited, 1993.

———. *The Baromashi Tapes*. Dhaka: Writer's Ink, 2011.

———. *Didima's Necklace and Other Stories*. Dhaka: Writer's Ink, 2005.

———. *A Divided Legacy: The Partition in Selected Novels of India, Pakistan and Bangladesh*. Dhaka: The UP Limited, 1999.

INDEX

*Aagariya*s, 161
Achebe, Chinua, 41
Ādittapariyāya Sutta (Fire Sermon Discourse), 124
*adivasi*s (aboriginal tribal people), 152, 156, 161
    treatment of, 158
Adorno, Theodor, 184
adult consciousness, 178
Advaita, 154, 198
Agamben, Giorgio, 71
agentic "feminine" nature, notion of, 13, 15
Agent Orange, 11, 18, 76–77, 79
agricultural economy, 183–184
agri-technologies, 184
Alaimo, Stacy, 101
    notion of "transcorporeality", 8
Alas Babylon (Pat Frank), 117
All Is Burning (Jean Arasanayagam), 24–25, 29, 36, 38, 190
    Sand Serpents, 29
Althusser, Louis, 47, 199–200
Ambedkar, B. R., 158
American soldiers, suicide of, 57
anatomo-politics, of the human body, 56, 194
Anderson, Benedict, 5
animality
    ancient belief systems in relation to, 59
    Blood of Leaves, The (Vo Thi Hao), 76–79
    Crocodile Fury, The (Beth Yahp), 59–76
    ecofeminism and animal rights, 58
    Heartless Forest (Khin Mya Zin), 79–86
    Maharlika (Sarmiento), 59–76
    Panchatantra, 58–59
    rhetoric of, 79
    women and, 55–58
animistic connections, loss of, 89
Anthropocene, 2, 44, 55
anthropocentrism, 28, 114, 154
anthropomorphism, 77
anti-Islamic sentiments, 135
anti-pastoral, ethos of, 135, 145
anxiety, production of, 179
apocalypse in literature, 116–117
    future and past, 118–120
    narratives by Asian women, 117–118
Arabian Nights, The, 59, 92
Aranyakandam, 161
Aranyakas (forest literatures), concept of, 6
Aranyani (forest goddess), 82, 84, 195
Archeological Survey of India (ASI), 111

Aristotle, 75, 178
Arthasashtra, 59
Asian
    blogs in English, 117
    ecocritical studies, 4, 6, 10
    ecofictions, 6, 18, 21
    women's relationships to non/human worlds, 2
Association of Southeast Asian Nations (ASEAN), 3
asura (demon), 161
Atharva Veda, 90–91
atman, 37
atomic bombing, of Hiroshima and Nagasaki, 117
at-risk-ecologies, 185
Attenborough, David, 1–2
attritional distress, 42
Atwood, Margaret, 101
Ayroso, Dee, 98

Babri Masjid violence (1992), 111, 113
Baines, Gary, 116
Bale, Kevin, 48
Baromashi Tapes, The (Niaz Zaman), 153, 179–186
Barry Lyndon (film), 119
Barthes, Roland, 70–71, 172
    para/doxical text, 71
Bataille, Georges, 73
Beck, Ulrich, 5, 13, 29
    "democratic" aspects of the new risks, 179
    idea of "risk society", 52, 179
Benjamin, Walter, 35
Bennett, Jane, 15
Bennett, Michael, 145
Berger, John, 78
Bhabha, Homi K., 15, 93, 170
    imagining of a cultural space, 23
    Third Space, idea of, 13, 15–16, 52, 170–171, 174, 179
Bhagavad Gita, 14
Bharatiya Janata Party (BJP), 111
Bhooma Devi (Earth Goddess), 7, 37
biocentric ethic, 17, 57, 68, 80
biocentrism, 60
biopiracy, 38
biopolitics, 44, 56–57, 70
    idea of population, 75
    triumph of modernity, 73
biopower
    idea of, 56, 87
    normalisation of, 76
    operations of, 65

Birkeland, Janis, 78
Blood of Leaves, The (Vo Thi Hao), 58, 190
  "ugliness" as peril in, 76–79
Blumberg, Hans, 113
boat people, 42, 45
Boccaccio, Giovanni, 92
Bonbibi stories, 18, 59, 81–82, 191
Bookchin, Murray, 3
Boromean knot, 77
Brahman, 154
Brahminism, 9
  nirguna brahman, 13
Braidotti, Rosi, 15
breach of trust, 50
British
  Empire, 22
  Raj, 27
Buddha's *Fire Sermon*, 12, 36–37, 124, 190
Buddhism, 6, 8, 10–11, 14, 37
Buddhist eschatology, 116
Budianta, Melanie, 138
Buell, Frederick, 127
Buell, Lawrence, 4, 77
Bulat Lat, 98
Burns, Charles, 34
Burns, Rose, 30
Butler, Judith, 41

Canterbury Tales, The (Geoffrey Chaucer), 92, 142
Carson, Rachel, 77, 90–91, 103
Cartesian dualism, 15
Cartesian mind/body dualism, 68
Caruth, Cathy, 99, 123
caste Hindus, 156, 165, 168–169
censorship, idea of, 70–71, 112
Chakrabarty, Dipesh, 41 102, 102
Chandler, Daniel, 73, 195
Chand, Meira, 17, 23
Chandragrohan (Lunar Eclipse, 2002), 112
Chatterjee, Partha, 45
China Relief Fund, 35
Christiansen, Allan, 13–14
Chua, Beng Huat, 46
civilization, enemies of, 169
civilizing mission, establishment of colonial rule
  as, 26
Clark, Timothy, 12, 134
Clean River Campaign (Singapore), 17, 24, 40, 42
  benefits of, 45
  human-rights issues, 46
  suffering faced by the river people during, 41
climate-change skepticism, 126
colonial tropes, of natives and jungles, 26–29
colonized other, 158
communal
  calamities, 120
  endeavor, 178
communist riot of 1927, 24
Conrad, Joseph, 26
Coole, Diana, 90

Corbett, Julia, 154
corporate globalization, 5, 17
corruption, problems of, 94
cosmic
  balance, 8
  imbalance, 111
Cottle, Simon, 13
COVID-19 pandemic, 1
Coward, Jonathan, 125–126
Cowper, William, 124, 168
crab-farm investments, 74
Crocodile Fury, The (Beth Yahp), 58
  artificiality of linear chronicling, 63
  idea of thanatopolitics, 71
  limits of the doxa, 71
  speciesism and anti-speciesism in, 59–76
Crosthwaite, Paul, 182
Cruz-Lucero, Rosario, 152
cultural differences, 94, 170
cultural identification, constructions of, 170
cultural imaginary, 154, 178
cultural structures and practices, narratives of, 105
culture/nature interconnection, 91
Currie, Mark, 98

daini (witch), 162, 164
Dalits (untouchables), 73, 158, 199
D'Ammassa, Don, 137
*Darśana*s, 14
Das, Bhagavan, 9
death
  of nature, 18
  politics of, 18, 56–57, 61
Death of Fray Salvador Montano, Conquistador of
  Negros, The (Rosario Cruz-Lucero), 153,
  169–175
Deckard, Sharae, 28–29
deforestation, 22
  caused by overpopulation, 29
delayed destruction, violence of, 22
Dening, Greg, 91
Derrida, Jacques, 73
desertification of the land, 22, 49
de-Shalit, Avner, 25
Devi, Mahasweta, 152, 154–169
  Bitter Soil, 168
  Little Ones, 162
  Witch, The, 162–164
de Wit, Michaël Dudok, 55
dharma, concept of, 8–9, 86
dhri, 9
Different Sky, A (Meira Chand), 23–24, 29, 35–36,
  51, 191
  awareness of colonial attitudes, 30
  colonial setting, 35
*diku*s, 156
dirty energy, legacy of, 98
dirty industries, shifting of, 21
Disability in Bangladesh (Titumir and Hossain),
  105

Index

disciplinary power
   normation of, 76
   notion of, 75
Discordant Harmonies (Daniel B. Botkin), 130
Discourse of Nature, The (Kate Soper), 189
disposable people, 48
divide and rule, colonial politics of, 17
domination
   logic of, 19
   social systems of, 161
Doubliago, Sharon, 7
doxa, limits of, 70–71
Dracula (Bram Stoker), 117
Dube, Saurabh, 48
Duertas, Fray, 172–173
duḥkha, 14
Dulce, Mamay, 95
Durai, Anna, 152
Duterte, Rodrigo, 72
dwelling
   in crisis, 127, 142
   notion of, 127
Dworkin, Andrea, 56

eco-cosmopolitanism, 12
ecocriticism, 3, 4–5, 9–10, 12, 15–16, 127
ecofeminisms, 3, 5, 7, 16, 53, 164
   and animal rights, 58
   discourse of, 58
ecofeminist
   ethics, nature of, 7
   spirituality, 151
ecofictions, 12–15, 17–18, 21, 90, 113, 190
eco-justice, 21, 40, 44, 47–51, 190
eco-localism, 69
ecological
   activism, 45
   awareness, 2, 4
   consciousness, 4
   destruction, 38, 141
   disputes, 40
   feminism, 7, 161
   feminist concepts of South and Southeast Asia, 6–10
   imperialism, 38
   justice, 38, 47–51, 74
   preservation, 7
eco-spiritualism, 5
enchantment, idea of, 19
"end-of-time" chronicles, 121
entrapment, phenomenon of, 144
environmental
   cleanup, 40
   colonialism, 38, 45
   hazards, 40, 41, 46, 50, 80, 153
   justice, 38, 77
   management, 40, 52
   sanitation, 41
environmentalism of the poor, 22–23, 39, 41, 154
Epic of Gilgamesh, 117

Escobar, Arturo, 45
ethics
   of control, 120–121
   lab, role of, 178
   of risk, 120–122
ethnocentrism, 69
Eurocentrism, 28
Evernden, Neil, 143, 149
exemplar virtutis, 26
export-dependent economies, 17
extrajudicial killing, of drug users and criminals, 72

Farid, Lily Yulianti, 118
Feinberg, Matthew, 126
female
   eco-empowerment, 8
   genital mutilation, 56
   sexual agency, 180
   sexuality, 100
Feminist Ethic of Risk, A (Sharon D. Welch), 120
feminization of nature, 18
feudalism, pitfalls of, 49, 52
Fish-Hair Woman (Merlinda Bobis), 92, 190
   characters and the storyline, 97–98
   postmodernist dimension of, 96
   postmodern stylistics and postcolonial angst in, 94–102
   Third Space between fact and fiction, 97
folk knowledge, 70
foot-binding, in China, 56
forest "spirit", 82
Foucault, Michel, 44, 56, 69
   concept of biopolitics, 71
   on disciplinary power, 75
   Discipline and Punish, 160
   on genealogy of race, 65
   general idea of population, 75
   governmentality, notion of, 93
   Homo Sacer, 71
   life, 71
   on power and techniques of punishment, 160
Freud, Sigmund, 145
Fromm, Harold, 142
Frost, Samantha, 90

Garrard, Greg, 77
Gautam, Pradeep Kumar, 59
Ghosh, Amitav, 2, 29, 94
   Sea of Poppies, 29
Gifford, Terry, 116
global
   chronicles of war, 95
   ecocracy, 41
   ecological crisis, 2
   literatures and ecocriticism, in South and Southeast Asia, 3–6
   risk, second modernity of, 179
   warming, 2, 40, 44, 126
global capitalism, 38, 183
   predatory theft of Asian natural resources, 23

226   Index

global economic
   hierarchy, 185
   imperialism, 183
God of Small Things, The (Arundhati Roy), 94
good karmic deeds (*punya*), 165
governmentality, notion of, 93
Great World Amusement Park, 34
Greimas, Algirdas Julien, 93
Gruen, Lori, 58
Gupta, Bina, 14

Halder, Ram, 167
Harris, Wilson, 174
Hashem, Dilara, 112
haunting trauma, depictions of, 86
Hazlitt, William, 26
Heartless Forest (Khin Mya Zin), 58, 79–86, 190
Heidegger, Martin
   "Being-in-the-world" (*Being and Time*), 184
   dwelling, notion of, 127
Heilmann, Ann, 97
Heise, Ursula, 5–6, 116, 126–127
Hekman, Susan, 101
Hindu
   caste system, 73
   cultural imaginary, 155
   *darshana*s (visions), 154
Hinduism, 5, 8–9, 37
Hindu–Muslim riots, 111
Hindu Quest for the Perfection of Man (Troy Wilson Organ), 154
Hindu religious festivals, 181
Hindutva movement, in India, 111
historical fiction, decline of, 119
Historical Novel, The (Georg Lukács), 119
Ho Chi Minh trail, 118, 123
homo sacer (sacred man), 71
hope, death of, 125
Hossain, Jakir, 105
Huey-li, Li, 4
Huggan, Graham, 44
human
   cultural formulations, power of, 71
   human-nature interactions, 4, 5
   human-rights violations, 98
   humans-at-risk, 120
   hunting, 87
   soul/self (*puruṣa*), notion of, 8
   spiritual evolution, 154
human bodies
   anatomo-politics of, 56
   control of, 56
human/non-human binaries, 60
   reevaluation of, 5
humility, idea of, 91
Hungry Tide, The (Amitav Ghosh), 94

"I am an Innocent Man" drama, 33, 38–39
ideal child, notion of, 103
Imaginary Maps (Chakravorty Spivak), 162

Imaginary Museum, 119
"imagined communities" of the nation, 5
imagined cosmopolitan communities of global risk, 5
Immersion, The (Dilara Hashem)
   liminal Third Space, 102
   real and the ideal in, 102–105
incremental violence, 22
Indian Iron Age, 1
Indic cultural substratum, 11
Indo-Aryan dynasties, 155
industrial society, first modernity of, 17, 22, 40, 179
intellectual diffusion, West-centric model of, 6
"intellectually challenged" children, 105
international capitalism, 50
intersubjective negotiation, 179
Iovino, Serenella, 15, 67, 81
irrefutability of logic, 178

Jameson, Frederick, 119–120
JanMohamed, Abdul R., 158
Jeffers, Robinson, 116
jñānamārgi, 107
jungles and civic spaces, in Singapore and Sri Lanka, 29–40
just-world hypothesis, 126

Kalki Avatar, coming of, 116
karmic hierarchy, 165
*kar sevak*s, 111
Katrina Ebora, 90
Khin, Mya Zin, 8
kleptocrat, 95
kshatriyas, 155
Kuan Yin, 8, 30
Kubrick, Stanley, 119
Kumar, Deepak, 22

Lake (Lily Yulianti Farid), 118, 135–148, 147, 190
   Zara's story, 136
land-grabbing, of tribal land, 162
Landscapes of Fear (Yi-Fu Tuan), 144
Lao, Tzu, 21
Last Man, The (Mary Shelley), 117
law and power, nature of, 71
Lee, Martha F., 125
Left Hand of Darkness, The (Ursula K. Le Guin), 61
LéLé, Wynn, 80
Lemm, Vanessa, 76
Leopold, Aldo, 7
Lessing, Doris, 28
life not worthy of being lived, 73
Lim, Suchen Christine, 24, 46
   advocacy on behalf of the "River People", 41
   River's Song, The, 24
Literary Fiction Influences Attitudes Toward Animal Welfare (Wojciech Małecki), 57
littoral literature, 91–94
Llewellyn, Mark, 97

Location of Culture, The (Homi K. Bhabha), 15–16, 23, 52, 93, 105, 148
logocentrism, 153, 173, 186
long dyings, notion of, 22, 77, 79, 83
Lukács, Georg, 119

Macey, David, 44
Macherey, Pierre, 47
Mahabharata (ancient Hindu epic), 12, 19, 152, 155, 189, 199
Maharlika (Sarmiento), 58
    process of indoctrination, 72
    speciesism and anti-speciesism in, 59–76
Mahasweta, *see* Devi, Mahasweta
Malayan emergency, in the mid-1950s, 24
Malecki, Wojciech, 57
male power fantasy, 31
malign jungle, 31
Manes, Christopher, 81
Manichean allegory, economy of, 158
Marfan syndrome, 78
mass conversion, of the natives in the Philippines, 153
material ecocriticism, 5, 12, 15, 67
matrix, creation of, 120–121
maya, 154
McDowell, Michael J., 143
Meeker, Joseph, 4
Mehta, Gita, 8, 112
Mei, Lan, 34–35, 51, 53
Mellor, Mary, 164
Merchant, Carolyn, 7
mestizaje (miscegenation), 69
metropolitanism, ethos of, 145
Mill, John Stuart, 9
Mindoran-Iraya tribe, 95
misogyny, 56
modernity
    in Asia, 48
    characteristic of, 89
    discourse of, 50
mokṣa, 8, 37, 82
Money Makers, The (Nita Umali-Berthelsen), 153, 175–179
Morton, Timothy, 86
Mother Earth, 37, 125, 127–128, 190
Mrovlje, Maša, 178
Mukherjee, Upamanyu Pablo, 6, 37
munsifbabbar, 185
murder, normalization of, 61, 72
Murray, S. J., 57
mysticism of Asia, 116

Naga baba, 110
Naicker, E. V. Ramasamy, 158
national progress, ideals of, 44
nation-building, idea of, 23, 191
natives and jungles, colonial tropes, 26–29
natural and cultural ecology, 121
natural environment, devaluation of, 3, 17, 22–23

natural laws, immutability of, 164
natural resources, management of, 3
natural world, colonial depictions of, 33
nature
    human atrocities against, 190
    idea of, 155, 189
    Mother Earth, 190
"nature/culture" hierarchical dualism, 71
Nazis, 73
neocolonial mentality, 45
neocolonial regimes, 23
    social justice and eco-justice in, 47–51
neoliberal politics, political right of, 57
nirguna brahman, 13
nirvana, 8, 37, 82, 133
Nixon, Rob, 22, 41
    idea of "slow violence", 52
    views about "the environmentalism of the poor", 39, 41
Nkrumah, Kwame, 22
non-human ecology, 33
North American intellectual heritage, 6
Nussbaum, Martha, 153

Oh Lovely Rock (Robinson Jeffers), 130
Ondaatje, Michael, 129
One Amazing Thing (Chitra Divakaruni Banerjee), 118, 135–148
one's identity, definition of, 158
Oppermann, Serpil, 67
Oreskes, Naomi, 41, 102
Organ, Troy Wilson, 8, 110
Ortner, Sherry, 6
Orwell, George, 27
othering, politics of, 153
Our Lady of the Immaculate Conception (Cruz-Lucero), 173

Pacification of the Primitive Tribes of the Lower Niger, The (Chinua Achebe), 41
pahaan (tribal priest), 162, 164
panchabhūtas, 25
Panchatantra, 12, 58–59, 92
Pandian, M. S. S., 158
Parkinson's disease, 183
pathetic fallacy, deployment of, 28, 164
Patterson, Wilfred, 30
Pearson, Michael N., 91
Pepperell, Robert, 146
Periyar, E. V. R., 152
Phillipine Daily News, 96, 100
place
    erotics of, 134
    sense of, 144
planetary management, 38
Plumwood, Val, 28
polygamy, 35
population
    biopolitical idea of, 75
    explosion of, 2

pornotropics, 35
postcolonial democracies, 23
postcolonial ecocriticism, 5
Posthuman Condition, The, 146
"post-industrial" societies, 40
post-traumatic stress disorder (PTSD), 133
power, concept of, 70
power relations, negotiation of, 41
prakṛti (nature), 8, 12, 14, 37, 81, 107
    Sāṃkhya system of, 190
Pralayaa (dissolution of the world), 116
predation, idea of, 38
predator and prey, division of, 75, 81
prelapsarian innocence, 175
Prithvi Sukta, 91, 189
puruṣa (purusha), 14–15, 37, 82, 107
    Sāṃkhya system of, 190

race, hierarchies of, 57
racial stereotyping, 77
Rai, Dakshin, 81
Rajan, Chandra, 59
Ramayana (ancient Hindu epic), 152, 163
    Aranya Kanda, 161, 164
    Bala Kanda, 155
    Chiatra Ratha, 161
    Javanese Ramayana, 10
    Kishkantha Kanda, 165
    Malay *Hikayat Seri Rama*, 10
    Tataka's land, 161
    Thai *Ramakien*, 10
    Uttar Ramayana, 7
    by Valmiki, 10, 155, 164
Ram Rath Yatra, 111
Rani in Search of a Rainbow (Shaila Abdullah), 118, 120–128, 141, 147
Reading for Wonder (Glenn Willmot), 103
redox-active heterocycles, 183
Red Turtle, The (2016), 55
re-enchantment of nature, 67
regional eco-consciousness, 180
Renn, Ortwin, 14
Repo, Jemima, 57
res cogitans (*puruṣa*), 15
res extensa, 15
Rhys, Jean, 27
right to live, 57–58
risk
    consciousness of, 147
    pervasiveness of, 77
    uncertainties of, 147
risk society in Asia, 13–14, 77, 179
    Beck's idea of, 52
    inhabitants of, 123
ritual ceremony, 71
river people, 40
    anti-pollution environmental campaigns, 45
    Lim's advocacy on behalf of, 41
    political and social issue of, 41
    quit notice for displacement of, 43
    suffering faced during the clean river campaign, 41
River's Song, The (Suchen Christine Lim), 24, 40, 51, 190
    as "consciousness-raising" effort, 46
    dialectics of, 42
River Sutra, A (1993), 92, 105–111, 113, 190
Road, The (Cormac McCarthy), 117
Roar of a Distant War, The (Viliya Ketavong), 118, 120–128, 147, 190
Roff, William, 26
Roman law, 71
Roosevelt, Theodore, 32
Ross, Andrew, 38
Roy, Arundhati, 94
Ṛta (ancient conception of the orderliness of the world), 9, 110
rubber plantations, in Malaya, 22
Rueckert, William, 4
Ruether, Rosemary, 8

Sachs, Wolfgang, 41
safe city, 31
Said, Edward W., 31
Salammbô (Gustave Flaubert), 119
Salleh, Ariel, 77
salt deficiency, 157
Salt Eaters, The (Toni Cade Bambara), 120
Sāṃkhya, philosophy of, 8, 12, 13, 14–15, 37, 82, 107, 190
Sanskrit, 6
Sarmiento, Irene Carolina A., 18
sati system, in India, 56
Saussure, Ferdinand, 73
"savage/civilized" forms, imperial binaries of, 31
savage native, 36
Save the Forests, 167
science-fiction, 117
    rise of, 119
"scriptural" tales, 156
Sea of Poppies (Amitav Ghosh), 29
Sebald, W. G., 72
self-consciousness, 92, 98
Sense of Place (Ursula Heise), 128
Sermon of the Seven Suns, 116
Sermon on the Mount, 124
Sesh Rater Songlap (Twin Towers, 2003), 112
Severance (Ling Ma), 117
sexes, segregation of, 35
sexual desire, 180
sexual division of labor, 13
Shahraz, Qaisra, 25
Shakta cults, practices of, 82
Shakti (Hindu goddess), 14
Shankar, V. V., 110
Sharma, Vishnu, 59
Shelley, Mary, 117
Shiva, Vandana, 4, 38, 177
Short History of Environmental Apocalypse, A (Frederick Buell), 147

Silent Spring (Rachel Carson), 77
Singapore
    civic spaces during World War II, 32
    Clean River Campaign of 1970s and 1980s, 17, 24, 40
    environmental management, 40
    environment *versus* subalterns in, 40–47
    fall of, 31
    Japanese invasion of, 31–32
    jungle laws, 32
    jungles and civic spaces in, 29–40
    national developmental schemes, 40
    political situation of 1970s in, 40
    savagery and mindless violence, 32
    unheimlich space, 32
    unsung heroes of, 40
    vegetable garden, 32
Singapore River, 42
Singer, Peter, 60
singulatim et omnis, 75
Slovic, Paul, 42
Slovic, Scott, 42–43, 130
slow violence, idea of, 17, 22–23, 39, 45, 49, 52
social
    consciousness, 139, 175
    discriminations, 155
    and environmental justice, 38
    identity, 158
social hierarchies, 155, 160
    justification of, 156
social justice, 43
    in neocolonial regimes, 47–51
socially disenfranchised, exploitation of, 155
social status, notion of, 165
sociopolis, 57
sociopolitics, 94
soil acidification, 22–23, 49
Soja, Edward, 15, 23, 92, 181
Solnit, Rebecca, 40
Soper, Kate, 9, 189
Sørensen, Mads Peter, 13
sor-hei ("comb-up" ceremony), 30
speciesism, obliteration of, 58
Spivak, Chakravorty, 155, 183
    Imaginary Maps, 162
Spivak, Gayatri Chakravorty, 152
Sri Lanka
    civil war in, 32–33
    devolution of post-independence, 38
    jungles and civic spaces in, 32
    as pearl in the Indian Ocean, 38
    as Venice of the East, 38
Stand, The (Stephen King), 117
Stoker, Bram, 117
Stone, Alison, 89
storytelling, 93, 104, 143, 160
Straits Times, 42
Structural Semantics (Algirdas Julien Greimas), 93
subjectivity, humanist concept of, 73
subsistence-based communities, 40, 41

sutra, 8
Suzuki, Toshio, 55

Tal, Kali, 131
Taoism (Daoism), 13
tawlar ratu, 8, 12, 59, 81, 190
technologies of self, 70
Tempest, The, 26
thanatopolis, 77
thanatopolitics, idea of, 17, 56–57, 71, 73
therianthropism (humans represented as animals), 58
Third Space, idea of, 13, 15–16, 23, 52, 92, 181
    consciousness, 181
    as space of resistance, 181
Thompson, Damien, 120
Tiffin, Helen, 44
Titumir, Rashed Al Mahmud, 105
topophilia, 144
topophobia, 144
toxic discourse, 77
toxic waste, management of, 21
"traditional" societies, 89
tragedy of the commons, 45
transcoding caste, act of, 158
transcorporeality, notion of, 8
transformative ideologies, 154
trauma
    definition of, 131
    place of, 133
tribes of India
    Agariya tribals, 162
    dignity and agency of, 168
    exploitation of, 156
    land-grabbing of tribal land, 162
    Oraon tribe, 156
    population of, 155
    Shabar tribe of Purulia, 166
    "tribal" rights, 19
    as "wageless" labor, 156
tropical decadence, themes of, 26
turbulence of life, 125

UNICEF's Water Sanitation and Hygiene program, 90
unity, idea of, 189
unrestrained instrumentalism, 154
"unsung heroes" of Singapore, 40
Upanishads, 154
    Maitrayanya, 14
    Svetasvatara, 14

valley of death, 35
vănarā (of the monkey tribe), 165
Vasudaiva Kudumbakam, 189
Vatter, Miguel, 76
Vedic Age, 1, 189
vegetable-garden city, 32
Velasquez, Lizzie, 78, 195
Verne, Jules, 119

Vietnam War, 77–78
violence against minorities, 57
virtue and evil, notions of, 158
Vishva Hindu Parishad (VHP), 111
von Schelling, Friedrich Wilhelm Joseph, 145

"wageless" labor, 156
Waites, Elizabeth, 131
Wallace, Molly, 40, 73
War of the Worlds (H. G. Wells), 117
Warren, Karen J., 7, 91, 151
Waste Land, The (T. S. Eliot), 124
water bodies, idea of, 94
Waugh, Charles, 76
Waugh, Patricia, 99
Wave (Sonali Deraniyagala), 118, 129–135, 147, 190
Weber, Max, 89
Wee, Jack, 32, 34
Weisman, Alan, 33
Wells, H. G., 117
Western environmentalist movement, 4
Wide Sargasso Sea (Jean Rhys), 27
Willer, Robb, 126
Wisner, Ben, 47

witch-hunting
  in Europe and America, 56
  in Salem, 56
Wolfe, Cary, 73
women and animality, 55–58
women–nature connections, 6–7, 191
women of color, 121
Woolf, Leonard, 28
World at a Distance, The (William Cowper), 124
World Bank, 21
World Conference on the Changing Atmosphere in Toronto (1988), 125
World War II, 23, 117
World without Us (Alan Weisman), 33
Wright, Laura, 5

Yahp, Beth, 18
Yajur Veda, 1, 116
Yama (Hindu and Buddhist God of Death), 37
yoga system, 107
Young, Robert J. C., 22, 102, 174

Zaman, Niaz, 153
Zemindar's Wife, The (Qaisra Shahraz), 17, 25, 47–51

www.ingramcontent.com/pod-product-compliance
Lightning Source LLC
Chambersburg PA
CBHW011755220426
43672CB00018B/2976